MOMENTS OF CAPITAL

CURRENCIES

New Thinking for Financial Times
STEFAN EICH AND MARTIJN KONINGS, EDITORS

Moments of Capital

World Theory,
World Literature

ELI JELLY-SCHAPIRO

STANFORD UNIVERSITY PRESS

Stanford, California

STANFORD UNIVERSITY PRESS
Stanford, California

©2023 by Eli Jelly-Schapiro. All rights reserved.

Printed in the United States of America on acid-free, archival-quality paper

ISBN 9781503634718 (cloth)
ISBN 9781503635432 (paper)
ISBN 9781503635449 (ebook)

Library of Congress Control Number 2022027850
CIP data available upon request.

Cover design: George Kirkpatrick
Cover art: *Strip* © Gerhard Richter 2022 (0159).

Typeset by Newgen in Janson Text 10/15

Table of Contents

Acknowledgments

Deep thanks:

To Liam Kennedy and Stephen Shapiro, for organizing the gathering in Dublin and editing the volume that provoked the initial articulation of the ideas that would become this book; to Stephen again, for being a generous and astute interlocutor over the course of this project's life; to Caren Irr, for including me in a stellar special issue of *Mediations*, which provided further opportunity to think through the questions at the heart of this project, and for supporting this work in many other ways.

To Laura Finch and Tony Jarrells, who both read an early draft of the book's conceptual template and discerned precisely what about it was worth elaborating, and what about it needed to change; to Daniel Hartley, who engaged the book's theoretical vocabulary and argument at two different stages, with clarifying erudition; to Greg Forter, who read the whole manuscript and brilliantly illuminated its proper shape and substance.

To all of my cherished friends and colleagues in South Carolina.

To Caroline McKusick, Erica Wetter, and Faith Wilson Stein, at Stanford University Press, for guiding the development of this book with wisdom and grace; to Stefan Eich and Martijn Konings, for their sharp and timely interventions, and for embracing this book in a series I'm honored to join; to Sarah Osment and Bryne Rasmussen, for their impeccable contributions to the book's final form; to the manuscript's anonymous reviewers, for their trenchant and vital insights.

To the Center for the Humanities at the University of California, Merced, and to the Office of the Provost and the Department of English at the University of South Carolina, for the gift of time.

To Alicia Schmidt Camacho, Hazel Carby, Michael Denning, and Paul Gilroy.

To Tamas, Krisztina, Pepi, Andrea, Matthew, and Ilona; to Mirissa and Pablo; to my parents, and to my brother; to Amália, Viola, and Zsofi, with love and wonder.

MOMENTS OF CAPITAL

Moments of Capital

IN *THE COMMUNIST MANIFESTO* (1848), Karl Marx and Friedrich Engels herald the imminent realization of the "world market," the universalization of capital and its social and political forms. But even as it renders, in floral terms, the consequence of that globalizing force, the *Manifesto* embeds a parallel history of capital in the age of its planetary projection, which places the accent on difference rather than sameness. Marx and Engels highlight, for example, the connection between the global ascendance of capital and the sharpening of the capital-labor antinomy. And that central contradiction is mirrored and magnified, they suggest, by the constitutive fact of spatial unevenness: "The bourgeoisie has subjected the country to the rule of the towns. . . . [And] just as it has made the country dependent on the towns, so it has made barbarian and semi-barbarian countries dependent on the civilized ones, nations of peasants on nations of bourgeois, the East on the West." In adjacent passages, meanwhile, Marx and Engels gesture toward the existence of several concurrent and conjoined processes within the age of the bourgeoisie's ascendance: patterns of colonization, inaugurated by the "discovery of America" and reprised by modern European empires; the "extension of industry," and its infrastructure of communication and transportation; and crises of overproduction, which compel the "enforced destruction of a mass of productive forces, . . . the conquest of new markets, and . . . the more thorough exploitation of the old ones."[1]

How to apprehend, or represent, both the global generality and differential composition of capital? From Marx onward, this problem has animated the practice of critical theory. It is likewise central, and increasingly so, to the production and study of "world literature." Responding to this fundamental question, *Moments of Capital* positions itself at the interface of these two fields.

In the *Manifesto*, Marx and Engels predict that the advent of the world market will occasion the advent of a "world literature." "As in material, so also in intellectual production," they write. "The intellectual creations of individual nations become common property. National one-sidedness and narrow-mindedness become more and more impossible, and from the numerous national and local literatures, there arises a world literature."[2] When viewed through the lens of culture, the creation of the world market, in Marx and Engels's narrative, does not produce difference but subsumes it. In its contemporary iteration, though, the project of "world literature"— a term that signifies at once a cultural form and hermeneutic orientation— evinces the heterogeneity of capitalist modernity, the manifold particulars that make it up. The various subdisciplines that shape the field of "world literature" deploy different analytic categories, or different theoretical vocabularies, to capture this unity and heterogeneity. Comparative literature privileges the differences of nation, region, language, or period. Postcolonial studies foregrounds the dialectical entanglement of colony and metropole, or the Global North and Global South. And a recent literary-critical tendency, borrowing the framework of world-systems theory, invokes the cartography of core, periphery, and semi-periphery. *Moments of Capital* is a work of comparative critique, which contributes to the postcolonial studies tradition, and which is indebted to world-systems approaches. This book sets out, though, to develop a new conceptual key for the mapping of the world market and world literature alike. Registering but moving beyond the differences of history and geography, I theorize, and examine the literary representation of, the unique "moments" that comprise global capital.

The term "moment" has for me a primarily synchronic rather than diachronic resonance. It refers, in this book, to a discrete moment in a dialectical process or totality. Contemporary global capital, I argue, is composed of three such synchronous moments, which are defined by distinct forms of accumulation and governance, and which correspond to distinct assemblages of theory and fiction. In the moment of primitive accumulation, ongoing processes of extraction, enclosure, and bondage are enabled by state violence. In the moment of expanded reproduction, the basic and constant movement of economic growth—the exploitation of wage labor, and the reinvestment of the surplus value thereby created—is guaranteed by ideology, or by what Max Weber termed "spirit." Finally, in the moment of what I call "synthetic dispossession," mechanisms of privatization and devaluation—the fabrication and subsequent assimilation of an outside to capital—and the general ascent of finance capital contribute to the waning power of ideology and heightened importance of state repression. Reading and integrating different works of theory and fiction, *Moments of Capital* both delineates the three moments of contemporary global capital and elucidates the dynamics of their concurrent combination.

*

Theorists and critics, whether their primary concern is the nature of capital itself or the problem of its representation, commonly use the term "neoliberalism" to denote the distinctiveness of the capitalist present. In scholarly and public discourse, "neoliberalism" refers to a series of transformations—provoked, in the first instance, by crises of energy and accumulation and the specter of economic decline—that have reshaped the world over the past four decades: the intensification of crude modes of dispossession, the innovation of various mechanisms of financial speculation and "flexible" production, the retrenchment of the welfare state, the clarification of new rationalities of the responsible and entrepreneurial self, and the extension of market logics to all realms of human social life.

The key plot points in the political history of neoliberalism are by now familiar. The first experiments in neoliberal political economy were conducted in the 1970s in Pinochet's Chile, under the remote advisement of University of Chicago economists.[3] The core precepts of neoliberal policy and thought were subsequently embraced, in the 1980s and 1990s, by the governments of the advanced capitalist world, the United States and the United Kingdom foremost among them. In the aftermath of the Cold War, neoliberal programs and ideas—from the privatization of public services, to the liberalization of trade and deregulation of usury, to the explosive expansion of consumer credit as a key driver of growth—acquired a global generality. Under the sign of "globalization," liberated financial capital seized upon the marketizing economies of the former Eastern Bloc, while "structural adjustment" initiatives led by the International Monetary Fund (IMF) in the developing world tied access to sovereign credit to the imposition of austerity measures and erosion of social and economic protections.

Around the turn of the millennium, the global pervasion of capital—the ultimate realization of the "world market" anticipated by Marx and Engels in the nineteenth century—was met, on both the left and right, with the declaration of a new historical age. Euphoric at the prospects of a global capitalist order ensured by the military power of the United States, intellectuals of the right or center—invoking the phrasing of Francis Fukuyama—announced the "end of history"; capitalism and liberal democracy had triumphed over all alternatives. Critical theorists such as Michael Hardt and Antonio Negri, meanwhile, used the term "Empire" to name the planetary articulations of capital and supranational bodies of political authority. This enunciation of the global also found expression in the literary-critical sphere, as the figure of "global literature" joined ongoing debates about "world literature," a concept that has itself acquired a resurgent discursive prominence in recent decades.

Moments of Capital shares with these diagnoses, and these cultural shifts, a fundamental recognition of the globality of contemporary political and economic forms. I am, though, especially concerned to emphasize the heterogeneous composition of contemporary global capital—the contradictions and unevenness that constitute the world market. In both Marxist and postcolonial theory, the unevenness of capital is habitually represented in spatial terms. The field of Marxist geography highlights the spatial dialectic of development and underdevelopment. And the work of certain anticolonial and postcolonial thinkers stresses the colonial origins and essence of that dialectic, the ways in which the economic advancement of the Global North has been made possible by the plunder of the Global South. I affirm this geographic approach. I argue, though, that our understanding of the spatial asymmetry of capitalist modernity is deepened when we attend, at the same time, to the multiple "moments" of capital. Doing so, for example, helps us resist the simple equation of particular modes of accumulation and particular spaces—primitive accumulation and the Global South, expanded reproduction and the Global North. The moments of primitive accumulation, expanded reproduction, and synthetic dispossession exist in synchronic combination, within specific national or regional geographies and in the broader context of the world-system.

The Marxist theorization of "uneven and combined development" does address the geographic co-belonging of different forms of accumulation. Leon Trotsky's treatment of "uneven and combined development," notably, focused on the concurrence of industrial and agrarian cultures of production within Russia.[4] Evading the assumption of a neat identity between different geographies and different modalities of capital, theories of uneven development, however, sometimes encourage the conflation of geographic and *historical* difference. Because capital presents itself, ideologically, as historically progressive, geographic differences are often read, by disparate discursive formations, as differences of time. This tendency is most pronounced in colonial mappings of the world. The authors and architects of empire imagine the (post)colony as "backwards," either premodern or belatedly and incompletely modern, confined to an earlier stage of economic and political development that Europe and North America long ago superseded. But the impulse to read geographic difference as historical difference is one feature, too, of the "stage theory" school of Marxist thought, which conforms to the teleological idea that all societies pass through discrete phases on their way to a common endpoint of industrial (or postindustrial) modernity. Abiding by this stadial conception of capital's historical unfolding, we might be tempted, for example, to identify primitive accumulation with the past, or regard as antiquated those spaces wherein crude methods of expropriation are pervasive or intensive. *Moments of Capital* resists the progressivist assumptions of these historicist tendencies, by illuminating the concurrence, and structural combination, of the three moments of capital. Primitive accumulation, expanded reproduction, and synthetic dispossession are equally present, and equally modern. They do not represent successive stages within, but compose the synchronic totality of, global capital.

In both the Hegelian and Marxian traditions, "moment" has a double meaning. It indicates, at turns or at once, a moment in history or time, and a moment in a dialectical process or totality. (In German, notably, these two meanings are accompanied by a differently gendered article: the masculine *der* for the former, and the neuter *das* for the latter.) My own treatment of the multiple "moments" of capital, while engaging the problem of time, aligns with this second resonance—"the reciprocal entailment and inseparability of the parts of a whole or totality," as Michael Inwood defines it in *A Hegel Dictionary* (1992).[5] The moments of primitive accumulation, expanded reproduction, and synthetic dispossession are inseparable "parts of a whole or totality." This understanding of "moment"—as one part of a dialectical unity—was taken up by Stuart Hall, a thinker whose work I engage often throughout this book. In particular, Hall's examination of the Introduction to Marx's *Grundrisse* (1939) includes an intriguing reflection on the "moments" of production, distribution, and consumption. Though implying a sequential movement—a commodity is produced and then distributed and then consumed—these activities, Hall observes, are all distinct moments of "a single act." Similarly, the three moments that structure my inquiry might initially suggest a kind of linear sequence: primitive accumulation founds expanded reproduction, the crises of which provoke rounds of synthetic dispossession. This abstract linearity—which the arrangement of the first three chapters of this book mimics—appears logical but is analytically limited and misleading. Primitive accumulation, expanded reproduction, and synthetic dispossession, I contend, do not unfold diachronically, but are synchronous and conjoined moments that constitute the singular act of capital's perpetual valorization.

This book demonstrates the synchronic unity of primitive accumulation, expanded reproduction, and synthetic dispossession. But I also acknowledge and grapple with their historicity. I attend, most significantly, to the historical conjuncture of the neoliberal present—the articulation therein of the three moments of capital. And I recognize, relatedly and more broadly, that the contours of each moment are especially defined—or attain a contingent, paradigmatic importance—in concrete spaces and times.

I am, all this is to say, attentive to the first meaning of "moment" outlined above, even as I focus on the second. Primitive accumulation is constant, but its emblematic political and economic forms have been emphasized in particular periods: the high point of modern European imperialism, in the decades surrounding the turn of the twentieth century; the anticolonial foment of the 1940s, '50s, and '60s, when the brutality of Europe's imperial history was exposed by intellectuals and artists from across the colonized world; and the twenty-first-century synthesis of market fundamentalism and permanent war, which has highlighted anew the enduring combination of state violence and primitive accumulation. The moment of expanded reproduction, meanwhile, appeared hegemonic to Marx and other European intellectuals in the nineteenth century, who were writing at the nexus of the first and second industrial revolutions; the political and economic machineries of expanded reproduction again attained a certain discursive primacy, in the advanced capitalist world, in the decades that followed from the Second World War—the apotheosis of the social democratic consensus, and the beginnings of its unraveling; and in the current conjuncture, the insidious nature of neoliberal ideas has provoked new inquiries into the "spirit," ideology, and modes of governmentality that ensure the reproduction of capitalist social relations, even in the context of heightened inequality and contradiction. The technologies of synthetic dispossession, finally, were crystallized, and provoked significant theoretical interventions, in the early decades of the twentieth century, following the ascent of finance capital and an associated series of economic cataclysms; and today, as the instruments of financialization are again dominant, and as the crises they occasion are both pervasive and acute, the moment of synthetic dispossession occupies the analytic and structural foreground.

These historical specificities betray, even as they might seem to belie, the synchronous interrelation of the three moments of capital, and the conversation, implicit or explicit, between their particular theoretical frameworks. Perhaps most tellingly, each moment corresponds to a unique strand of *contemporary* critique. But the simultaneity of the three moments of capital is evidenced as well by the historical-theoretical archive. For example, at the same time that Louis Althusser was meditating on the problem of ideology, the soft power of the capitalist state, anticolonial intellectuals such as Frantz Fanon were chronicling the outright violence of colonial depredation. Reading these two thinkers alongside one another—and staging other such critical encounters, across the spatial and temporal fault lines—helps to illuminate the concurrence, and dialectical interrelation, of capital's multiple moments.

My approach to both theory and fiction is necessarily comparative. The theoretical archive that this book marshals is composed, in large part, of different trajectories of Marxist thought—theories of primitive accumulation and imperialism, expanded reproduction and the problem of ideology, financialization and crisis, and the differential unity of the capitalist world-system. I also examine, though, the investigations of Max Weber and Michel Foucault, and their contemporary exponents, into the mechanisms of capitalist power. The juxtaposition of ostensibly disparate theoretical vocabularies and methodologies elucidates the broad shape and internal complexity of global capital. The dialogue between Marxist theories of racialized dispossession and Weberian theories of capitalist "spirit" is marked by tension rather than intuitive agreement. But such discordances, I contend, reflect how the different questions posed, or different diagnoses made, by different theoretical interventions are an effect of the different moments those interventions emerge from.

Capital's global generality and internal heterogeneity is also demonstrated by the corpus of novels that this book engages. Since the eighteenth century, when the establishment of new relations of production coincided with the innovation of new cultural forms, capitalism and the novel have been intimately entwined. The modern novel, in its inception, was one cultural expression of a nascent bourgeois consciousness and ideology; but what would become its dominant form, realism, also made possible the critical revelation of capitalism's constitutive contradictions. Joining or juxtaposing realist and more experimental techniques of representation, the contemporary novel, I argue, is a privileged site for identifying and deconstructing the differential composition of global capital—the modes of governance and accumulation, and cultures of critique and resistance, that inhere in the three moments of capital, and the dynamics of their interrelation. The works I analyze are manifold in form. And they range across space and time—from a mineral mine in Central Africa to a corporate office in midtown Manhattan, from a plantation in eighteenth-century

Jamaica to a shipyard in contemporary Seoul. Placing, for example, bourgeois realist novels in close analytic proximity to speculative postcolonial fictions, my literary readings make vivid the uneven texture of lived experience under capital.[6] This book's literary excurses, that is, limn the particular "structures of feeling," to invoke Raymond Williams's phrase, that mark the different moments of capital—the affective atmospheres, and figures of thought, within and through which individual and collective subjects register existing social and political realities and, perhaps, intimate new ways of organizing human community. The concept of "structures of feeling," Williams avowed, describes "meanings and values as they are actively lived and felt . . . practical consciousness of a present kind, in a living and interrelating continuity." It is, Williams wrote, a "cultural hypothesis," which is often signaled by the aesthetic artifacts of art and literature, and which is irreducible to, but exists in dialectical relation with, "more formally structured hypotheses of the social"—such as those advanced by the theory I engage throughout *Moments of Capital*.[7]

The basic argument of this book—that global capital is composed of three distinct moments, which correlate to distinct modes of governance and accumulation, and distinct modalities of theory and literature—is reflected by its structure. The first three chapters outline in turn the moments of primitive accumulation, expanded reproduction, and synthetic dispossession—their historical and contemporary theorization, and their literary figuration. The fourth chapter, meanwhile, considers, in dialogue with theorists and novelists, the synchronous combination of capital's multiple moments. My conceptualization of the three moments of capital, and the problem of their interrelation, functions as a key for the mapping of contemporary theory and contemporary world literature—while also acting, in itself, as a new "world theory," a new way of capturing the unity and difference of capitalist modernity.

*

Marx's reflections on primitive accumulation, in the concluding chapters of *Capital*, volume 1, trace several concurrent histories: the forcible separation of the worker from the means of production, a process of expropriation achieved, in Europe, through acts of enclosure and other "terroristic laws"; the theft, by Europe's imperial powers, of the natural resources of the

New World and other colonized spaces; and the enslavement of Africans by those same European powers, another instance of radical deracination that founded the plantation economies of the Americas, which—because of the raw commodities and general wealth those economies produced— accelerated the advent of the industrial proletariat, and industrial capitalist, within Europe. The capital generated by colonial plunder and chattel slavery combined with the "free and rightless" proletariat born of domestic histories of enclosure. This alchemy of the two primary sites or instances of primitive accumulation, Marx observed, made possible the genesis of industrial capitalism.

Though highlighting the combination of colonial and domestic instances of primitive accumulation, Marx's focus, in *Capital*'s final pages, is on the metropole—the history of enclosure and creation of the proletariat within England. This subtle myopia prefigured later interpretive elisions: the pervasive historiographic premise, for example, that the "transition" to the capitalist mode of production was initially and paradigmatically a European event; and the related assumption, propagated in the first instance by liberal political economists but faintly echoed by Marx himself, that primitive accumulation is a specific and finite stage in the history of capitalism. Both of these truisms have been subjected to trenchant scholarly critiques. Eric Williams's *Capitalism and Slavery* (1944), for example, chronicled how the combination of chattel slavery and plantation agriculture in the Americas made possible the explosive growth of industrial civilization and political emancipation of the bourgeoisie within Europe. Williams's intervention, which elaborated Marx's reflections on the relationship of slavery to capitalism, furthered the broader anticolonial reassessment of the origins of modernity at large. Writing, like Williams, in the middle of the twentieth century, C. L. R. James, Frantz Fanon, and Aimé Césaire illuminated the centrality of the periphery, the ways in which the essential political and economic forms of capitalist modernity—modes of accumulation, apparatuses of powers, and narratives of racial difference—were innovated in the space of the colony, or through colonial processes.

This anticolonial anatomization of capitalism's history, and the legacy of that history in the present, entered into implicit or explicit dialogue with

Marxist theorists of imperialism, who had sought, in the decades around the turn of the century, to grasp capital's expansionary imperative. Rosa Luxemburg, notably, advanced the crucial insight that the moment of primitive accumulation is not simply originary but constantly reprised. To avoid crises of accumulation, capital must relentlessly find and assimilate "non-capitalist strata"—land, resources, markets, and people outside of its domain. The idea that primitive accumulation is ongoing—not merely the precondition of the capitalist mode of production but a basic feature of its mature and even late form—is today largely taken for granted by historians and theorists of capital. It has informed, for example, the analysis of neoliberal mechanisms of enclosure. And it is also a core premise of the critique of settler-coloniality, which bears witness to the cultural and political persistence—within settler nations such as the United States and Brazil and indeed within the global context of colonial modernity—of racialized depredation, exclusion, and dominance.

The critical theorization of primitive accumulation, I argue in Chapter 1, seeks to excavate what Étienne Balibar has termed the *real history* of capital—to counter the mythologies authored by classical political economists and the "bourgeois historians" (Marx's term), and the amnesia of the commodity form itself. This central ambit compels and sanctions two intersecting routes of inquiry. On the one hand, empirical and theoretical treatments of primitive accumulation reveal the *history of the present*. Venturing into the "hidden abodes" of extraction, Marx and Luxemburg (et al.) bring into evidence the terror of capital's birth, and the necessarily ceaseless repetition of that foundational synthesis of state violence and "simple robbery" (as Hannah Arendt put it).[8] On the other hand, the critique of primitive accumulation directs our attention to the *presence of history*, the reverberation, throughout the social and political spheres, of deeper histories of dispossession—the "slow violence," for example, of slavery, indenture, and ecological destruction. In recent years, scholars such as Nikhil Pal Singh, Glen Coulthard, and Silvia Federici—joining the work of Luxemburg and other earlier Marxist thinkers to critical race and feminist theory—have explored the protracted effects of acute instances of extraction and expropriation, the structural entrenchment and cultural assimilation of putatively "primitive" accumulation. The history of primitive accumulation endures both because the act of dispossession is constantly reprised, and because past instances of destruction and theft continue to shape social and political life in the present.

The dual attention to the history of the present and presence of history is likewise a feature of the contemporary novel of primitive accumulation, and indeed of postcolonial fiction broadly conceived. Postcolonial literature both redresses the erasure of colonial history and makes vivid its endurance, the haunting of the present by unacknowledged imperial pasts. The novels I consider in Chapter 1 undertake this project of historical recovery, revealing the residue, in the present, of longer histories of primitive accumulation. Marlon James's *The Book of Night Women* (2009), Amitav Ghosh's *Sea of Poppies* (2008), Hernan Diaz's *In the Distance* (2017), Fiston Mwanza Mujila's *Tram 83* (2014), and Michael Ondaatje's *In the Skin of a Lion* (1987) chart the genealogic routes between the colonial past and present—the advent and contemporary reproduction of colonial modes of depredation and unfreedom, and the subjective experience of history as repetition. Together, I suggest, these formally diverse novels model the critical efficacy of narratives that occupy or address multiple spatial and temporal frames—unique histories of primitive accumulation, and their global location and lasting resonance. These novels also indicate various traditions and possibilities of critique and resistance—from counterviolence, to vernacular expressions of anticapitalist cosmopolitanism, to the enunciation of indigenous cultures of ecological reciprocity—which might expose, and perhaps even arrest or transcend, the relentless movement of primitive accumulation.

Marx's reflections on primitive accumulation chronicle the inception of two conjoined figures, the capitalist and the wage laborer. Where did the foundational capital possessed by the capitalist come from? And how was the worker dispossessed of the means of subsistence and thus compelled to sell their labor for a wage, in order to purchase the commodities necessary for survival? A greater part of *Capital*, though, is devoted to another question: How is capital, and the relationship between the capitalist and the wage laborer, reproduced? What economic laws govern the expansionary reproduction of surplus value? And what political rationalities maintain the essential relationship of capital and labor?

"Expanded reproduction" refers, for Marx, to an economic movement wherein the surplus value derived from any given advancement of capital is not simply consumed (or hoarded) by the capitalist but reinvested in the key factors of production—the fixed capital of machinery or the variable capital of labor power. Like the other moments of capital, though, expanded reproduction is distinguished by a particular culture of governance, and not just a particular mode of accumulation. In the moment of primitive accumulation, Marx contended, the birth of capital is made possible by violence—by the barrel of a gun, as by the "bloody legislation" of enclosure and other state-sanctioned acts of expropriation. But the expansionary reproduction of capital, Marx noted, is ensured rather by the "silent compulsion" of economic relations—forms of soft power that guarantee a basic, if always vulnerable and incomplete, level of popular consent, the willful submission of the "free" worker to a relationship and system that is founded on their exploitation. The abiding problem of this "silent compulsion," I argue in Chapter 2, has given rise to several cognate critical vocabularies—from Weberian conceptualizations of "spirit," to Foucauldian treatments of "governmentality," to Marxist theorizations of "ideology."

Weber's fundamental insight, in *The Protestant Ethic and the Spirit of Capitalism* (1905), is that capitalist society flourishes where and when individuals invest a certain ethical and moral faith in the system. Without those ethical and moral commitments, the process of expansionary reproduction would fail to take hold, and the relationship between the capitalist and the worker would break down. Bringing Weber's vocabulary to bear on the neoliberal present, the French sociologists Luc Boltanski and Eve Chiapello define "spirit," in simple terms, as "the ideology that justifies engagement in capitalism."[9] While Weber focused on the exceptional yet paradigmatic attributes of the Calvinist entrepreneur, Boltanski and Chiapello center the figure of the manager, and the broader vocabulary of managerialism: self-organization, flexibility, creativity, and intrinsic motivation. The insidious nature of this rhetoric, Boltanski and Chiapello submit, makes managers of us all.

Contemporary cultures of self-governance and self-management are captured as well by the concept of governmentality. Governmentality, for Foucault, signifies the "conduct of conduct"—the assimilation and enactment, by the individual, of particular logics of governance, logics that uphold capital and the state but operate by way of invisible diffusion, rather than emanate directly from the mouth of the sovereign. In his lectures at the Collège de France in the later 1970s, Foucault developed a theory of a specifically neoliberal governmentality. In the neoliberal context, Foucault observed, the market determines the state (an inversion of the classical liberal dynamic); and the subject of economic order, *homo oeconomicus*, is no longer a pretext or precondition of government, but something that must be produced by specific governmental practices. Wendy Brown, reckoning with the decades of neoliberal devastation that Foucault could only anticipate, suggests that the very distinction between the market and its outside no longer obtains. The habitat of *homo oeconomicus* is boundless, as market rationality presides over all realms of human social and political life; we are always and exclusively market actors. Correlatively, *homo politicus*, and the space of the demos, are at risk of imminent extinction or disappearance.

The imposition of neoliberal policies, though, has engendered acute and deepening *crises* of capitalist ideology, which have amplified what Raymond Williams termed "emergent" ideologies and occasioned the tentative formation of what Antonio Gramsci described as a new "historical bloc."[10] The theories of ideology composed by Williams and Gramsci, as by Stuart Hall and others—which are genealogically related to Marx's own work, most notably *The German Ideology* (1932 [1846])—possess an attention not only to the dominance of the ideas of the ruling class, but to the possibility of their denaturalization and displacement. The contest between dominant and emergent ideas plays out in myriad forums—schools, universities, media institutions, and other ideological state apparatuses; at Occupy Wall Street encampments and Black Lives Matter demonstrations. And it is dramatized in the narrative worlds of various cultural forms, including and especially, I contend, the modern novel. The novel is, at turns or at once, a site of naturalization and denaturalization. In the dialogic encounters it stages—within individual texts, and in the act of intertextual comparison—competing ways of representing the world are clarified, and subtle but materially significant moves are made in the broader and perpetual war of ideological position.

When Marx and Engels prophesied the imminent realization of a "world literature," they imagined the global generalization of a quintessentially bourgeois form—which might, precisely because of its globality, be transmuted into a medium of proletarian internationalism.[11] The dialectic of world literature, then, dovetailed, in the nineteenth century, with the dialectic—or "antinomies," in Fredric Jameson's phrasing—of realism. Terry Eagleton has famously argued that the nineteenth-century rise of realism—and specifically its heightened emphasis on interiority—was a symptom of, and complicit with, the ascendance of capitalist individualism. That interiority, moreover, was mirrored by the claustrophobic settings of many realist novels, the overlapping domestic spheres of home and nation. But the carefully delimited surrounds of the bourgeois-realist novel, its gardens and manor houses, could never quite erase the world beyond the hedgerow or sitting room walls. There is always a Bertha Mason in the attic, whether or not they make an actual appearance. In *The Afterlife of Enclosure* (2021), Carolyn Lesjak chronicles how the realist novel of the nineteenth century indexed the histories of dispossession that conditioned its evolution as a paradigmatic cultural form—the profound social and ecological transformations, at once immediate and "slow," wrought by the enclosure of common lands in Britain. Lesjak's intervention evokes Georg Lukács's classic defense of realism's critical and political efficacy. Reading Honoré de Balzac and Thomas Mann, and reflecting back on the high point of a form then being displaced by various modernisms, Lukács argued that realism possesses a certain revolutionary potentiality. The realist novel, he avowed, is uniquely capable of grasping "social totality," the objective reality of capitalist social relations—precisely because realism, whether proletarian or bourgeois in its orientation, brings into relief the disjuncture between consciousness and reality, appearance and essence, or, to invoke Althusser's definition of ideology, "the imaginary relationship of individuals to their real conditions of existence."[12]

In a corpus of contemporary fictions, bourgeois in setting and psychology, ideology is not merely a formal feature or effect, but a narrative thematic. The novels I engage in Chapter 2—Jennifer Egan's *A Visit from the Goon Squad* (2010), Jonathan Franzen's *Freedom* (2016), Benjamin Kunkel's *Indecision* (2005), and Ben Lerner's *10:04* (2014)—reckon with the problem of history and totality: the means of its concealment, and the possibility of its revelation. These novels undertake this critical work in provisional and uneven ways. All four texts, though, depict the capitalist present as marked by the declension of various publics, and by the foreclosure of historical possibility. The "end of history" is experienced, by the economically secure and socially privileged characters who people these novels, as a kind of collective depression. Resisting that malaise, the protagonists of Lerner's *10:04* and Kunkel's *Indecision*, in particular, expose the workings of capitalist ideology and begin to recover, or at least register the existence of, the histories and realities—including figments of radical futurity—that that ideology has so successfully obscured.

Today, processes of expanded reproduction unfold in the context of what Robert Brenner has termed "the long downturn"—a period, beginning in the latter part of the 1960s, marked by declining rates of profit and stagnant productivity growth (in the advanced capitalist world especially).[13] This protracted decline, which has been punctuated by acute economic shocks, has shed renewed light on both the crisis tendencies that are intrinsic to capitalism and the mechanisms that capital deploys to exploit or defer them. It has once again brought to the political-economic and conceptual fore, that is, the moment of "synthetic dispossession," which I consider in Chapter 3.

Rosa Luxemburg's *Accumulation of Capital* (1913) examined the conjoined crises of overproduction and underconsumption that roiled the Euro-American world in the decades surrounding the turn of the twentieth century. The capitalist state attempted to resolve these crises, Luxemburg discerned, through imperialism—the opening up of new markets, and the initiation of new rounds of primitive accumulation in the colonies. Observing the necessity of "non-capitalist strata" to the imperative of growth, Luxemburg argued that because the world is finite, there are intrinsic limits—spatial and therefor temporal—to both capital and capitalism. When all existing "non-capitalist" strata have been assimilated into the world market, accumulation will cease. The apparent limits of capital, though, are challenged, if never transcended, by finance capital and other instruments of synthetic accumulation. In the latter decades of the twentieth century, the architects of neoliberalism enabled the forces of financialization while working to fabricate new outsides to capital—through the privatization of public resources, services, and spaces, and calculated methods of devaluation and reacquisition.

David Harvey has used the term "accumulation by dispossession" to capture the continuities between crude and synthetic forms of depredation. My own account echoes Harvey's attention to the historical and formal connections between these two moments of capital—primitive accumulation and synthetic dispossession. I am also keen to insist, though, on their distinction. When we focus on the moment of primitive accumulation, our analysis might privilege, for example, the enactments of state and extrastate violence that accompany the mining of cobalt, copper, and tantalum in the Congo, or the violent histories of expropriation that are enshrined in the juridical apparatus of the settler-colonial state (and that permit therein the continuous extraction of resources). When our attention is instead directed toward the moment of synthetic dispossession, we might rather investigate the distinctive combinations of coercion and consent that governs the spaces and subjects of incipient or chronic precarity—the denizens of the unemployment line; the assembly line of a new, nonunion auto plant, where workers who lost their United Auto Workers (UAW) jobs to outsourcing earn a fraction of their former wage; the "tent cities" on the margins of the capitalist metropolis, occupied by the casualties of eviction and foreclosure.

When the bubbles created by emboldened financial capital burst, the subsequent crisis is used, by policy makers, as a pretext to reaffirm the state's commitment to austerity and accelerate the selling off of public infrastructure. In the advanced capitalist world, the combination of austerity and the regressive redistribution of wealth increases inequality, exposes ever-more people to insecurity, and occasions crises of consent. When the market ceases to offer even the most modest promise of material comfort, its "silent compulsion" becomes rather less compelling. But the breakdown of capital's ideological efficacy coincides with the resurgent importance of more violent forms of state power. The decline of the welfare state and growth of the police state are reciprocal processes. As Stuart Hall and the coauthors of *Policing the Crisis* (1978), writing at the neoliberal end of the 1970s, put it, in the moment of crisis, "the masks of liberal consent and popular consensus slip to reveal the reserves of coercion and force on which the cohesion of the state and its legal authority depends."[14]

The explicit mobilization of these "reserves of coercion and force"—the militarization of public and private and police, the expansion of the prison industrial complex, the police occupation of poor Black communities—has prompted new inquiries into the longer history and contemporary expressions of racialized police brutality and carceral regimes. The essential political and economic forms of synthetic dispossession have also engendered a somewhat more abstract theoretical conversation, which centers on the politics of "precarity." The principal contributors to this conversation are concerned in the first instance not with the longer history of racial capitalism, and the state violence that has always accompanied it, but with the epiphany of bourgeois insecurity—the exposure of previously secure populations to the quotidian realities of contingency and vulnerability. Neoliberalism instills, in the spheres of culture and politics and in the individual subject, the basic tenets of managerial ideology; but it also, Lauren Berlant argues, generalizes the structural realities and quotidian experiences of working-class life. What Berlant and other theorists of precarity identify is a social-political realignment—the becoming-precarious of certain segments of the middle classes, which might compel the newly insecure to recognize the connection between their own vulnerability and that of others (those for whom insecurity is not a novel condition), and to work toward the construction of alternative social formations founded on the ideal and practice of mutual care.

Though its invocation implies the possibility of futurity, the precariat is—relative to cognate terms such as the "proletariat," or the "multitude"—a tentative collective subject. The magnitude of its world-historical agency, and the precise shape of the society it might bring into being, is uncertain, even for its theoretical authors. It is, perhaps, the paradigmatic figure of the impasse of the present—the aporia that we inhabit, as the old world dies and the new one struggles to be born. The feeling of that impasse, or that indeterminacy, is, I contend in Chapter 3, made vivid by a distinct corpus of contemporary fictions. The novel of synthetic dispossession is marked by the dialogue between two narrative modalities, and two "structures of feeling." Texts such as Dave Eggers's *A Hologram for the King* (2013) and

Rafael Chirbes's *On the Edge* (2016) occupy the expanding time-space of crisis and index the waning force of capitalist ideology therein. The protagonists of these two texts—white men, in each case—have been made redundant, by financial crises or the changing geography of industrial production. Underemployed, financially unstable, they struggle to hold on to some sense of agency or purpose, within the market, and within history. Novels such as Eugene Lim's *Dear Cyborgs* (2017) and Barbara Browning's *The Gift* (2017), by contrast, trace not only decline and disappointment, but the creation of cultural and political newness, by the growing ranks of the "precariat," or by a collective subject that has yet to be named. Abjuring the pull of nostalgia—the longing for a bygone age of security and its associated hierarchies—*Dear Cyborgs* and *The Gift* approach the political horizons that come into view in the context of capitalism's diminished spirit, the intimacies and solidarities that take root within the wreckage of crises that are both located and general.

An important strand of contemporary critique—developed by scholars such as Anna Kornbluh, Leigh Claire La Berge, Annie McClanahan, Elizabeth Holt, Alison Shonkwiler, and Arne De Boever—examines the relationship between crisis (crises of finance in particular) and cultural form, across a range of periods and geographies.[15] This critical current is concerned with the intimacy between fictitious capital and fiction itself, the technologies that represent value—money, debt and credit, stocks and bonds—and various modes of literary or cultural representation.[16] The affinity between capitalism and the novel, that is, is formal as well as historical. Just as the value of the S&P 500 acts as a metonym for "the economy," the novel distills into narrative shape—or allegorizes—the complexity of capitalist social relations. The metonymic function of the novel, moreover, is especially pronounced in contemporary financial fiction. Therein, La Berge observes, finance often stands in for capital broadly conceived; it acts, in other words, as a figure for an economic totality that remains obscure.[17] My own account registers the paradigmatic status of finance capital within the current capitalist conjuncture. But I also set out to resist the tendency that La Berge identifies—the metonymic reduction of global capital to financial processes and instruments. My comparative approach, in this book, locates the fictions of finance—the mechanisms and mediations of synthetic dispossession—in relation to the political, economic, and literary forms that mark the moments of primitive accumulation and expanded reproduction.

The critique of the current crisis, and of capitalist crises in the abstract, is sharpened when it attends to capital's essential heterogeneity and unevenness. That unevenness was analyzed, in the aftermath of the Russian Revolution, by Leon Trotsky. His account of the revolution's trajectory, and the crises that made it possible, included an intensive treatment of the concept of "uneven and combined development." In pre-capitalist societies, Trotsky concluded in *History of the Russian Revolution* (1932), the introduction of capitalist rationality rarely prefaces its immediate and total ascendance. In the colonies, and in other peripheral or semi-peripheral spaces, emergent capitalist forms combine with non-capitalist ways of organizing social and economic life. The Russian Revolution, Trotsky asserted, demonstrated that the advent of communism in unevenly developed capitalist societies would necessarily be brought about by an alliance between the peasantry and the immature proletariat, which would preempt the rise of the bourgeoisie and seize the levers of political and economic power.

Though focused on Russia, Trotsky presented the theory of "uneven and combined development" as a universal law of capital, one that could be brought to bear on specific national case studies, and on the broader world-system. Writing at the same time as Trotsky, Marxist thinkers such as Antonio Gramsci and José Carlos Mariátegui analyzed the unevenness of capital within Italy and Peru, respectively, while situating those national geographies in relation to global patterns of uneven development. In the middle and later decades of the twentieth century, meanwhile, a coterie of anticolonial and postcolonial thinkers—among them C. L. R. James, Aimé Césaire, Frantz Fanon, Walter Rodney, and Stuart Hall—documented the specifically colonial nature of capital's geographic asymmetry. This anticolonial tradition, I argue in Chapter 4, is a crucial resource for the project of theorizing the unity and difference of global capital. Redressing the parochialisms of much Euro-American Marxist thought, the anticolonial apprehension of capitalist modernity as colonial modernity discerns the dialectical interrelation of different forms and sites of political and economic power within a global frame. And this critical effectiveness is magnified, I contend, when the multiple *moments* of capital are afforded analytic prominence.

Of special utility to my theoretical framework is the concept of "articulation." For Althusser, "articulation" signified an interrelation wherein the component parts maintain their distinctive form. His invocation of the concept—and the related idea, borrowed from Marx, of "complex unity"—highlighted the contingent combination of capital's constitutive contradictions. This understanding of "articulation" was later elaborated by Stuart Hall. In "Race, Articulation, and Societies Structured in Dominance" (1980), Hall considered the interplay between the combination of different modes of production and the intersection of different modes of social differentiation. Summoning Trotsky's theory of uneven and combined development, Hall observed that the capitalist sector in apartheid South Africa relied upon putatively non-capitalistic economic practices and relations; the persistence of subsistence agricultural production, and the existence of a nonproletarianized population, allowed capital to remunerate waged workers below the cost of their reproduction. Concomitantly, the degradation of Black labor helped guarantee the ideological enlistment of the white working class. Racism, that is, functions, ideologically, as a primary means through which the "white fractions" of the working class imagine and "live" their relationship to nonwhite workers and capital itself.[18]

The concept of "articulation" models a critical approach that is attentive to difference as well as sameness, and that perceives how the whole is structured in unevenness and contradiction. Addressing the combination and convergence of different moments of capital compels, too, a treatment of the complex interrelation of differentially raced, gendered, and classed subjects—within national spaces and within the capitalist world-system. The cultural and structural substance of that interrelation was anatomized by Fanon. In a suggestive passage in *The Wretched of the Earth* (1961), Fanon contrasted the prevailing modes of capitalist governance in the metropole and in the colony. In the metropole, the exploitation of labor was enabled by the "structure of moral reflexes . . . [and] aesthetic expressions of respect for the established order," which create around the worker an "atmosphere of submission." In the colony, "the policeman and the soldier, by their immediate presence and their frequent and direct action maintain contact with the native and advise him by means of rifle butts and napalm not to budge."[19] Put slightly differently, the primitive accumulation of capital in the colonies was conditioned by the "language of pure force" (also Fanon's phrase), while the reproduction of capital in the metropole was made possible by ingrained moral sentiments. Fanon's account, though, implied the interrelation of and not simply the distinction between colony and metropole. Primitive accumulation in the colonies fueled processes of expanded reproduction within the metropole, including the social democratic construction of the ideological state apparatuses. And the racialized negation of the colonized subject helped facilitate the interpellation of the white worker back home; that interpellation was further secured by the social exclusion and super-exploitation of racial others within the metropole itself.[20] In the putative aftermath of the colonial period, these interrelations mutated in pace with the exigencies of accumulation, as synthetic methods of dispossession—advancing what Henri Lefebvre termed the "colonization of everyday life"—joined with neocolonial processes of extractive industry, and enduring relations of expanded reproduction, to renew the ideal and reality of economic growth.[21]

In the late-neoliberal present these patterns of interconnection persist. Expanded reproduction continues to be enabled by outright theft. And the power of capitalist ideology continues to be made possible in part by the enactment of crude state violence, in the Global South, and in spaces of marginality and exclusion within the Global North. That the "reserves of coercion and force" are applied with such severity on the other side of the tracks ensures the potency of the "structure of moral reflexes" on this side. But the integrity of that structure, the efficacy of capitalist ideology, is today threatened by the heightening of inequality and generalization of insecurity. And as the spirit of capital continues to fade, new political possibilities—new routes of solidarity, for example, between the dispossessed migrant, alienated or exploited wage laborer, and newly proletarianized middle class—might come into view.

In addition to Marxists from the (semi)-periphery such as Gramsci and Mariátegui, and theorists of colonialism and its afterlives such as Fanon and Hall, there are other reservoirs of critique to which we might turn, in our effort to grasp the interrelation of different forms of political and economic power, and different languages of resistance. Informed by the anticolonial and postcolonial reading of capitalist modernity's colonial fundament, the tradition of world-systems theory maps the contradictions and asymmetries that define the relationship between three structural positions: core, periphery, and semi-periphery. Immanuel Wallerstein, in accord with thinkers such as Walter Rodney, examined the dialectic of development and underdevelopment, the ways in which the wealth of the core derives from the depredation of the periphery. He observed, too, echoing Fanon among others, how the strength of the "state machinery" in the core—including its ideological apparatuses—corresponds to the prevalence of extralegal violence on the periphery.

World-systems theory maps the geographic differences that constitute capitalist modernity at large. It implies at the same time, however, the synchronization of different moments of production. The problem of synchrony and nonsynchrony, or simultaneity and nonsimultaneity, is an abiding concern of Marxist thought. Marx himself gestured toward this dialectic, in the *Grundrisse*, when he referred to the "annihilation of space by time"—and the imperative of synchronizing the various activities of the productive process—while acknowledging that capital "moves in contradictions which are constantly overcome but just as constantly posited."[22] The drive to surpass spatial and temporal barriers is countered by the fact that the creation of capital requires the production and exploitation of difference—differences of productive modality that have a spatial character, and that might appear as differences of history or time. The historical implication of this tension—between the universalizing drive of capital and the perpetual reproduction of its fundamental contradictions—was explored, in the early twentieth century, by Ernst Bloch. Reflecting on the residue of pre-capitalist social forms in interwar Germany, Bloch invoked "the simultaneity of the non-simultaneous" (a phrase that is sometimes translated as the "contemporaneity of the non-contemporaneous").[23] This idea, which resonated with theories of uneven and combined development, was later engaged by thinkers such as Étienne Balibar, who diagnosed, in *Reading Capital* (1965), the "coexistence of several modes of production," in periods of "transition" most especially.[24] Althusser's related conceptualization of the "conjuncture" captured the notion of a structuralist unity that is historically contingent. It sought to reconcile, in other words, the synchrony of capital and the immutable fact of history (or, the two meanings of "moment" that I outline above).

Another way of thinking about the relationship between capital's historical evolution and dialectical totality has been advanced, more recently, by Giovanni Arrighi. The global history of capital, Arrighi contended in *The Long Twentieth Century* (1994), can be divided into four "systemic cycles," which correspond to particular geographic loci: Genoese (fifteenth to early seventeenth century), Dutch (late sixteenth through eighteenth century), British (latter eighteenth to early twentieth century), and US (late nineteenth century through to the present). Adapting Marx's M-C-M' formula—for the logic of capital's valorization—to the movement of history, Arrighi argued that each cycle contains two successive phases: MC, the phase of material expansion, in which money capital "'sets in motion' an increasing mass of commodities"; and CM' (or, simply, MM'), the phase of financial expansion, in which accumulated money capital severs its ties to the process of commodity production and is invested in purely financial speculation.[25] Arrighi registered the dialectical unity of productive and financial capital; but his account privileged the diachronic shape of each cycle of accumulation and the diachronic progression from one cycle to another—the linear enlargement of the capitalist world-economy. According to this framework, we currently inhabit the late financial "autumn" of the US systemic cycle. Arrighi's historical theorization of capitalism remains luminous. And I agree, to join my own conceptual vocabulary to Arrighi's, that the moment of synthetic dispossession is today archetypal (in the advanced capitalist world, in particular). But the moments of primitive accumulation and expanded reproduction are very much extant. This or any previous capitalist conjuncture is distinguished, I argue, not merely by the dominance of one moment of capital above others, but by the dynamics of their synchronization.

Over the past decade or so, some of the foremost venues for Marxist theory—Verso, for example, and the journal *Historical Materialism*—have curated discussions of capitalist modernity's temporal multiplicity and synchronic unity. Notable interventions in this conversation include Massimiliano Tomba's *Marx's Temporalities* (2014) and Stavros Tombazos's

Time in Marx: The Categories of Time in Marx's Capital (2013). These works propose an important new critical vocabulary for detailing the structures or experiences of time that mark, for example, the spheres of production, circulation, and consumption, or the concurrent combination of specific mechanisms of valorization. "The categories of the capitalist mode of production," Tomba writes, "do not unfold in diachronic succession, but present themselves as a unitary constellation within which each concept, as a monad, is enclosed."[26] Tomba notes that "the unilinear conception of historical time," which characterized many twentieth-century Marxist theories of history, "[allows] different social forms to be pigeon-holed as advanced or backward."[27] This tendency, as I have discussed, is a pitfall of stadial historical approaches; but it also colors invocations of the "simultaneity of the non-simultaneous," which imagine the coincidence of the archaic and the modern. "The juxtaposition of a plurality of historical times," Tomba writes, "where forms of peasant-slavery exist alongside high-tech production in the superannuation of the dualism between centre and periphery, not only explains nothing, but is obfuscatory. . . . The real problem," he continues, "is their combination by means of the world-market's mechanisms of synchronization."[28] Emulating this important observation, but ranging beyond *Capital* and Marxist thought, I demonstrate how diverse theoretical traditions—from Weberian inquiries into the "spirit" of capitalism to postcolonial critiques of the relationship between capitalist accumulation and racial thinking and practice—heighten our understanding of the synchronous combination of capital's multiple moments.

The project of apprehending the sameness and difference of global capital, and the collective subject that might transform this world into another one, is central not just to theory but to world literature. And in the literary sphere as in the theoretical one, the contributions of anticolonial and postcolonial thought have been decisive. In its nineteenth-century enunciation—by Goethe in the first instance, and by Marx and Engels—"world literature" (*Weltliteratur*) pointed to the correspondence between global political and economic forces and global cultural forms; the accent was on the universalizing effects of capital, rather than the differences—inequalities—it both produced and exploited, the oneness of the world rather than the fractures and divisions that make it up. Synthesizing

Marxist and postcolonial approaches, the contemporary critique of world literature—in the work of scholars such as Rey Chow, Pascale Casanova, Emily Apter, Franco Moretti, Sarah Brouillette, and the Warwick Research Collective, among many others—addresses instead the implication of literary production in global relations of uneven and combined development: the circulation of literary texts through global markets, and the formal strategies performed by literary texts to represent the totality and contradictions of global capital.

Moretti's influential essay "Conjectures on World Literature" (2000) defined world literature as a planetary system that mirrors the world-system of capital.[29] In recent years, critics have explored various aspects of that fundamental interrelation. To cite just two significant examples: Brouillette's *UNESCO and the Fate of the Literary* (2019) uses one cultural institution as a lens onto the uneven global determinants, and uneven global consequence, of the production and consumption of contemporary world literature. The Warwick Research Collective's *Combined and Uneven Development: Towards a New Theory of World Literature* (2015), meanwhile, examines how the literary forms of the periphery and semi-periphery register the "singularity . . . and internal heterogeneity" of capitalist modernity.[30] My own invocation of "world literature" stresses the imperial conditions of possibility for that generality and that difference. Herein, "world literature" signifies a cultural and critical formation that renders the "complex unity" of the global capitalist order brought into being by empire and its afterlives—the entanglement of different spaces of capital, and the synchronic combination of different moments of capital, within the historical and geographic frame of colonial modernity.

In dialogue with contemporary theorists and practitioners of world literature, I consider in the latter part of Chapter 4 how three contemporary novels illustrate the multiple moments of global capital. Pitchaya Sudbanthad's *Bangkok Wakes to Rain* (2019) illustrates how the entwined histories of capital and empire continue to shape the precarious present and antediluvian future of one global city. Inhabiting a national frame, Neel Mukherjee's *The Lives of Others* (2014) reckons with the Naxalite resistance to modes of primitive accumulation in contemporary India, while self-reflexively incorporating the formal strategies of concealment that keep long and enduring histories of expropriation out of view. Rachel Kushner's *The Flamethrowers* (2013), the novel with which I conclude, is more planetary in its scope. Set in the late 1970s, as the advent of neoliberalism coincided with the introduction of post-Fordist relations and cultures of accumulation, *The Flamethrowers* connects processes of synthetic dispossession in deindustrializing Manhattan to the dialectics of exploitation and revolt in the Italian auto industry and the brutal harvesting of rubber in Brazil. Evincing the three moments of contemporary capital—their articulation within three spatial scales—each of these novels makes audible as well the unique languages of critique that are invented and enunciated therein, by distinct collective subjects. They contribute, that is, to the central objective of my investigations in this book—the illumination of the essential unity and differential composition of global capital.

CHAPTER 1

Primitive Accumulation

IN THE CONCLUDING CHAPTERS OF *Capital*'s first volume, Marx undertakes a suggestive meditation on the history of primitive accumulation: the forceful "divorcing of the producer from the means of production," and "the extirpation, enslavement and entombment in mines of the indigenous population of [America], . . . the conquest and plunder of India, the conversion of Africa into a preserve for the commercial hunting of black skins."[1] In the metropole and the colonies, the birth of capital, Marx wrote, was "written in the annals of mankind in letters of blood and fire."[2]

Though chronicling the terror of capital's birth, Marx shared with classical political economy an understanding of primitive accumulation as a *specific* phase in the emergence and evolution of the capitalist mode of production. He did not, in other words, devote a great deal of attention to the not simply primordial but perpetual importance of primitive accumulation to the process of valorization.[3] In *Capital* ([1867] 1990), the foundational terror of primitive accumulation gives way to the "silent compulsion" of economic relations. This is a protracted transformation, unfolding over decades and even centuries, but a definite one. "In its embryonic state, in its state of becoming," Marx wrote, "capital cannot yet use the sheer force of economic relations to secure its right to absorb a sufficient quantity of surplus labor, but must be aided by the power of the state." In time, however, "the 'free' worker, owing to the greater development of the capitalist mode of production, makes a voluntary agreement, i.e. is compelled by social conditions to sell the whole of his active life."[4]

Later thinkers, however, did develop empirical and theoretical treatments of primitive accumulation's ongoing centrality to the maintenance, and continuous reinvention, of capitalism. "The original sin of simple robbery," Hannah Arendt observed, "must be repeated lest the motor of accumulation suddenly die down."[5] Arendt's insight borrowed from Rosa Luxemburg, who observed capitalism's dependence on "non-capitalist social strata." In order to survive, Luxemburg argued, capital must constantly find and claim spaces outside of its dominion. Luxemburg was responding to an epoch in the history of capitalism that Marx himself did not live to witness—the late-nineteenth-century height of modern European imperialism, which highlighted the "spatial fix" to crises of accumulation, the tendency of surplus capital to seek out and occupy new sites of production and new markets for consumption. This period and the theoretical interventions it provoked illustrated the continuing importance of primitive accumulation and coercive state violence within a mature stage of capitalism that Marx imagined as defined by expanded reproduction and the "silent compulsion" of the market.

The advent and deepening of neoliberal methods of dispossession has occasioned a renewed critical interest in the endurance of primitive accumulation. Joining the work of Luxemburg and other earlier Marxist thinkers to theories of coloniality, race, and gender, scholars such as Glen Coulthard, Nikhil Pal Singh, and Silvia Federici have explored the routes of continuity between original and modern histories of primitive accumulation. The contemporary theorization of primitive accumulation examines how specific instances of expropriation—for example, the enclosure of common lands or theft of indigenous resources—dovetail with the protracted effects of depredation, and the structural constancy of the raced and gendered relations of dominance that are formed in and reproduced by the genesis of capital. Primitive accumulation is an extant phenomenon, that is, not only because the act of dispossession is constantly reprised, but because ostensibly historical instances of extraction or enclosure continue to shape the structure and lived experience of social and political order in the present. The critique of and resistance to primitive accumulation, I contend, directs our attention to both the history of the present and the presence of history.

This twofold ambit is likewise enacted by a growing strand of contemporary fiction. Historical novels of slavery, indenture, and settler-colonialism, such as Marlon James's *The Book of Night Women* (2009), Amitav Ghosh's *Sea of Poppies* (2008), and Hernan Diaz's *In the Distance* (2017), bring into view the longer history of primitive accumulation. Fictions of latter-day extractive industry such as Fiston Mwanza Mujila's *Tram 83* (2014) and Michael Ondaatje's *In the Skin of a Lion* (1987), meanwhile, reveal the continuity between original and contemporary modes of crude dispossession—the essential coloniality of capital. Together, these five novels clarify how, in the moment of primitive accumulation, time is experienced, and history is imagined, as repetition; and if that repetition evokes, in the present, the apparent intractability of the apparatuses of primitive accumulation, it also signals the abiding urgency of resistance. The critical vocabularies and narratives that guide that resistance, which these novels model in their form and content, are addressed to and operate within multiple spatial and temporal frames—the located instance of extraction or expropriation and its planetary context and reverberation. And they indicate, however gesturally, the immanence of other ways of imagining, relating to, and constructing the world: from indigenous cultures of ecological reciprocity, to the possibility of demotic and cosmopolitan movements against the local and global authority of primitive accumulation.

The Origins of Capital

The placement within *Capital* of Marx's reflections on primitive accumulation is counterintuitive. Where one might expect to find the prehistory of capital at the beginning of the volume it is in fact deferred to the end. *Capital* opens instead with Marx's analysis of the commodity form—its internal logics and social conditions and effects. In his brief introduction to the concept of commodity fetishism, Marx outlined the process—defined by the objectification of labor in the commodity, and the related transmutation of use value into exchange value—through which "the definite social relation between men assumes . . . the fantastic form of a relation between things,"[6] an instance of reification that corresponds to an inverse transformation, the personification of things. Together, the thingification of persons and the personification of things obscure the history of the unique commodity and the surplus value embedded therein—the individual labor and contingent social relations from which the commodity emerged. *Capital*'s entire opening chapter—and these crucial paragraphs perhaps most especially—foreground the problem of *history*, even as it presents a distinctly ahistorical account of capital.

The commodity, Marx demonstrates at the outset of *Capital*, conceals its own history—in particular the exploitation of labor that produces the surplus value that is latent in the commodity and actualized by its sale. But this intrinsic technology of erasure is compounded, Marx's reflections on primitive accumulation suggest, by externally authored narratives—the mythology of capital's beginning authored by liberal political economists. Countering the liberal assumption of capital's pacific origins, Marx chronicled, in the concluding chapters of *Capital*, the originary modes of expropriation that made the expropriation of labor possible. The creation of capital, he observed, is the consequence of a meeting—the coming together of "the owners of money, means of production, means of subsistence" and "free workers, the sellers of their own labor power."[7] The history of primitive accumulation, that is, is the history of the formation of two classes: the wage laborer and the industrial capitalist. How was the worker "robbed of all their own means of production" and thus forced to sell their labor for a wage? And how did the capitalist acquire the surplus that enabled them to purchase the labor power of others?

The expropriation of the agricultural population in Europe took several forms, over the course of several centuries (from the fifteenth to the nineteenth, in England). "The spoliation of the Church's property, the fraudulent alienation of the state domains, the theft of the common lands, the usurpation of feudal and clan property . . . under circumstances of ruthless terrorism." All of these instances of dispossession, Marx wrote, "were just so many idyllic methods of primitive accumulation. They conquered the field for capitalist agriculture, incorporated the soil into capital, and created for the urban industries the necessary supplies of free and rightless proletarians."[8] This "free and rightless" proletariat, though, "could not possibly be absorbed by the nascent manufactures as fast as it was thrown upon the world." The forcible separation of the people from the land, and from the means of production more broadly, created not only a class of factory workers but masses of "vagabonds and paupers"—a wageless *lumpen* that depressed the compensation of the industrially assimilated proletariat, and that was disciplined by "bloody legislation," anti-vagabondage laws that penalized the landless and unemployed for their largely enforced condition.[9] Laws governing the movement, and ways of being, of the newly "freed" class of men cooperated and coincided with the state regulation of wages and the length of the working day, and with more immediate coercive measures—internal to the factory—that heightened the rate of exploitation. Such laws and disciplinary codes are not, of course, unique to the moment of primitive accumulation. Marx was, however, careful to highlight their importance in the context of the proletariat's genesis, when the "consent" of the wage laborer is far from guaranteed, when "grotesquely terroristic laws" are still the primary instrument through which the "discipline necessary for the system of wage-labour" is established.[10]

If the expropriation of the agricultural producer at home created a mass of "free and rightless" workers, the birth of the industrial capitalist was made possible, in large part, by the depredation of the colonized world. In India, the English East India Company enjoyed exclusive monopolies of the tea trade, as well as the trade in "salt, opium, betel, and other commodities." Because company officials fixed the price of these commodities, "trade" was a mere euphemism for theft, and "great fortunes sprang up like mushrooms in a day; primitive accumulation proceeded without the advance of even a shilling."[11] In the Atlantic world, meanwhile, the traffic in African slaves, and the wealth those slaves produced on the plantations of the Americas, further conditioned the commercial advances of Europe's imperial powers, and the establishment therein of the emerging capitalist class, the bourgeoisie. The wealth generated by these histories of primitive accumulation, in the colonial theater, combined with new methods and institutions of securitization—public debt, international credit, the banking system—and the nascent proletariat to catalyze the ascendance of industrial capital and the industrial capitalist. "The treasures captured outside

Europe," Marx wrote, "by undisguised looting, enslavement and murder flowed back to the mother country and were turned into capital there."[12]

Marx's treatment of primitive accumulation recognized the structural interrelation of endogenous and exogenous histories of dispossession. "The veiled slavery of the wage-labourers in Europe," Marx observed, "needed the unqualified slavery of the New World as its pedestal."[13] The problem of the precise relationship between the institution of chattel slavery in the Americas and advent of capitalism within Europe continues to occupy a prominent place within historiographic debates about the origins of political and economic modernity. Was slavery internal to the nascent capitalist mode of production or one essential element of its constitutive outside? This question bears upon how we periodize, or locate historically, the moment of primitive accumulation. Does the moment of primitive accumulation belong to the time of the capitalist mode of production broadly conceived? Or does it rather correspond to the liminal juncture of *transition*? Responding in affirmation to the first question compels an inquiry into the ways in which primitive accumulation is perpetual, fundamental to capital's mature and not merely embryonic form. When we respond in affirmation to the second question, meanwhile, we are more likely to confine primitive accumulation to the *prehistory* of capital, its past rather than its present. As Louis Althusser, Étienne Balibar, and others have argued, Marx himself was clear to mark the distinction—both historical and categorical/conceptual—between primitive accumulation and the capitalist mode of production. The moment of primitive accumulation gives rise and gives way to the moment of expanded reproduction, wherein the "silent compulsion" of the market—rather than crude state violence—governs economic relations. And the laws of capital that Marx describes in *Capital*'s first seven parts cannot be brought to bear on the concept of primitive accumulation introduced in its eighth. "The production of this original capital," Balibar writes, "constitutes a threshold and crossing this threshold cannot be explained by the action of the law of capitalist accumulation alone."[14] My intention is not to dispute Balibar's reading. But I am interested, throughout the course of this book, in revealing the synchronic interrelation of these ostensibly discrete and diachronic moments—along with a third moment, "synthetic dispossession"—and perhaps even arriving at a new theory of how their respective rationalities comprise one unitary logic of accumulation and governance.

Repetition and Reverberation

Rosa Luxemburg's *Accumulation of Capital* was published in 1913, in the wake of the financial upheavals that shook the capitalist world around the turn of the century, and against the backdrop of a global geopolitical order shaped by European imperialism. Attempting to work through the connections between these two historical circumstances, Luxemburg's critical elaboration of Marx's theorization of capital illuminated the central role played by imperialism—the constant assimilation or appropriation, by the imperial state, of non-capitalist spaces and entities—in resolving, or deferring, domestic crises of overproduction and underconsumption. Luxemburg argued that primitive accumulation remains a central component of capitalist generation beyond the time-space of foundation. And relatedly, she insisted that state violence does not recede in importance once the rationalities of the market have been naturalized, but continues to facilitate the extension and expansion of capital.

"For Marx," Luxemburg noted, "the processes [of primitive accumulation] are incidental, illustrating merely the genesis of capital, its first appearance in the world; they are, as it were, travails by which the capitalist mode of production emerges from a feudal society. As soon as he comes to analyse the capitalist process of production and circulation," she observed, "he reaffirms the universal and exclusive domination of capitalist production." Resisting the assumption of that "universal and exclusive domination"—and the historical rupture it implies between the moment of primitive accumulation and the moment of expanded reproduction—Luxemburg contended that "capitalism in its full maturity also depends in all respects on non-capitalist strata and social organisations existing side by side with it."[15] Such "non-capitalist strata" are, in other words, a structural imperative within the modern capitalist world-system. Their purpose is threefold: they function as a potential market for finished commodities, when the demand of the home market cannot keep pace with supply; they act as a source of raw materials, when demand increases or reserves of raw materials are diminished; and they contain reservoirs of unfree—enslaved or otherwise violently coerced—labor, the seizure of which enables the expansionary reproduction of capital to continue. In short, the existence and expropriation of non-capitalist strata ensure that the surplus is not simply realized as value but turned back into productive capital.

To illustrate the central import of "non-capitalist" forms of labor to mature capitalist processes, Luxemburg invoked the English cotton history of the nineteenth century. Her brief rehearsal of this classic example betrays an interpretive disjunction. Echoing Marx, Luxemburg recalled that "[t]he emancipation of labour power from primitive social conditions and its absorption by the capitalist wage system is one of the indispensable historical bases of capitalism." But her very next sentence highlights a different historical movement, "the millions of African Negros who were shipped to America to provide the labour power for the plantations." This population of slaves was, of course, later "incorporated in the class of wage labourers in a capitalist system"—a transition, some historians have argued, that was required if the broader capitalist economy of the United States was to avoid stagnation.[16] In the historical example that Luxemburg cites, however, it was the act of enslavement rather than emancipation that provided the necessary fuel for the English cotton industry to flourish. In other words, the crucial moment is when capital joins itself to, and exploits, the "primitive" social form of chattel slavery, and not when it encourages the transformation of slaves into "free" wage laborers. The relationship between the plantation and the industrial factory, moreover, was not ephemeral, a contingent combination always destined to lead toward emancipation, but endured for centuries. And the eventuality of its undoing, while determined in part by economic imperatives, was also an effect of slave struggle and other political pressures that cannot be reduced to the hidden logics of capitalist progress.

Luxemburg, all this is to say, identified and grappled with one of the core contradictions in Marx's theory of accumulation—"the dialectical conflict that capitalism needs non-capitalist social organisations as the setting for its development, [but] it proceeds by assimilating the very conditions which alone can ensure its own existence."[17] If, as Marx suggested, the accumulation process endeavors "to establish the exclusive and universal domination of capitalist production in all countries and for all branches of industry," the realization of this universalizing tendency would mean the disappearance of those conditions required for the continuing genesis of capital. Although the "non-capitalist strata" are "indispensable for accumulation, the latter proceeds at the cost of this medium nevertheless, by eating it up."[18] Capitalism "strives to become universal," but it is "immanently incapable" of doing so: "In its living history it is a contradiction in itself, and its movement of accumulation provides a solution to the conflict and aggravates it at the same time."[19] The instant of capital's achieved universality is also the instant of its death (if, crucially, an alternative social-economic formation is ready to assert itself, intellectually, culturally, and institutionally). In her efforts to revise and expand Marx's theory of capitalist subsumption, Luxemburg thus highlighted the need to counter two "fictions": the idea that the moment of primitive accumulation is merely foundational, and the notion that the movement of reproduction is narrowly defined by the "internal relationship between the branches of capitalist economy," in a context in which the commodity has eclipsed all non-capitalist social and economic forms. She sought to arrive, alternatively, at a theory of the laws of accumulation that would more fully explicate the dialectical interrelation of capital and its outside.

Central to this critical revision of Marx's framework is a heightened recognition of and engagement with the importance of outright violence to the imperative of accumulation. Marx's reflections on primitive accumulation chronicle the violence of capitalism's beginnings. But they depict that violence as limited to the time of foundation, and as a necessary negation of more "primitive" social and economic relations—feudalism, for example—that would hasten the development and ultimate negation of capitalism itself. When Marx writes, in relation to primitive accumulation, that "force is the midwife of every society pregnant with a new one," one can hear the romantic hint in his voice. Luxemburg's inquiry resisted these teleological implications, by accenting the fact that primitive accumulation is not a finite stage of capitalist becoming, which is always destined to be surpassed, but a central component of capitalism's mature form.[20] And the constancy of primitive accumulation implies the constancy of state violence. "Militarism," Luxemburg observed, "fulfils a quite definite function in the history of capital, accompanying as it does every historical phase of accumulation"—from the plunder of land and raw materials, to the enslavement and proletarianization of colonized populations, to the forcing open of non-capitalist markets and protection of European investment capital therein, to the inter-imperial contest for control over what remains of the non-capitalist world.[21]

Luxemburg's accounting of the constancy of dispossession, and the violence that facilitates it, prefigured the contemporary theorization of primitive accumulation in several ways. Her insights into the *repetition* of putatively original methods of expropriation have informed a concomitant investigation into the *reverberation*, across time, of longer histories of depredation. And her intimation of the spatial and racial logics of capitalism's "dual character"—the dialectical interrelation of freedom and unfreedom, security and insecurity, rights-based belonging and rightless vulnerability—anticipated the historical-theoretical reappraisal of the distinct modes of social differentiation that the genesis of capital produces and exploits. Joining these two routes of inquiry, contemporary thinkers such as Coulthard, Singh, and Federici anatomize, respectively, the cultural and structural expressions, in the present, of the principal histories of racialized and gendered dispossession—the settler-colonial conquest of Native lands, the institution of chattel slavery, and the foundational expropriation of women's bodies.

Contemporary theories of primitive accumulation, that is, privilege those spaces, histories, and subjects that are not precisely apprehended by the classical Marxist account of the capital–labor antinomy. Coulthard's *Red Skin, White Masks*, for example, argues for the need to foreground the colonial relation—rather than the merely capitalist one—in our critique of historical and contemporary enactments of primitive accumulation. "The history and experience of dispossession, not proletarianization," Coulthard observes, "has been the dominant background structure shaping the character of the historical relationship between Indigenous peoples and [the state]"—in Canada, the object of his inquiry, and in other settler-colonies.[22] Examining indigenous struggles against enduring forms of settler-colonial power, Coulthard reveals the complex rationalities and technologies of governance that enable historical and contemporary

processes of primitive accumulation—the state theft of indigenous territory and resources. Though acknowledging the "persistent role that un-
concealed, violent dispossession continues to play in the reproduction
of colonial and capitalist social relations in both the domestic and global
contexts," Coulthard is preeminently concerned with those apparatuses of
power that *are* concealed and apparently nonviolent.[23] More specifically,
Red Skin, White Masks outlines how the Canadian state deploys narratives
of liberal multiculturalism and the politics of "recognition" to silence by
assimilating indigenous rights to the commons and indigenous articulations of free and autonomous selfhood.

The title of Coulthard's book refers to Frantz Fanon's *Black Skin, White
Masks*, a text, as Coulthard notes, that analyzed the "specific modes of colonial thought, desire, and behavior that implicitly or explicitly commit the
colonized to the types of practices and subject positions that are required
for their continued domination."[24] This understanding of colonial governance evokes C. L. R. James's epic account of Toussaint Louverture and
the Haitian Revolution, *The Black Jacobins* (1938; 1963). In the appendix
added to that volume's 1963 reissue, James contended that chattel rationality did not simply negate the humanity of the enslaved; the space of the
plantation also *produced* particular, and particularly modern, subjects and
subjectivities. James's depiction of the productive powers of the plantation
system noted that the enslaved were forced to enunciate their claim to
personhood and freedom in the very Enlightenment vocabulary that had
sought their enslavement. David Scott, in his postcolonial rereading of *The
Black Jacobins*, names this intractable contradiction "the tragedy of colonial
enlightenment."[25] When Coulthard asserts that the politics of recognition
are less a route toward indigenous self-determination than a crucial technology of colonial power, he is highlighting a similar problematic. It is
instructive, though, that in James's narration Toussaint's fateful error is his
conviction that the French will be moved by the radical invocation, on the
part of the enslaved, of the Enlightenment ideals—recently given a concrete political instantiation in the context of the French Revolution—of
man and citizen, liberty and equality. Toussaint, James suggested, arrived
too late to the Fanonian conclusion earlier reached by the masses—that
the system of chattel slavery would only respond to the language it most

fluently spoke, that of violence. In the concluding chapters of *Red Skin, White Masks*, Coulthard traces a similar, if less dramatic, transformation of consciousness and strategy: the recent turn—in the wake of the Conservative government's violation of indigenous treaty rights in 2012—away from the institutional levers of recognition and accommodation, and toward more militant practices of direct action against the ongoing theft of indigenous land and resources. The "Idle No More" movement, for example, has deployed a variety of tactics, including the blockade of roads, railway lines, and bridges. Though not violent in a corporeal sense, these instances of resistance are forms of economic destruction. And in beginning to peel away the layers of ideology and juridical right that today disguise the government's looting of indigenous communities, such actions have shed renewed light on the state violence—the state's monopoly on legitimate force—that has always attended the primitive accumulation of capital.

Perhaps what is required is a more expansive definition of state violence, one that might privilege the contiguity between performances of military and police repression and the more mundane workings of the law. Antonio Negri has observed that violence "constitutes the vehicle between accumulation and right. It has no problem presenting in legal terms, or better, making law a subsidiary element of accumulation."[26] The law does not represent the conversion of direct violence into noncoercive means of discipline or control, but is, rather, *the* "direct expression" of the revolutionary violence of the bourgeoisie.[27] The law, that is, occasions the structural realization of capital's essential violence, the institutionalization and perpetual reproduction of the "state of exception" under which capital enters the world. "Constituent power," Negri writes, "has become a constituted power, a sort of average level of violence that overdetermines every social relationship."[28] The presence of primitive accumulation is not only defined by recurring rounds of naked expropriation, but by the enshrinement as law of extra-economic—and indeed extra-juridical—violence.

The legal codification and structural constancy of that violence is clarified by racial thought and practice. The "configuration of capitalism" that is founded on chattel slavery, Nikhil Pal Singh suggests, "develops racism as a dimension of its general form."[29] Race marks the "divisions between (re)productive humanity and disposable humanity," and mediates the shifting interrelations of waged and wageless life, fracturing the proletariat and honing the instruments of state violence that manage "spatiotemporal zones of insecurity and existential threat" (the abode of the reserve army of labor, the part who have no part).[30] In dialogue with and expanding upon Luxemburg, Singh examines the racial character of the dialectic of inside and outside, the co-belonging of exploitation and dispossession, incorporation and exclusion. The degradation of blackness establishes whiteness as a "wage," which is haunted by the specter of wageless life (qua slavery). And the "valuation and devaluation" of Black lives—through, as Singh puts it, "medical experimentation, crime statistics, debt peonage, labor market manipulation, rent harvesting, infrastructural exclusion, and financial speculation"—continues to underpin capital's expansionary reproduction.[31] Blackness functions, for capital, as ideology—a mode of social representation that provides the "white working class" with the ballast of racial superiority, and thereby disables the possibility of anticapitalist solidarities between the free and the unfree, waged and unwaged—*and* as a key technology of accumulation. At the ever-shifting limits of capital, the racial logics of outright exclusion and differential inclusion cooperate and coincide. And the fluid boundaries between inside and outside—the "primitive" other who yesterday lacked the capacity for industry, for example, may tomorrow be required as a cheap source of labor power—must be constantly policed by the state, whose security apparatuses deploy a combination of regulative and coercive violence.

The centrality of chattel slavery to the development of the capitalist mode of production demonstrates how unpaid labor makes possible the exploitation of wage labor. This fundamental condition of surplus-value creation is likewise clarified, as Marxist-feminist theory instructs, by the capitalist appropriation of women's unpaid social and biological labor—on the plantation, where the children of enslaved women entered the world as property, and in the home of the "free" worker, where the unpaid labor of women heightens the rate of exploitation in the sphere of formal commodity production (by reducing the wage required for basic subsistence). In the context of the plantation, the expropriation of female reproductive labor was secured by a regime of quotidian brutality, which itself was legitimated by the law. The devaluation and assimilation of women's unpaid work in ostensibly "free" domestic spaces, meanwhile, is underwritten by various legal mechanisms—from welfare state provisions that only recognize waged workers, to laws (and juridical precedents) that establish the home as a space of quasi exception, a site of privatized violence wherein men can abuse women with impunity.

The gendered division of labor that prevails in the present has its roots, Silvia Federici has argued, in the early-modern transition from feudalism to capitalism. Tracing the prehistory of capital's gendered origins and effects, Federici's *Caliban and the Witch* (1998) focuses on three interlocking transformations: "(i) the development of a new sexual division of labor subjugating women's labor and women's reproductive function to the reproduction of the workforce; (ii) the construction of a new patriarchal order, based upon the exclusion of women from waged work and their subordination to men; [and] (iii) the mechanization of the proletarian body and its transformation, in the case of women, into a machine for the production of new workers."[32] While Marx described the "terroristic laws" that sought to discipline the expropriated peasant into the institution of wage labor, Federici notes an adjacent objective of such legal violence—the "radical transformation of the person," the redefining of the human body as a mechanical source of labor power rather than as a sacred repository of the soul.[33] As a part of this broad process, women were dispossessed of their reproductive autonomy and turned into "machines" for the production and reproduction of living labor.

Marx understood primitive accumulation as a moment that produces the wage laborer and the capitalist. Federici offers an immanent revision of this narrative framework, by demonstrating how primitive accumulation "was not simply an accumulation and concentration of exploitable workers and capital. It was *also an accumulation of differences and divisions within the working class*, whereby hierarchies built upon gender, as well as 'race' . . . , became constitutive of class rule and the formation of the modern proletariat." And it is "in great part because of these imposed divisions," she insists, "that capitalist accumulation continues to devastate life in every corner of the planet."[34] Federici's treatment of primitive accumulation departs from Marx's in one other significant way: if Marx imagined the brutality of capital's genesis giving way to the "silent compulsion" of market relations,

Federici, in accord with Luxemburg and many others, emphasizes instead the persistent centrality of primitive accumulation and the violence that enables it. "The continuous expulsion of farmers from the land," she writes, "war and plunder on a world scale, and the degradation of women are necessary conditions for the existence of capitalism in all times."[35] Primitive accumulation—the expropriation, in particular, of women's bodies and un-waged labor—is not only an extrinsic precondition of capitalism but one of its core and abiding features.

As the theorists whose work I engage above collectively convey, the moment of primitive accumulation is at once acute and perpetual. Discrete instances of dispossession dovetail with what Singh has described as "the repetitive, incremental, often slow or concealed violence of appropriation."[36] Addressing this duality, contemporary struggles against the violence of primitive accumulation emerge from, and are directed toward, multiple temporal scales. The Standing Rock Sioux's resistance to the Dakota Access Pipeline connects the pipeline's destructive ecological effects to the longer history of settler-colonial plunder and the "slow violence" of climate change.[37] Communal struggles against the extraction of oil in the Niger Delta enunciate a cognate critical vocabulary—revealing the relationship between contemporary forms of petro-imperialism (enabled by the corruption of the postcolonial state) and the longer history of colonial dispossession in the region. And the Black Lives Matter movement articulates latter-day patterns of police brutality, incarceration, and exploitation—and other cutting-edge technologies of enforced precarity—to the deeper violence of a society structured in racial violence.

Like the critical theorization of primitive accumulation, each of these movements is attuned at once to the history of the present and the presence of history—the longer history of primitive accumulation, which gave birth to the intersecting modalities of class, race, and gender, and the contemporary reenactment (as repetition and reverberation) of putatively original modes of depredation. Even as they imagine and work toward the transcendence of these extant histories of dispossession, that is, struggles against primitive accumulation also perform the work of memory and memorialization, registering both what has been lost or negated and the history of its erasure. The literary texts that I engage below help elucidate this dialogue—between the violence of primitive accumulation and the strategies of resistance and witness to which that violence continually gives rise.

Literature: The History of the Present, the Presence of History

There is a profound and abiding intimacy between capitalism and the novel. The social form of capitalism and the aesthetic form of the novel evolved in concert. The realist iteration of the novel, in particular, was conditioned by the crystallization of capital's social and economic contradictions. The birth of the modern realist novel was joined to the birth of the bourgeoisie—a class that occupied, in the time of its origin, a liminal social position, between the aristocracy and the proletariat, while claiming and exercising growing political and economic power. Beginning in the eighteenth century, the novel modeled new forms of representation, including, according to Franco Moretti, *prose itself*, which gave voice to this emergent bourgeois consciousness—an ideological orientation, or way of being in the world, that Marx and Weber alike identified as revolutionary in its effects.[38] But if the novel is a quintessential bourgeois form, it has never been exclusively bourgeois in its orientation or focus. Different novelistic traditions accent different aspects of capitalism's history and social consequence; and they do so from disparate political positions, which might be defined, alternatively or at once, by, for example, unconscious complicity, immanent critique, or manifest opposition. From its inception, Bashir Abu-Manneh observes, the modern novel has represented capitalism as a complex "social system." And there are myriad instances of novels that foreground less the rich inner world of the bourgeois subject than the histories of expropriation, and violent modes of social differentiation, that created the bourgeoisie as a class. "Sir Walter Scott," Abu-Manneh writes, "charted the dispossession of the highlands; James Fenimore Cooper ruminated on the dispossession of the Native Americans; Naguib Mahfouz captured the new social differentiation of the Arab capitalist city; Abdul Rahman Munif captured the transition to capitalism in the Gulf"; and, in a more contemporary context, manifold fictions, including the works I analyze in this chapter, attempt to grasp the systemic shape and quotidian experience of capitalist transformations—the extension of capitalist forms across space, and their intensification within specific geographies.[39]

What is often identified as the first modern novel in English, Daniel Defoe's *Robinson Crusoe* (1719), is, appositely, a parable of primitive accumulation. Crusoe's adventures involve several circuits of capital. He acquires his initial wealth on the Guinea coast, via a favorable trade of assorted commodities for a quantity of gold that he later translates into money savings. On a subsequent voyage to Africa, Crusoe's ship is seized by Moors, who enslave Crusoe. When he escapes from captivity, accompanied by the Black slave Xury, Crusoe reenters the sphere of exchange by selling his companion—along with the boat that enabled their flight—to a Portuguese captain, who offers Crusoe passage to Brazil. Once there, Crusoe uses the proceeds derived from his sale of Xury (and the boat) to purchase a plot of land, on which he builds a plantation. But Crusoe soon realizes that his own labor is not enough to make the plantation flourish. Summoning half of his savings from England, in the form of merchandise, Crusoe uses the profits gained from the sale of those commodities to acquire a slave and indentured servant. On the back of this unfree labor, Crusoe's plantation begins to yield a steady surplus and Crusoe himself becomes a respected member of the planter class. His growing wealth and status, though, does not lead to a sense of contentment. Personifying capital's expansionary compulsion, Crusoe joins a slaving expedition to Africa that meets with disaster and leaves him stranded on an island between Venezuela and Trinidad. There he constructs a domesticated kingdom of plenty from the island's bountiful natural gifts, with the help of the tools and provisions he salvages from the wrecked ship.

Of foremost importance among the instruments Crusoe sources from the wreck is a gun and stock of ammunition. It is the gun that guarantees the initial submission of Friday. Its fantastical powers, which Friday beholds, endow Crusoe with a kind of godlike authority. And the threat of its application against Friday himself, should he contradict that authority, is implicit. With the specter of the gun established in Friday's consciousness, Crusoe sets about constructing his servant's ideological subservience—his acceptance of, even gratitude for, the master-slave relationship. When this party of two grows, after Friday and Crusoe liberate—by subjugating—two further captives of the natives that periodically visit the island, Crusoe's dominion is complete. He possesses not only productive land but subjects that ensure its perpetual improvement. The moment of primitive accumulation has been joined to that of expanded reproduction. Crusoe sits idly by as others grow his wealth, and his monopoly on the means of violence is accompanied by more subtle cultures of governance, from religion to the habitus of work. Toward the end of the narrative, the arrival of a British ship in mutiny—to which Crusoe helps restore order—permits Crusoe to reenter the world beyond the island. He is happy to learn that his plantation in Brazil has generated, in his absence, significant wealth. And so too does his island continue to prosper; divided in parcels and peopled with women as well as men, the institutions of private property and the family are able to firmly take root.

Published in 1719 but set in the years 1651–87, *Robinson Crusoe* is a historical novel. And in keeping with Lukács's theorization of that form, *Crusoe* depicts a society and world in the throes of epochal change—a transformation driven by the revolutionary consciousness and practice of the nascent bourgeoisie. But if Defoe's novel extols the radical consequence of bourgeois ingenuity, the world-making potentialities of the individual capitalist, it also contains within it a parallel narrative that contradicts the bourgeois myth of capitalism's conception. Crusoe's wealth is less the outcome of his own diligent industry—a capacity to work and propensity to save and wisely reinvest—than an effect of two things: his ownership over and application of technologies of crude violence, and his privileged location in global relations of uneven and combined development.

In the aftermath of the age of revolutions—from the French and Haitian Revolutions of the late eighteenth century to the paroxysms of 1848—the terror of capital's origins began to find greater literary expression. Writing in the early 1800s, Sir Walter Scott chronicled the transition from feudalism to capitalism in Britain—including the "clearances" that severed the small producer from the means of production, and thereby created the conditions for a mass proletariat. In the latter decades of the nineteenth century, meanwhile, writers such as Émile Zola documented how primitive accumulation persisted beyond that moment of foundation—because processes of enclosure were (and are) ongoing, and because the proletariat found employ not only in the factories but in the mines, where the exploitation of living-labor was joined to the exploitation of other forms of nature. Set in the 1860s in northern France, Zola's *Germinal* tells the story of a coal miners' strike that builds in radicalism, culminating in an explosion of violence. The workers' revolt is a response most immediately to the exploitation of their labor and degradation of their lives. But it summons as well deeper and related histories and structures of domination, from the counterrevolutionary terror of 1793, to the alienating effects of the human destruction of the earth, to the brutalities—public and private—of patriarchal order. The miners' uprising evidences the tenuousness, the incompleteness, of their capture by the market's "silent compulsion." When their strike turns violent in its tactics, that violence is met with the violence of the state. The mask of ideology is thrown off, and the crude force that underlies the origins and reproduction of capital is laid bare.

Germinal's attention to the imbrication of various relations of power—the domination of labor, women, and the natural world—anticipates the intersectional concerns of the contemporary novel of primitive accumulation. *Germinal* also prefigures contemporary narratives of primitive accumulation in its distinctly historical consciousness, its engagement with the reverberation—across decades and centuries—of prior instances of capitalist terror. The contemporary novel of primitive accumulation works, analogically or genealogically, to trace the connections or routes of continuity between historical and present-day forms of crude expropriation. All of the novels I consider below—Marlon James's *The Book of Night Women*, Amitav Ghosh's *Sea of Poppies*, Hernan Diaz's *In the Distance*, Fiston Mwanza Mujila's *Tram 83*, and Michael Ondaatje's *In the Skin of a Lion*—make audible the echoes in the postcolonial present of colonial mechanisms of accumulation and technologies of governance—highlighting the modes of unfreedom that prevail in the current conjuncture, and the "language of pure force" (to again invoke Fanon's phrase) that continues to enable primitive accumulation. Each of these novels also illuminates the distinctive languages and tactics of struggle that bear witness to, and work toward the overcoming of, long and extant histories of dispossession. Representing the presence of the past, these novels indicate how history is experienced and imagined, in the moment of primitive accumulation, as repetition; and they reveal how the violence of that repetition, its immediacy, charges the present, the perpetual "now-time" of primitive accumulation, with the urgency of revolution.

James's *The Book of Night Women* is set in Jamaica in the closing years of the eighteenth century, in the aftermath of the Haitian Revolution. The world-historical implications of that event have begun to reverberate throughout the region, inspiring Jamaica's slaves and terrorizing its planter class. Haiti's slaves in revolt have enacted, in particular, the possibility of a radical rupture with the histories of violence that gave birth to colonial modernity and define its enduring rationalities of race and labor.[40] "Every Negro walk in a circle" is a refrain that reverberates throughout the novel, signaling the seemingly immutable violence of that modernity's perpetual reproduction. Indeed, the violence of reproduction is introduced in the novel's opening lines, which describe the birth of its protagonist Lilith:

> People think blood red, but blood don't got no colour. . . . Not when blood spurt from under the skin, or spring from the axe, the cat-o'-nine, the whip, the cane and the blackjack and every day in slave life is a day that colour red. . . . Two black legs spread wide and a mother mouth screaming. A weak womb done kill one life to birth another. A black baby wiggling in blood on the floor with skin darker than midnight but the greenest eyes anybody ever done see.[41]

The birth of Lilith is a negation. She enters the world as chattel, as the property of another. And this negation is compounded by the death of her mother, who perishes at the very moment her reproductive—property-bearing—capacities are realized.

That Lilith has "the greenest eyes anybody ever done see" is a sign that she, like many of the slaves on the Montpelier estate—and all the members of the "night women" rebel collective—is the daughter of the overseer Jack Wilkins. Lilith's early life is defined by her fraught relationship to the blackness that signifies her infrahumanity, and to the whiteness that is her dual inheritance. A domestic slave, Lilith spends her days working in the master's house and seeking the master's affections. She labors, there, alongside Homer, an older slave who guides Lilith toward self-recognition and political radicalism. Regarding the network of scars on Homer's back, Lilith perceives that blackness is inscribed through violence. Nothing, Lilith reflects, "make a nigger more black than whip scars."[42] This impression is affirmed when she herself becomes the object of the whip's lash—her punishment for spilling a bowl of soup on Miss Isobel, Master Humphrey's lady in waiting:

> Lilith know that each day getting darker and darker for her. After a week, negroes stop coming to her whipping, even them that glad she get what was coming to her. Everybody just know the scream. The frighten wild beast scream that ring throughout the estate and the field and the boiling house and the kitchen, twice a week at around the two o'clock hour. The negro scream that white people don't hear because it never stop late lunch or afternoon tea. A negro scream be like a pig scream. A negro scream be like a dog whistle. A negro scream be like wind.

Surviving this terror, Lilith undergoes a transformation of consciousness; her disidentification with blackness (as infrahumanity) is displaced by a newfound identification with blackness as resilient and dignified human being.

> Soon she stop scream. When the time come for the whipping she don't even need nobody to get her. She go to the tree early and raise her hands up. She stop cry and only wince when the lash too hard. When they cut the rope, she drop to the ground and pick herself up. She stand and stagger a little, but still stand. . . . Every three or four step she limp, and one time she nearly drop, but her chin still raise.[43]

These lines recall the opening chapter of C. L. R. James's *Black Jacobins*: "though one could trap them like animals, transport them in pens, work them alongside an ass or a horse and beat both with the same stick, stable them and starve them, they remained, despite their black skins and curly hair, quite invincibly human beings."[44]

The affirmation and realization of the slave's innate humanity, Lilith and Homer together discern, will require the total destruction of the powers that refuse it. "We not getting free," Homer insists, "we taking free." Homer understands freedom not as a question of formal rights or interpersonal recognition, but as the reflexive affirmation of human self-hood that follows from the negation of a negation. "Sometimes," the novel's narrator reflects, "a negro get tired of white man stomping so he grab the foot, twist and break it." As Homer instructs Lilith, "we goin' kill them . . . every single white son of a bitch within hundred mile. We goin' kill them all."[45] When news of the events in Saint-Domingue arrives to the plantation, this conviction—in the urgency of revolution and its necessarily violent method—is reinforced: "You hear about Saint-Domingue, Lilith? That be the all-negro republic. Nigger want freedom and they take it. Nigger want land and they take it. Nigger want blood and they take that too."[46] Importantly, the violence of revolution is redressing both the immediate violence of the plantation and the deeper violence of the middle passage: "Lilith have a quilt on her back, but there be a bigger quilt, a patchwork of negro bones that reach from the Africa to the West Indies."[47] Prior to the night women's revolt, Lilith performs her own spontaneous act of violence, when she kills Isobel's family and burns down their estate. That this fire does not spare the lives of the family's young children is indicative of its broader, structural—world-systemic—object. Lilith is not merely seeking vengeance for the brutality visited upon her by the Rogets, but a cessation of slavery's reproduction.[48] If the experience of being whipped altered Lilith's consciousness of her own human being—and its relationship to her racialized body—the experience of enacting a violent reply has a similarly transformative effect: "That was the first time she feel darkness. True darkness and true womanness that make man scream."[49]

In one sense, this "darkness" is a form of alienation. Through the act of violence, Lilith loses something of herself. If a means toward liberation, violence also occasions the waning of autonomy and will. When Lilith revolts, she is channeling a power that exists beyond herself, and that, in the moment, overwhelms and controls her. But that loss of the self—that transmission of some extrinsic power—doubles as a kind of connection, to a community or history of resistance. The "true darkness" she feels in the instance of revolt signals the more metaphysical dimensions of the struggle against slavery—in particular the spiritual tradition of Obeah/Myal, which inspires and guides the night women's conspiracy. Plotting their rebellion, the night women retreat, under cover of darkness, to a cave that lies beyond the reach of the plantation's agents of surveillance. There the women combine reflection on the philosophy and praxis of revolutionary violence with rituals that ward off any hostile forces: "not even the massa dog can find this place," and its location can only be detected by those who possess some intimacy with Obeah/Myal. Lilith is compelled toward the cave by "her own insight map"; but her path is illuminated too by "Olokun," the Yoruba deity of the oceans and its greatest depths.[50] Lilith is led to the cave, in other words, by a West African deity who resides with and watches over the untold victims of the middle passage, whose bodies rest at the bottom of the sea, concealed by its dark fathoms. She and the other night women carry within themselves, and are moved by, what Toni Morrison memorialized as the "sixty million and more." Like the "quilt of bones" that connects the scars on Lilith's back to a collective history of loss, Obeah is a link to Africa, to the world beyond the plantation and to the time before bondage. In Marx's formulation, primitive accumulation proceeds by way of two negations—the negation of pre-capitalist life-worlds, and the subsequent historical erasure of that negation. The deployment of Obeah/Myal by the night women works to counter each of these erasures, recalling while resisting—attempting to re-member—the radical rupture of the middle passage.

Lilith's role in the night women's rebellion, though, is ultimately ambivalent. She is haunted by the spirit of violence that animated her murder of the Rogets, however justified her actions may have been, politically and philosophically. And she retains a complex attachment to her own divided racial inheritance. In the event of the revolt, she drugs in order to protect her white lover—the Irish overseer Robert Quinn—and runs too to shield her father, the father of all the night women, Jack Wilkins. As the insurrection rages around them, though, Lilith reflects to Wilkins's wife that "day like this he damn well cause."[51] Wilkins's rape of so many slaves has served to reproduce the structures of racial and sexual violence that found the plantation's social order; but it has also given birth to a collectivity of sisters that are committed to destroying the chattel rationality that claims by negating their bodies and humanity. The book's narrator, we discover in its final paragraphs, is Lovey Quinn—the daughter of Lilith, and of Robert (who is killed during the revolt, despite Lilith's intervention). Taught to read and write by her mother, Lovey has taken up the task of recording Lilith's life and memorializing as well all of the night women (her "aunts") and their revolt. In the aftermath of the rebellion, as words of its protagonists and plot circulate around and beyond the island, the women themselves are elided from the story. Because a woman-led uprising is unthinkable, it becomes known as the Great Atlas Revolt (as Atlas "was the first man name anybody remember").[52] *The Book of Night Women's* final chapter recites the "songs" of remembrance that were composed to redress that archival absence—the vernacular cultures of memory that testify to the night women's resistance and to the fully human lives that inspired it. In writing her mother's story Lovey is adding her own voice to that chorus of songs. The refrain "every negro walk in a circle" signifies the reproduction of slavery's essential violence; but it also evokes, Lovey's narrative insists, the long and extant struggle to bear witness to, and perhaps one day finally overcome, that history of domination and loss.

In *The Book of Night Women*, the faith of Jamaican planters in the infrahuman being of their slaves is shook by the news of revolution emanating from Saint-Domingue. The reverberation of that event across the West Indies and world at large, coupled with the subsequent abolition of the slave trade by the empires of Britain and France, encouraged the innovation of new forms of capitalist bondage. Ghosh's *Sea of Poppies* traces this transformation, shifting the focus from the late eighteenth century to the mid-nineteenth, from the Caribbean to the Indian Ocean, from the slave plantation to the trade in coolies and opium.

The novel begins with the apparition of a "tall-masted ship, at sail on the ocean"—a vision of the future, of the vessel that will transport the novel's motley cast from India to their common fate as indentured laborers in Mauritius. This eventual journey is prefaced, in the narrative, by a vivid rendering of the social world the migrants will leave behind. When the image of the ship appears to Deeti, a small farmer in northern Bihar, she is preoccupied with the lateness of that year's poppy crop. The plants are holding on to their blossoms, and "for mile after mile, from Benares onwards, the Ganga seemed to be flowing between twin glaciers, both its banks blanketed by thick drifts of white-petalled flowers."[53] This pastoral scene, though, belies the violent relations of production within which the

fields of poppies are bound up. In the India of *Sea of Poppies*, the British reliance on opium—to balance its trade deficit with China and fuel its imperial
expansion—has displaced practices of subsistence farming with monocul-
tural production. The transition toward this market-driven agriculture is
not voluntarily embraced by the farmers themselves but imposed by the
English sahibs, who force cash advances on small producers, demanding
they exclusively grow poppies to fuel the factory's "never sated" appetite
for opium.[54] Many farmers struggle each year to repay this compulsory
credit. Others who fail to do so exchange one form of indenture for another, joining the growing ranks of migrant workers bound for southern
Africa and the West Indies. It had not always been so:

> When Deeti was her daughter's age, things were different: poppies had
> been a luxury then, grown in small clusters between the fields that bore the
> main winter crops—wheat, masoor dal and vegetables. Her mother would
> send some of her poppy seeds to the oil-press, and the rest she would keep
> for the house, some for replanting, and some to cook with meat and vege-
> tables. As for the sap, it was sieved of impurities and left to dry, until the sun
> turned it into hard abkari afeem; at that time, no one thought of producing
> the wet, treacly chandu opium that was made and packaged in the English
> factory, to be sent across the sea in boats.[55]

In the present, the well-being of Deeti's family is entirely dependent on
the poppy crop's fickle annual yield. And her husband, Hukam Singh, who
wounded his leg while fighting for the British, is subjected both by opium
itself (he is an addict) and by the draconian regime of the nearby factory
where it is produced, prior to its implication in Britain's networks of imperial trade. In pursuit of her husband one afternoon, Deeti regards the factory with a Dickensian eye: "her eyes were met by a startling sight—a host
of dark, legless torsos was circling around and around, like some enslaved
tribe of demons. . . . [These] bare-bodied men, sunk waist-deep in tanks of
opium, tramping round and round to soften the sludge . . . had more the
look of ghouls than any living thing she had ever seen."[56] And Deeti grasps
that the factory's social order—and the broader international relations of
dominance it fuels—is conditioned by violence, by "white overseers . . .

armed with fearsome instruments: metal scoops, glass ladles and long-handled rakes."[57]

The agents of British empire in India attempt to cloak the brutality of colonial dispossession in the rhetoric of freedom and liberty. Benjamin Burnham, a British merchant who once trafficked in slaves and now facilitates the trade of indentured workers and opium, offers especially floral tributes to the virtues of imperial accumulation, slavery included. "The African trade," he remarks in earnest, "was the greatest exercise in freedom since God led the children of Israel out of Egypt." He laments that "the doors of freedom were closed to the African," but takes solace in the fact that "the Lord opened them to a tribe that was yet more needful of it—the Asiatick."[58] Like slavery, indenture is freedom. And the war with China looming on the horizon, he insists, will be waged not for opium but "for a principle: for freedom—for the freedom of trade and the freedom of the Chinese people."[59] One can hear, in Mr. Burnham's words, an echo of ideology's preeminence in other moments of capital—the conjoined ideals of "free labor" and "free trade" that mask the violence of the wage relation and assimilate the individual subject to the rationalities of the commodity form. But in the immediate context of *Sea of Poppies*, his paeans to the liberatory powers of capital are drowned out by the lash of the whip and report of the rifle.

The migrants that come together on board the *Ibis*—Burnham's vessel, and the concrete manifestation of Deeti's vision—hail from different social backgrounds and are compelled toward the ship by disparate circumstances and events. In one sense, their common status and destiny works to dissolve the caste distinctions that governed their lives on land. As one migrant puts it, "from now on, and forever afterwards, we will be ship-siblings. . . . There'll be no difference between us."[60] But if the ship enables processes of individual reinvention and the formation of new collectivities, it is also a space of rigid hierarchies and exceptional violence. "While you are on board the *Ibis* and while she is at sea," the captain avows, "I am your fate, your providence, your lawgiver. This chabuk you see in my hands is just one of the keepers of my law"; the others are the noose and above all the whip, which "coiled out to make a crack that split the overheated air like a bolt of lightning."[61] In this sense, then, the ship is utterly contiguous with the extra-juridical violence that founds and defines colonial order on land. In either context, it is the overseer's lash rather than his rhetoric that ensures in the last instance the conditions of capitalist unfreedom. And as in *The Book of Night Women*, freedom—for the indentured or imprisoned—is, in *Sea of Poppies*, realized by the absolute negation of an absolute negation. In the novel's penultimate scene, the whip is snatched from midair by the coolie Kalua and returned to the subedar who wields it, coiling around his neck and ending his life—an act of violence that compels and allows Kalua's escape from the ship, along with three companions.

Sea of Poppies is narrated from an indeterminate point in the future, and the story's recorded presence is made possible by the memory work performed by Deeti herself and by her descendants. In the book's opening pages, the narrator refers to "the legions who came to regard the *Ibis* as their ancestor."[62] This feeling of ancestral connection is encouraged by the mobile shrine that Deeti constructs and reconstructs—at home by the Ganga, on board the *Ibis*, and in Mauritius. In the shrine, individual stories gather and commingle, constituting a broader archive of collective survival and resistance. In this way, the shrine functions similarly to the "songs" of *The Book of Night Women*—forms of remembrance that evidence elided histories, while testifying at the same time to the technologies of erasure, the structures of blindness, that create the need for such alternative practices of memorialization. The past and its presence is further registered in the novel by the poppy seed, "this minuscule orb—at once bountiful and all-devouring, merciful and destructive, sustaining and vengeful."[63] As a repository of memory, the poppy seed captures the dialectic of the history contained in Deeti's shrine—a history of radical and traumatic rupture, of exceptional imperial violence, and a history of survival and resistance. As the *Ibis*'s voyage nears its end, Deeti is given a pouch of poppy seeds by her friend Sarju, another migrant:

> Deeti thrust her fingers into the pouch and rubbed the tiny, speck-like seeds between her fingertips. The familiar grainy feel transported her back to the environs of Ghazipur; suddenly it was as if she was in her own courtyard, with Kabutri beside her, making posth out of a handful of poppy

seeds. How was it possible that after spending so much of her life with these seeds she had not had the foresight or wisdom to bring some with her—as a keepsake if nothing else?[64]

The poppy seeds evoke another life and world—not, in this instance, the brutality of the opium factory and the routes of imperial plunder to which is joined, but an intimate connection to family, to the landscape, to the cycle of seasons, that exists outside the logics of the commodity form. The poppy seed, though, is more than just a connection to the past; it is also a sign of the future and its manifold possibilities. Sarju instructs Deeti to "make of them the best use you can. . . . Keep them hidden till you can use them; they are worth more than any treasure."[65] The specific promise they contain is unelaborated. But the seed, perhaps, will hasten the manifestation of the egalitarian social forms invoked and rehearsed on board the ship—a liberatory desire and vision articulated in the starkest possible terms by Kalua's murder of the subedar.

Marx's theory of primitive accumulation, Balibar suggests, replaced the fictive *memory* of capital's birth—the myth of capital's peaceful origins composed by classical political economy—with its *real history*. *The Book of Night Women* and *Sea of Poppies* chronicle capital's "real history," the violence of its perpetual emergence. Both of these novels, moreover, dramatize Fanon's insistence that the violence of colonialism—the violence of capital's origins—will only yield when confronted with a reciprocal violence. Even as they excavate capital's "real history," though, James and Ghosh offer an alternative figuration of that other term deployed by Balibar, "memory." Counter-histories of capital, *The Book of Night Women* and *Sea of Poppies* redress the false memory of capital's auto-historiography; but they also demonstrate the world-making possibilities of the memory—individual or collective, possessed by the slave or indentured migrant—of the time before primitive accumulation, and of the generations of resistance to its advent.

This literary project of recovery and reimagination is likewise undertaken by Diaz's *In the Distance*, which locates the story of capital's beginnings in the American West, in the nineteenth century. The novel's protagonist, Håkan Söderström, is a poor kid from Sweden's feudal hinterlands, a physical giant whose almost mythic proportions mark him as a person apart. His migration to the New World is inspired not by a will toward conquest or accumulation, but by the fantastical tales of distant lands imparted by his elder brother. Håkan arrives on the west coast determined to make it east, to New York, where he imagines his brother—from whom he was separated in England, on the eve of their Atlantic crossing—is bound to land. He is moving, in other words, against the current of the continent's settler-colonization. But he is unable to evade the forces of exploitation and racial violence that define the space of the frontier and govern the colonizer's relationship to the land and its indigenous inhabitants. Håkan's indeterminate journey spans untold decades—the novel includes few references to specific historical markers—but his time in the New World, begun as young man and ended as an old one, is marked by two close and edifying encounters with the space and moment of primitive extraction. Observing the process and apparatuses of extraction, the relations and instruments of violence that enable it, Håkan apprehends the essence of capital in its imperial form.

Upon disembarking in San Francisco, Håkan falls in with an Irish family, the Brennans, whose patriarch, James, is in zealous pursuit of gold. Before long, he finds it:

> Suddenly pale, panting and stumbling stiffly like a flightless bird, [James] went to his children, dragged them to the hillside, and seemed to explain to them what he had just found. With eyes shut, he pointed first to the sky, then to the ground, and finally to his heart, on which he tapped while repeating the same phrase over and over again. The only word Håkan understood was "father."[66]

James's children are frightened by this rapture, by how the discovery of gold disfigures and possesses their father. In the coming weeks, the family's existence deteriorates in pace with the gold's accumulation. In contrast to the abstract wealth the gold represents, they have no proper shelter and insufficient provisions. James himself, "working uninterruptedly and hardly feeding himself, was becoming a gaunt specter, his eyes . . . bulging in his haggard, angular visage."[67] James's alienation and degradation are not the result of exploitation; he owns the product of his labor. Rather, he is alienated because his labor is invested wholly in the production of exchange value, and in the incessant repetition of the originary act of extraction. This is Håkan's inaugural lesson in the nature of the commodity form.

The insight it gives him into the intimacy of violence and capital is reinforced when several inhabitants of the nearby settlement of Clangston arrive to dispossess James of his mine. Their proprietary claim, Håkan perceives, is legitimated solely by their superior and more numerous weapons. As James himself is dismissed from the premises—a sack of money tossed at his feet as a gesture toward a more pacific and voluntary exchange—Håkan is taken captive by, and becomes a sort of sex slave of, the woman who owns and presides over Clangston. When first escorted into her chambers, Håkan is struck by the superfluity of the objects that populate the room:

> Wherever he looked, Håkan saw an ivory statuette or an old bibelot, a fading goblin or some gewgaw. Gleams of gold and hints of crimson came trembling out of the darkness, blurred by waves of gauze and chintz. Layers of curtains, festoons, and fringes smothered every window. . . . Diptychs, cameos, enamel eggs encrusted with jewels, and all other sorts of baubles were on dim display behind the beveled glass of the convoluted cabinets. A case with a greening saber, dusty epaulets, ribboned medals, wax-sealed letters, frayed aiguillettes, and an embossed snuffbox occupied a place of honor.[68]

For the first time in his life, Håkan is fully immersed in commodity culture. And his reading of these unfamiliar—strange and estranging—surrounds is attuned to the animate qualities of the objects, the way they "tremble" and "smother" and occupy space. He immediately intuits, that is, the fetishism of the commodity—the personification of things. And this personification, it is implied, is the flip side of his own objectification; the woman possesses him, just as she possesses the "enamel egg encrusted with jewels."[69] Struck by the violence of this reification, Håkan flees—into the desert, into the wilderness, a space ostensibly ungoverned by commodity rationality, where the unforgiving sun and barren land diminish him to the point of near death.

Resigned to this gradual fading away, Håkan is discovered and brought back to precarious health by a naturalist named Lorimer, who is traversing the continent not to claim or dominate some part of it, but to study the diversity of its life forms and to listen to the "constant sermon of things," in order to arrive at a deeper understanding of where life comes from and our connection to all living beings. Teaching Håkan his craft—the arts of collection, dissection, and preservation—and the cosmology that underlies it, Lorimer endows his pupil with a new view of the world and his place therein, one explicitly opposed to the commodity rationality he perceived and was objectified by in Clangston. "The hare," Lorimer professes, "like a blade of grass or a piece of coal, is not simply a small fraction of the whole but contains the whole within itself. This makes us all one. . . . Our flesh is the debris of dead stars, and this is also true of the apple and its tree, of each hair on the spider's legs, and of the rock rusting on planet mars. Each minuscule being has spokes radiating to all of creation." Once this knowledge, this "marvelous congruity," is assimilated, Lorimer argues, "man can no longer examine his surroundings merely as a surface scattered with alien objects and creatures related to him only by their usefulness," can no longer treat the external world as something to be exploited or wasted.[70]

This vision aligns with the ethos of a healer that Lorimer and Håkan encounter, an indigenous man who is laboring to save the few surviving members of his village, after it was looted and razed by a band of white settlers. The unnamed healer and other survivors embody a way of mourning that testifies to the continuity of life, the constant and "almost inaudible hum" of a lullaby that "had no refrain" but "flowed forward in an ever-changing rivulet." And when the deceased are laid to rest atop the earth, Lorimer finds confirmation of his faith in the interconnectedness of life: "What greater tribute than to be feasted upon by one's fellow creatures? What monument could be nobler than the breathing tomb of a coyote or soaring urn of a vulture? . . . This is true religion—knowing there is a bond among all living things."[71] Lorimer's philosophy of interdependence resonates, too, with the critical vocabulary of indigenous struggles against settler-colonial extractivism. "Colonialism and capitalism," Leanne Simpson observes, "are based on extracting and assimilating. My land is seen as a resource. My relatives in the plant and animal worlds are seen as resources. My culture and knowledge is a resource. . . . The act of extraction removes all of the relationships that give whatever is being extracted meaning. . . .

The alternative," Simpson avows, "is deep reciprocity."[72] Moved by the truth of such sentiments, Håkan is ever more sensitive to how the violence of property is manifesting itself in this new world, the imperial rationality that is remaking the continent in the image of capital. The desert lands that almost staged his death, and that were also the site of his revivification, are, Håkan perceives, bound up in rather than the absolute antinomy of the commodity culture that prevailed in Clangston. He begins to reckon, too, with his complicity—however accidental—in the settler-colonization of this apparently vacant land:

> Håkan realized now that he had always thought that these vast territories were empty—that he had believed they were inhabited only during the short period of time during which travelers were passing through them, and that, like the ocean in the wake of a ship, solitude closed up after the riders. He further understood that all those travelers, himself included, were, in fact, intruders.[73]

In subtle opposition to the geographic trajectory of that intrusion, Håkan recommits to an eastward course, in the hopes that he might find his now long-lost brother on the other edge of the continent.

Lorimer outfits Håkan with a pony and a burro, some basic tools and supplies, a small amount of currency and gold, and a compass. The compass has a particularly transformative effect. "Despite its unbending sameness, the desert was now entirely different in Håkan's eyes. From the compass warming in his pocket, invisible beams radiated in every direction. The plains were no longer blank but traversed by lines of certainty, as solid and unquestionable as avenues and thoroughfares." This spatial orientation is, in one sense, a welcome revelation, as it turns the plains into "an actual territory that could be traversed and exited instead of a suffocating void from which everything, including space itself, had been drained."[74] But if Håkan feels, for the first time, that he might one day belong in this place—or find a route beyond it—the "lines of certainty" that the compass exposes carry the danger of a different alienation, the possibility that he might come to feel some possession over the land, or some proprietary desire for it (like the extractive interests reshaping the landscape of the continent at large, and like the settlers who are moving west as he moves east).

Exposed to the trail of emigrants trekking across the plains, who destroy and discard the living things they encounter, Håkan grasps again the fundamental brutality of the settler-colonial project. So he retreats, with the exception of several fleeting human encounters, to a life of "silence and solitude." At times, this withdrawal is akin to a kind of surrender, the displacement of purpose and will by the unthinking mechanics of mere survival in the present—a kind of animate death that is mirrored by the landscape itself. Approaching a deep canyon, Håkan reflects that "some great force had tried; it had broken the ground up like a loaf; it had, at some point, poured water into those ravines; it had even arranged the gulches and streams in pleasing patterns; and then, for some reason, it had desisted and withdrawn. The rivers dried up. The dirt hardened, yellowed, and crimsoned. All that was left was a majestic hopelessness." The deserts he has wandered, though, "were wastelands, yes, but they had been created that way, and perhaps their emptiness was only the first stage of a long process toward a lush future."[75] The landscapes that Håkan passes through evoke, at turns or at once, what has been lost—the extermination of the continent's indigenous inhabitants; the despoliation of the land—and the urgent possibility of what is to come.

Reclaiming some authorial power over his own existence, and some belief in the future, Håkan decides to give up the search for his brother and take leave of the New World. On his way back to the Pacific, Håkan returns to Clangston, hoping to recover James Brennan's hidden store of gold, in order to pay for his ocean-bound passage. But the city and the mine are utterly transformed. In the city itself,

> [a]ll constructions, from stables to taverns, looked new but also worn by constant activity. There were many elaborate houses, some of which reminded him of the ornate dresser he had found in the desert years ago. Almost every building was some sort of shop. Many sold goods, while others were simply full of rows and rows of desks at which groomed clerks in shirtsleeves toiled away on large sheets of paper. Despite stillness reigning in these places, it was plain that the anxiety and the strain of those scriveners bent over their ledgers exceeded that of any man yelling or fighting on a corner.[76]

The city is marked by a superfluity of commodity culture. The sphere of exchange appears limitless: "The commercial frenzy overflowed the confines of the stores and poured out on the streets in the form of stalls and stands with wares of every sort."[77] Håkan's new insight into the manifold excesses and alienations of capitalist culture, in its urban form, is confirmed when he confronts the mine itself: "Vast, frantic, intricate, terraced, roaring, twisting, the quarry was an insane city for an unknown species. . . . This inhuman place, with its filthy pits, abrupt walls, and tiered plateaus descending into the broken earth like a gigantic staircase, extended beyond the reach of the eye. Wherever Brennan's hoard was," Håkan concludes, "it had been swept away like dust."[78] The mine is a quintessential site of primitive accumulation, a wound in the earth that bares capital's violent origins; and the mine is contiguous with the metropolis, the space of expanded reproduction, that is itself structured in unevenness and dominance. "Just like Clangston never really ended, the mine never really started." And its vast workings are defined by the synthesis of human and natural degradation: "Almost every flatbed wagon was packed with gangs of chalky men leaning on their pickaxes and shovels. The ground itched with the rumblings of distant explosions. Cracks and holes, many of them framed and supported by beams, interrupted the ochre monotony of the land. Out of nowhere, the heavy hands of iron tools would emerge from the ground in different points only to dive back in immediately."[79] Håkan discerns that the modest gash in the earth forged by James Brennan, and the localized alienation it engendered, had deepened, and had led to the generalization of a monstrous social and economic order. The mine would keep expanding into and across the earth. So he resolves again to continue his journey toward the coast, to abandon this place.

He resolves, too, to depart America as he arrived, with no possessions. "What would he have done with the gold? How was gold even used? How much did one give and what could one expect for it? . . . Much better, he thought, to end his journey as it had started—with nothing."[80] As he approaches the coast, and as the density of human settlement increases, Håkan passes through a vast and immaculate estate, "like nothing he had ever seen. The triumph of man over nature was complete. Every plant had been forced into some artificial shape; every animal had been domesticated;

every body of water had been contained and redirected. And all around, Indians in white made sure that each blade of grass stayed in place."[81] The grounds act as a metaphor for or microcosm of the domestication of the continent at large—the precise process from which Håkan is eager to sever himself. But he is intercepted by the estate's proprietor, Captain Altenbaum, a Finnish vintner who pours Håkan his first glass of wine and pledges to help him get to Alaska, from where he might reach Russia and eventually Sweden. Before they part, the Captain shows Håkan Alaska on a globe: "Håkan, who had never seen a globe before, walked around it, trying to track his journey and seeing how all those lands came together in a circle."[82] Håkan marvels at the representation of territories he has inhabited, crossed and re-crossed, for so many years. But he also recognizes that to represent the world is a gesture of imperial authority and control, of ownership—and this contrasts with his way of being in the world, his desire to live beyond the logics of property and possession. When we last see him, he is on an ice field in Alaska, poised to embark on a long walk home: "He looked at his feet, then up again, and set off into the wilderness, toward the sinking sun."[83]

Håkan ends the novel marching west, not in rhythm with the trajectory of the settler-colonial project but in an attempt to outpace it. The frontier, viewed through Håkan's estranged but lucid gaze, is a space not of national vitality and civilizational progress but of depravity and terror—the site of the exceptional racial violence that facilitated the primitive accumulation of wealth in the New World (and other colonized lands), which conditioned the formation, and continues to enable the reproduction, of the capitalist world-system. Diaz's supple and defamiliarizing descriptions of the landscape of the West—at once realist and ethereal, lyrical and stark—summon what colonialism has destroyed; the emptiness that Håkan inhabits is the product of a genocide. But that emptiness, or that vastness, as Diaz renders it, also contains within it manifold figments or fragments of alterity, the other worlds that are already present within this one. The novel's recovery of the "real history" of capital, in other words, simultaneously restores the possibility of other destinies, which might evade or even counter the manifest brutality of primitive accumulation. The final steps Håkan takes in the novel anticipate that futurity. From the perspective of the twenty-first

century, though, we know that Clangston, and the extractivism it crystallizes, will pursue Håkan to the ends of the globe. The mining metropolis
will become the world.

The planetary generalization of extractive modernity is evinced by
the "City-State" that stages Mujila's *Tram 83*. The City-State resembles
Mbuji-Mayi and Lubumbashi, the mining metropolises of the contemporary Congo; but its depiction gestures as well to broader continental
or global realities. The corporate, governmental, and artisanal mines that
surround and pervade the City-State clarify a political-economic order—
coterminous with capitalist, colonial modernity at large—defined by the
ascendance of exchange value and corresponding degradation and objectification of human life and labor. The novel begins in the City-State's central train station, "an unfinished metal structure, gutted by artillery, train
tracks, and locomotives that called to mind the railroad built by Stanley."
According to popular mythology, "the seeds of all resistance movements,
all wars of liberation, sprouted at the station, between two locomotives";
and "the same legend claims that the building of the railroad resulted in numerous deaths attributed to tropical diseases, technical blunders, the poor
working conditions imposes by the colonial authorities—in short, all the
usual clichés."[84] The station elucidates the thematic of colonial dominance
and anticolonial revolution. But that neat narrative framework, Mujila implies, does not precisely capture the unique expressions of colonial rationality that guide the primitive accumulation of capital in the postcolonial
present. *Tram 83* is searching for a language and narrative form that might
bring into stark relief the endurance of colonial culture in the time of its
putative negation, and the persistent centrality of extractive industry—
underwritten by violence—in the time of "progress" and "development."

Tram 83 begins in a train station, but it centers on the nightclub that
lends the novel its title. In the world of the novel, as Mujila has put it in an
interview, "everyone wears themselves out . . . despite their excessive desire
to hold tight to life."[85] The social and cultural effects of this exhaustion are
on graphic display in the nightclub, where the superfluity of wealth and the
superfluity (disposability) of human life produce a tragic yet intoxicating
synthesis—an aesthetic of excess that is mirrored by the linguistic superfluity of the novel itself.[86] During the day, the "tourists" that "blew into town

from the four corners of the globe . . . wandered zombie-like through the mining concessions they owned by the dozen, and at night they ended up in Tram 83 to refresh their memory"—joined by "all sorts of tribes," from "Pentecostal preachers and students resembling mechanics" to "polka dancers and pirates of the high seas and seekers of political asylum and organized fraudsters and archaeologists . . . and explorers searching for a lost civilization and human organ dealers and farmyard philosophers."[87] Each night, Lucien—an aspiring writer and former denizen of the City-State, just recently returned after interludes in Paris and the "Back-Country"— converges on Tram 83 with his old friend and adversary Requiem, a local hustler who raids the mines and presides over the club's motley assemblage, its underclass of "diggers" in particular. The real governors of Tram 83, though, are its many sex workers. And their favored line of introduction, "Do you have the time?", which resounds throughout the book, signals the temporal confusion that pervades the City-State, a society and a world that is exhausted by—unable to orient itself in—history.[88]

The people of the City-State, and the patrons of Tram 83—from diggers to rumba musicians—only know one tense, the relentless "is" of the perpetual present, wherein the tragedy and brutality of all history is collapsed and heightened. In one sense, this can feel like a sort of transcendence. "The city state is one of those territories that have already broken through the barrier of internal suffering." Because "you share the same destiny as everyone else, the same history, the same hardship, the same trains, the same rot, the same Tram beer . . . [because] your fate is already sealed . . . like that of the locomotives carrying spoiled merchandise and the dying . . . death holds no meaning."[89] But death is only meaningless "since you've never really lived." Escaping "the monotony, fever, sleeping sickness, earthquakes, cholera, and cave-ins" requires devising "a life that's bogus," a life based on fakery and the kinds of fantasy—pornography, above all—that are about immediate gratification rather than any vision of the future and its possibilities. Lucien's interest in both history and the future is derided. When he informs a new acquaintance, at Tram 83, of his degree in history, "the interlocutor slammed his glass down on the table and erupted into laughter." And crucially, this man assumes that Lucien's historical impulse is accompanied by a romantic investment in what is to come. In the City-State, he guffaws, "we need doctors, mechanics, carpenters, and garbage collectors, but certainly not dreamers!"[90] It turns out, though, that Lucien's companion is a publisher ("Joy-Train Publications"), who is actually keen, despite his initial hilarity, to hear the young writer's pitch. "Literature," Lucien submits, "deserves a pride of place in the shaping of history. It is by way of literature that I can reestablish the truth. I intend to piece together the memory of a country that exists only on paper. To fantasize about the City-State and the Back-Country with a view to exploring collective memory."[91] More than his intellectual bearing, it is this concern with the conjoined problems of history and memory that marks Lucien as other than his context, as much a foreigner in Tram 83 as the "tourists" themselves.

In the world of the novel, the term "tourist" refers to prospectors from abroad, as well as NGO workers and others with a specific or vague neocolonial claim on the City-State. The publisher, Ferdinand Malingeau, is a "nonprofit tourist," among those who "arrived with the hope of living in a world, a continent, as yet unpolluted by the excrement of globalization." Such tourists are blind to the fact that the modernity of global capital was constituted by the extraction of wealth in the colonized—and thus underdeveloped—world; the City-State is a space of globalization par excellence. And if Malingeau arrived with ambiguous motivations—"In a town erected solely upon guile, resourcefulness, Kalashnikovs, and the stone, it had become hard to discern the precise identity of the tourists. Which countries did they hail from? Why had they come to Africa?"—it wasn't long before he, too, was compelled toward the mines, to excavate, in order to survive.[92] A "nonprofit" tourist that participates in the economy of the stone, Malingeau symbolizes the contiguity between the colonial and postcolonial periods, and the indeterminacy or aporia of the postcolonial condition. Malingeau is granted title to a derelict mine ("abandoned in the aftermath of decolonization") by the "dissident General," an old acquaintance. His interest in Lucien's writings, moreover, highlights the process through which the *history* of colonialism—of primitive accumulation and the exceptional violence that accompanies it—might itself be commoditized.

Lucien confronts the paradox of representing a place that is composed of myriad signifiers: "Tourist Street, Independence Street, International

Armistice Street, Gravedigger Street, Mineral Street, Copper Street, First Revolution Street, Third Revolution Street, True and Sincere Revolution Street." He has taken it upon himself, in the epic "stage-tale" he aspires to write, to counter the false narratives of colonial heritage and postcolonial triumph inscribed from above, by capital and the state. But he must negotiate, too, the fact that the histories authored by and for the official sites of power are already contradicted by myriad counter-narratives: "The City-State was written by her gigolos, her baby-chicks, her diggers, her four-star whorehouses, her dissident rebels ready to imprison you, her prospectors, her semi-tourists." What place is there for a writer such as Lucien, in a place that doesn't need literature precisely because it is literature?[93] Requiem poses this problematic in slightly different terms: "The tragedy is already written, we merely preface it. So let us preface."[94] Requiem dismisses futurity, any possibility of redemption. And his call to "preface" is not an appeal to the history of the present—an affirmation of the need to register and narrate the origins of the tragedy we inhabit. He is, rather, arguing for a way of being in the world that acknowledges our immersion in, and avows our role in the reproduction of, a tragedy that cannot be transcended. The intractability of the tragedy is symbolized by the ceaseless excavation of metals and minerals. "IN THE BEGINNING THERE WAS THE STONE," the novel's opening lines avow.[95] And the colonial modernity founded in the act of extraction, which introduces exchange value into the world, is extant. The time of primitive accumulation has no evident end.

The principal mine of the City-State is Hope Mine, which is a city or a world unto itself. "A high wall studded with barbed wire ran around it, enclosing an area twenty-one miles by twenty-five. It contained warehouses, prefabricated sheds, old locomotives, boxcars, and jalopies from the Second Republic."[96] Hope Mine recalls the vast mine that extends from Clangston in Diaz's *In the Distance*—a seemingly limitless site of subterranean accumulation that is contiguous with the metropolis. In either case, the indistinction of the mine and the city analogizes the imbrication of colony and metropole—the ways in which the plunder of the former conditions the development of the latter—and the concurrence of primitive accumulation and expanded reproduction. And in either case, the space and culture of primitive accumulation threatens to overwhelm, utterly submerge, all other modes and forms of life. Primitive accumulation pervades space as well as time. The region around Hope Mine is so rich in mineral deposits, "the inhabitants of the City-State dug up their gardens, their houses, their living rooms, their bathrooms, their bedrooms, and even the cemetery. . . . They even dug at the station whose metal station recalled the 1885s . . . sometimes even with the collusion of the local mayor, who wielded a pickax in his own offices, and busily scoured public buildings from top to bottom."[97] The apparatuses of the public sphere are literally taken apart by the instruments of primitive accumulation.

Compelled by Requiem, who argues that "the more there are of you, the more sacks you can carry away," Lucien reluctantly joins an illicit expedition to the mine. He fulfills his role, under the threat of death—"I'll shoot anyone who drops the merchandise," Requiem warns—but on the way out of the mine realizes he left his notebook behind, by an old boxcar. His attempt at recovering it meets with disaster, as he is detained by a crew of "desperados" who escort him to the nearest police station.[98] There, Lucien is subject to the requisite performances of state terror (torture) before his release is negotiated by Émilienne, a female acquaintance from Tram 83. Back at the club once again, Lucien melds with the Diva, the Tram's foremost frontwoman. Her voice, "long like the rain," has moved Lucien toward an epiphany, the concept of "locomotive literature." "In my sentences," Lucien explains, "I desperately seek the breath of life that those trains have, the trains from here. The poise, the pride, the fury of a rabid dog, the dilapidation, and the rust they bear." The Diva is in rhythm with Lucien's aesthetic revelation. "I was born on a train, so my adopted mother told me. Train tracks, the road, train tracks, exile, you see what I mean? . . . Later there grew in me a kind of rage to devise my own genealogy." The recorded sounds of the train, Lucien reflects in response, "are historical monuments, works of literature, poems, tragedies. Through the rust and other elements, you feel the history, the history of peoples, the memory of migration."[99] For the colonized, Mujila has suggested, trains "symbolized the taming of African nature, deportation, forced labor, exploitation, the transport of minerals, looting."[100] The train is a quintessential technology of primitive accumulation—the vehicle that hastens the violent dislocation of people and resources.[101] But its literature, Lucien insists, might also point to a way beyond the City-State and the extractivism that defines it.

One of *Tram 83*'s fundamental insights is that the time-space of coloniality, and of primitive accumulation, is an abiding planetary condition. The City-State is the world in which we live. But the form of the novel, the urgency of its musical rhythm, enacts the imperatives of movement. Its kinetic meter, and the *jouissance* of its language, imply the endurance of struggle as well as suffering. And music, in the novel, is not simply a formal effect, but a quotidian mode of liberation. Lucien testifies to the transporting qualities of a singer's voice that "lacerates you," instilling the feeling that "time had lost all purpose, we were in 2069 or 1735 or 926 or the Paleolithic era." Here the exhaustion of history does not preclude either witness or futurity. Listening to the Diva, Lucien writes in his notebook that "joy means drowning your tears, your failures, your languor in a little music that is simply human."[102] In *Tram 83*'s closing pages, this music plays in the background as the novel returns to where it began, the train station.

> Stepping from one [rail] to the next, the music reached them, a delicious conversation between saxophone, drums, and trumpet. . . . [It] echoes through the station with its unfinished metal structure, gutted by artillery, train tracks, and locomotives, that called to mind the railroad built by Stanley, cassava fields, cut-rate hotels, greasy spoons, bordellos, Pentecostal churches, bakeries, and noise engineered by men of all generations and nationalities combined.[103]

The railroad built by Stanley evokes the originary violence of colonialism, and of primitive accumulation in particular. The modernity that colonialism brought into being is defined by asymmetry, fracture, and contradiction. But it is also global, and the fact of that globality—the entanglement of different moments and spaces—expresses the potentiality of immanent and vernacular forms of cosmopolitanism, defined by their heterogeneous sources and composition, which arise in opposition to the ubiquity of capital and the violence of its extraction.

In the Distance and *Tram 83* represent the globality and continuity of primitive accumulation. Both novels, though, simultaneously illuminate the imminence, or immanence, of alternative ways of imagining, relating to, and constructing the world—from the ethos of ecological cosmology that Lorimer imparts to Håkan, to the "locomotive" aesthetic of Lucien and the Diva, which gives voice to the possibility of a vernacular counter-movement to the local and global authority of extractive rationality. Such figments are not prescriptive, in any absolute sense. They will join with other vocabularies and narratives of survival and overcoming, emanating from the differential spaces and moments of contemporary capital. But if Requiem suggests that all we can do is preface a tragedy that has already been written, Lorimer's cosmological revelation that "each minuscule being has spokes radiating out to all of creation," and Lucien's vision of a radical and ecstatic noise "engineered by [people] of all generations and nationalities combined," are fitting epigraphs for the post-extractivist planet yet to come.[104]

In *In the Distance*, the Clangston that Håkan encounters upon his return, after decades traversing the continent's interior, is wholly determined by the logics of capital and the commodity form. All wealth is private, and there is no evident pretense of its accumulation serving the "public good" or "common stock of humanity." There are hints of the market's "silent compulsion" taking hold—the scriveners bent over their desks in anxious concentration. But the state that might join the ideology of capital to that of a coherent political community, and its "indivisibility," still appears wholly absent. Ondaatje's *In the Skin of a Lion* tracks the emergence of that national imaginary and form, the process—chronicled by Glen Coulthard—through which the exceptional violence of the continent's settler-colonization is refined and concealed by the mature institutions of the bourgeois state.

Patrick Lewis is a young boy in backwoods Ontario, "in a region which did not appear on a map until 1910."[105] Up at dawn, he watches a procession of Finnish loggers march to the forest, the workers "already exhausted." He has observed them before, working among the trees, "has heard their barks, heard their axes banging into the cold wood as if into metal.... The sweat moves between their hard bodies and the cold clothes. Some die of pneumonia or from the sulfur in their lungs from the mills they work in during other seasons. They sleep in the shacks behind the Bellrock Hotel and have little connection with the town."[106] The labor of these migrant workers—the destruction of their bodies and lives—makes possible the primitive accumulation of capital, and the concomitant construction of Canadian modernity. But they themselves remain outside society, unincorporated by the narrative or material fact of national progress. Later, Patrick's father will join the ranks of those killed by their work, when a section of feldspar mine collapses and crushes him.

Nicholas Temelcoff is a Macedonian immigrant in Toronto, working, in 1917, on the construction of the Bloor Street Viaduct—the bridge that will carry water and electricity and trains across the Don Valley. Nicholas "is famous on the bridge, a daredevil. He is given all the difficult jobs and he takes them. He descends into the air with no fear," suspended, guiding steel through the fog. His work is not wholly alienated; he takes pride in the skill it requires, and in the courage. But his story is not included in the official record of the viaduct's completion: "Even in archive photographs it is difficult to find him. Again and again you see vistas before you and the eye must search along the wall of sky to the speck of burned paper across the valley that is him, an exclamation mark, somewhere in the distance between bridge and river."[107] *In the Skin of a Lion* holds up a magnifying glass to that exclamation mark, that glimpse or fragment of a life—while memorializing, at the same time, the many workers who died during the bridge's construction, those who are not even faintly visible in the photographic archive.

In the 1920s, Patrick himself migrates to Toronto, the metropolis that absorbs the surplus produced by the spoliation of his home region. He works at various jobs and falls in love, in succession, with two women, Clara and Alice, who are best friends. Alice was once a nun, whose life was saved by Nicholas Temelcoff when a gust of wind threw her off the Bloor Street Viaduct. Patrick falls in with the Macedonian community and befriends Nicholas, who has opened a bakery. After a few years, Patrick follows in Nicholas's footsteps, joining the crew of workers constructing another of the city's major public works projects—a tunnel under the lake, two miles long, that will house the intake pipes for the new waterworks. Ondaatje's descriptions of this work are vivid: "Exhaustion overpowers Patrick and the other tunnellers within twenty minutes, the arms itching, the chest dry. . . . For eight hours a day the air around them rolls in its dirty light. From somewhere else in the tunnel there is the permanent drone of pumps attempting to suck out the water, which is constantly at their heels. . . . They have all imagined the water heaving in, shouldering them aside in a fast death."[108] As a child Patrick watched the Finnish loggers bring down the forest. And he and his father, on occasion, themselves worked as dynamiters on the river, exploding logjams, freeing the water. Not uncommonly, he saw "a twenty-foot log suddenly leaping out of the water and side-swiping a man, breaking his chest."[109] Now, working as a dynamiter underground, he is once again subject to the violence and folly of the human will to dominate nature. But like Nicholas, he finds a certain tranquility amid the danger: "Nobody else wants the claustrophobic uncertainty of this work, but for Patrick this part is the only ease in this terrible place where he feels banished from the world."[110]

Like the Bloor Street Viaduct, the waterworks were imagined by Rowland Harris, the commissioner of Toronto's public utilities: "Harris had dreamed the marble walls, the copper banded roofs . . . the brass railings curved up three flights like an immaculate fiction." To journalists, Commissioner Harris extolled the jobs he was providing, "the men hired daily for grading, clearing brush, removing stumps, and rip-rapping the sides of streams."[111] The workers, though, see Harris with utter clarity. Nicholas, for example, "knows Harris. He knows Harris by the time it takes him to walk the sixty-four feet six inches from sidewalk to sidewalk on the bridge and by his expensive tweed coat that cost more than the combined weeks' salaries of five bridge workers."[112] Unbeknownst to Harris, the unfinished waterworks are occupied, beyond the working day, by an alternative, more radical, vision of public life. "An hour after dusk disappeared into the earth the people came in silence, in small and large families, up the slope towards the half-built waterworks," for a performance, a party, a political meeting.[113] "Forty puppets moved into the light, their paws gesturing at the air . . . before each exaggerated step was taken on this dangerous new country of the stage."[114] The stage—and the motley, polyglot composition of the audience that surrounds it—is a space where new social forms, publics that exist beneath and in opposition to the national imaginary prescribed by the state, might be glimpsed and enacted.

Patrick is unnerved, and unmoored, by the spectacle, which he can't assimilate to the reality of the world as he occupies it. But Alice is one of the performers, and beyond these waterworks bacchanals she labors to radicalize Patrick's "passive sense of justice," to expose the limits of his sentimentality and compassion.[115] Of the workers in the audience, she notes that whatever affects guide their family lives—from romantic love to paternal care—"they must turn and kill the animals in the slaughter-houses. And the smell of the tanning factories goes into their noses and lungs and stays there for life. They never get the smell off their bodies. Do you know the smell? You can bet the rich don't know it. It brutalizes."[116] When Patrick gets a job at a tannery, he acquires a more intimate insight into the brutality that Alice invokes. "They had consumed the most evil smell in history, they were consuming it now, flesh death, which lies in the vacuum between flesh and skin, and even if they never stepped into this pit again—a year from now they would burp up that odour. . . . they would die of consumption and at present they did not know it." Patrick asks Alice what is to be done. "You name the enemy and destroy their power. Start with their luxuries—their select clubs, their summer mansions."[117] Patrick carries this idea with him, but his politicization announces itself in the first instance through an impulse toward historical recovery.

In the Riverdale Library, searching for stories about the construction of the Bloor Street Viaduct, Patrick "reveled in this room, the tiny desks, the smell of books."[118] But the articles and images he pores over disrupt this archival idyll; they depict "every detail about the soil, the wood, the weight of concrete, everything but information on those who actually built the bridge."[119] Patrick sees that "official histories and news stories were always soft as rhetoric, like that of a politician making a speech after a bridge is built, a man who does not even cut the grass on his own lawn."[120] He feels the violence of the archival elision of people like himself, his comrades underneath the lake and in the tannery. The absences he discovers, though, endow him with a certain purpose, the possibility of composing his own counter-history of how the city and nation were constructed—a corrective to the fictive "memory," the auto-historiography, of the capitalist state. And his initial efforts at historical reclamation have a profound effect on a friend:

> Temelcoff in his grey clothes talks with Patrick about the bridge and the nun. . . . Nicholas is aware of himself standing their within the pleasure of recall. It is something new to him. This is what history means. He came to

this country like a torch on fire and he swallowed air walked forward and he gave out light. Energy poured through him. That was all he had time for in those years. Patrick's gift, that arrow into the past, shows him the wealth in himself, how he has been sewn into history. Now he will begin to tell stories.[121]

Patrick's archival practice includes an accounting of the life and death of Cato, Alice's former lover, and the father of her daughter—a logger and radical trade unionist who was murdered by the lumber bosses. When Alice herself is killed by a bomb, after picking up the wrong satchel at a demonstration, Patrick turns toward the violence that she advocated—less to avenge her death, which was accidental, than to pay tribute to the ideals and commitment that guided her and Cato's lives. In his first act of revolt, Patrick burns to the ground the luxury Muskoka Hotel—a solitary gesture of resistance that leaves him feeling "fully alive, feral, exhilarated," but also somewhat detached from the world, "unhistorical."[122] After a term in prison, Patrick plans, with the help of the thief Caravaggio and his wife, Giannetta, a second, grander, act of violence—the destruction of the waterworks. Under cover of darkness, on a "night of no moon," Patrick dives into the lake and enters the intake pipe before blasting his way into the pumping station. Taking his time, he sets the explosives in place and carries the blasting box to the office of Commissioner Harris, who, ever vigilant in guarding his creation, is awake. Patrick runs his hands over Harris's desk, noting, to himself, that it's made of feldspar, a textural fact that summons the death of his father. Patrick testifies to Harris about the forgotten people who built the waterworks, killed in the tunnels or erased from the official narrative of their construction. Harris responds with a brief lecture on the nature of power and Patrick's fear of it. Patrick's testimony, his description of the degradations of his working life, renders him weary and he falls asleep, reverting to his "passive sense of justice." The unrealized potentiality of the blasting box seems to dismiss the possibility of absolute transcendence or negation. The waterworks exist, for Patrick, as reminder of toil, exploitation, and death; they are also, though, a monument to his own labor and that of so many others, the workers with whom he joined in a "falling together of accomplices." And they archive and evoke too the counter-publics that gathered there, the performances that hastened and revealed the other worlds in this one. In the end, all this is to say, Patrick privileges his work of historical excavation above the practice of radical destruction, without disavowing the urgency of the latter. Like the poppy seed in *Sea of Poppies* and memory songs in *The Book of Night Women*, the waterworks, as a symbol, functions in a dialectical way—representing both the violence of primitive accumulation, and the fragments of utopian possibility that belong to the past as well as the future.

Conclusion

Primitive accumulation is a structural constant—not merely the precondition of the capitalist mode of production but an essential feature of its mature form. The constancy of primitive accumulation corresponds to the constancy of state violence, which makes processes of expropriation, enclosure, and extraction possible, and which polices the lines between inside and outside, incorporation (qua exploitation) and exclusion. Marx narrated the terror of capital's birth in stark terms, but he devoted less attention to the necessary repetition of the original instance of dispossession. Later Marxist thinkers, such as Rosa Luxemburg, responding to the tumults of financial capital and intensification of European imperialism in the decades around the turn of the century, developed a more sustained treatment of the enduring centrality of primitive accumulation. That line of inquiry has been further advanced by contemporary theorists of primitive accumulation, who highlight the reprisal, and lingering residue, of "past" instances or practices of depredation. The reverberation in the present of deeper histories of primitive accumulation has likewise been made audible by a growing body of novels. *The Book of Night Women*, *Sea of Poppies*, *In the Distance*, *Tram 83*, and *In the Skin of a Lion*—and many other works that I do not discuss above—bring into evidence the continuity, across space and time, of intersecting forms of raced and gendered unfreedom. These novels also, though, make audible the various languages of critique and resistance that inhere in the moment of primitive accumulation—methods of historical recovery, vocabularies of ecological reciprocity, cultures of demotic cosmopolitanism, and practices of militant struggle against capital's machineries of destruction and theft. The paradigmatic lived experience of the moment of primitive accumulation, that is, is captured by the phrase that echoes throughout James's *The Book of Night Women*: "every negro walk in a circle"—a refrain that signals at once the ceaseless reenactment of racialized dispossession and the enduring tradition of resistance to it, which bears witness to what has been negated by, and works toward the negation of, the violence of capital and empire.

CHAPTER 2

Expanded Reproduction

MARX'S THEORIZATION OF PRIMITIVE accumulation, in the latter pages of *Capital*, is a response to one basic question: If capitalism is defined by the relationship between labor power and capital (the wage laborer and the capitalist), where did these two figures come from? What historical transformations conditioned their emergence, and guided their convergence? The chapters that precede Marx's reflections on primitive accumulation, though, largely assume the existence of this essential relationship, and thus pose a different question: What laws govern the reproduction of labor power and capital?

Addressing the technical implications of this guiding question, Marx outlines the distinction between "simple" and "expanded" reproduction. In the hermetic cycle of "simple" reproduction, the capitalist consumes all of the surplus value yielded by any given advancement of capital. If the surplus value derived from the productive process—the purchase of labor power that produces a commodity that is then sold on the market for a profit—"serves the capitalist only as a fund to provide for his consumption, and if it is consumed as periodically as it is gained, then, other things being equal, simple reproduction takes place."[1] For "expanded" reproduction to unfold, some part of that surplus value must be reconverted into capital. Otherwise, when the capitalist has consumed surplus value equal to the original capital investment—after five years, say, if an initial advance of $1,000 yields $200 annual returns, which are consumed each year—"not a single atom of the value of his old capital continues to exist" (even if the quantity and material fact of that old capital is unchanged).[2] The "whole character of capitalist production," Marx writes in *Capital*, volume 2, "is determined by the valorization of the capital value advanced, thus in the first instance by the production of the greatest possible amount of surplus value." For expanded reproduction to be achieved, this accumulated surplus value must, in the second instance, be transformed into capital.[3] Once the capitalist "hoards" enough money capital, he uses it to acquire more productive capital—the fixed capital of machinery and/or the variable capital of labor power.

The movement of expanded reproduction, moreover, necessarily involves not just the acquisition of labor power but its sustenance and renewal. The reproduction of the worker is "the absolutely necessary condition for capitalist production."[4] Marx explicates this movement, the perpetuation of labor power, by delineating two forms of consumption: one, the consumption, by the worker, of the means of production—a "productive consumption," which converts the means of production into commodities that possess a higher value than the capital advanced, and which doubles as the consumption of labor-power by the capitalist; and two, the worker's consumption of the means of subsistence—an "individual consumption," wherein the worker converts the wage extended for his labor power into the materials that will enable his survival. "The result of the first kind of consumption," Marx concludes, "is that the capitalist continues to live, of the second, that the worker himself continues to live."[5] When the capitalist purchases labor power, he "kills two birds with one stone"— appropriating the surplus value embodied in the commodity, and enabling the endurance and reproduction of the worker whose exploitation produces that surplus value.[6] And it is not merely the case that the capitalist, by purchasing labor power, produces labor power and encourages its reproduction; the "individual consumption" of the worker also ensures her continued submission to the labor-capital relation, by "annihilating" the means of subsistence, which compels the "continued reappearance [of the worker] on the labour-market."[7]

That reappearance is determined by economic logics, the imperatives of capital's expansionary valorization. But it is facilitated by particular rationalities of governance. If "the Roman slave was held by chains," Marx wrote, "the wage-labourer is bound to his owner by invisible threads."[8] Once the primitive accumulation of capital has been achieved, Marx suggested, the machineries of growth are guaranteed not by crude violence but by the "natural laws of production," and by the workings of culture—"education, tradition, and habit"—which ensure the willful participation of the worker in a system that is premised on their exploitation.[9] Over the course of the past century or so, the vocabulary that guides the theorization of capital's "silent compulsion"—the "invisible threads" that bind the worker to the capitalist, and the capitalist to the pursuit of profit—has been various: from Max Weber's concept of "spirit," to Louis Althusser's critique of "ideology," to Michel Foucault's elaboration of "governmentality." These intersecting critical strands share a fundamental concern with the soft power of capital, the invisible and totalizing hand of the capitalist state. But certain theorists of ideology, such as Raymond Williams and Stuart Hall, and certain works of contemporary fiction, identify the possibility of ideological counter-movements—emergent patterns of thought that cut through the screens of fetishism and reification, reveal the "hidden abodes" of expropriation and exploitation, and imagine alternative ways of organizing social and economic life.

The contest between the naturalization of capital and the possibility of its denaturalization is central to the history of the novel, its realist form in particular. One prominent line of critique chronicles how the bourgeois-realist novel of the nineteenth century, and its descendants, worked to naturalize capitalist social relations—by emphasizing the mundane "filler" of domestic life, by marginalizing the public sphere, and by concealing the spaces of production.[10] Another critical tradition, summoning the insights of Georg Lukács, argues that realism—its attention to the disjuncture between appearance and essence, consciousness and reality—in fact possesses a unique ability to grasp social totality. What Fredric Jameson terms the "antinomies of realism" describes not merely the discordance of two hermeneutics, but a kind of formal ambivalence. In other words, any given realist novel might, simultaneously, both occlude history and meditate on the possibility of its revelation, or privilege the domestic sphere while avowing the need to occupy and nurture public spaces and subjectivities. This ambivalence is central to the contemporary bourgeois-realist novel, as the texts I examine in the latter part of this chapter—Jennifer Egan's *A Visit from the Goon Squad* (2010), Jonathan Franzen's *Freedom* (2010), Benjamin Kunkel's *Indecision* (2005), and Ben Lerner's *10:04* (2014)—demonstrate. All four of these novels feature bourgeois characters who experience the "end of history," the ascendance of capital in apparent perpetuity, as a sort of depression, and who understand market choice as a form of power that diminishes more meaningful democratic subjectivity. Highlighting a growing crisis of ideology among the middle classes, these novels make the "silent compulsion" of the market audible. *Indecision* and *10:04* in particular, meanwhile, begin to recover something of the history such ideology conceals.

Ideology, Spirit, Governmentality

Marx's most focused consideration of the problem of ideology is found in *The German Ideology* ([1846] 1932). In that text, Marx and Engels differentiate their materialist understanding of history—and the operations of ideology therein—from the idealism of the "young Hegelians." Bruno Bauer and others, Marx and Engels wrote, "attribute an independent existence . . . [to] conceptions, thoughts, ideas, in fact all the products of consciousness."[11] Defining their methodology, Marx and Engels insist, by contrast, that if German philosophy "descends from heaven to earth . . . we ascend from earth to heaven. That is to say," they continue, "we do not set out from what men say, imagine, conceive, nor from men as narrated, thought of, imagined, conceived, in order to arrive at men in the flesh. We set out from real, active men, and on the basis of their real life-process we demonstrate the development of the ideological reflexes and echoes of this life-process."[12] This somewhat crude framing of the relationship between the economic basis of social life and its ideological superstructure is lent a greater nuance, and dialectical complexity, in Marx's later work. But *The German Ideology* is useful precisely because of its polemical clarity. It crystallizes one of the core assumptions of historical materialism, the idea, as

Marx put it in "The Eighteenth Brumaire of Louis Bonaparte" (1852), that "men make their own history, but they do not make it as they please; they do not make it under self-selected circumstances, but under circumstances existing already, given and transmitted from the past."[13] And it renders as well the ways in which the ideas of the ruling class become the ideas that govern society at large: "The ruling ideas are nothing more than the ideal expression of the dominant material relationships, the dominant material relationships grasped as ideas."[14]

Marx's provisional reflections on the question of ideology were elaborated by a series of thinkers in the decades that followed from the Second World War, the high point of the social democratic era. Louis Althusser, Raymond Williams, and Stuart Hall, among others, were writing within and responding to that ephemeral period, in the advanced capitalist world, wherein the state sought, to imprecisely paraphrase Marx, "not [to do away with] two extremes, capital and wage labor, but [to] weaken their antagonism and transform it into a harmony."[15] Althusser's essay "Ideology and Ideological State Apparatuses," for example, was composed in the immediate aftermath of the tumults of 1968. The events of that May in France brought into relief creeping fractures in the fragile capital–labor compromise. Successive cycles of rapid inflation and enforced deflation— originating in the debt financing of the Algerian War—had culminated in conjoined crises of underemployment and underconsumption. The general strikes that followed the initial student demonstrations, though, won significant wage increases, which restored—if fleetingly—the ideal and reality of working-class consumerism.[16] The capitalist state responded to labor protest not with heightened repression but with newly brokered terms of consent. Born of this conjuncture, Althusser's essay highlighted the forms of unfreedom that define the figures of "free" labor and the "free" subject— even and especially in situations of ostensibly diminished contradiction.

Though shaped by a particular historical conjuncture, Althusser's theorization of ideology was distinctly *a*historical. "Ideology has no history," he avowed. Though ideolog*ies* vary across space and time, the form of ideology—and the function of that form—is unchanging. "All ideology," Althusser argued, "interpellates concrete individuals as concrete subjects." Althusser understood ideology as a proprietary technology of the capitalist state, which facilitates the reproduction of capitalist social relations.[17] But the definition of ideology he advances permits a more dialectical, and more historical, approach. "Ideology," he wrote, in terms both expansive and precise, "is a representation of the imaginary relationship of individuals to their real conditions of existence."[18] And that representation is not necessarily "false," but might in fact critically illuminate the real, or hasten its material transformation.

This dialectical understanding of the problem is already present, in a limited form, in *The German Ideology*, where Marx anticipated the proletarian capture of the state, which would enable the proletariat as a class to universalize its interests, and its ideas—to assert its hegemony. Gramsci's treatment of the problem of "hegemony," departing from Marx in ways, imagined the formation and assertion of new ideas—new cultures of imaginative representation—as an essential component, and not only an after-the-fact consequence, of class struggle. In dialogue with Gramsci, Raymond Williams later outlined the distinction and contest between the "residual," "emergent," and "dominant" ideological formations present in any given historical conjuncture, in any given social order. "Ideology," as Williams defines it, is a "formal and articulated system of meanings, values, and beliefs," which inheres in and emanates from particular classes. The concept of "hegemony," for Williams, incorporates the question of ideology but also goes beyond it, encompassing "not only the conscious system of ideas and beliefs, but the whole lived social process as practically organized by specific and dominant meanings and values."[19] "Hegemony," that is, signifies the articulation of ideology and "culture" (a "whole social process") within a social field structured by "specific distributions of power and influence."[20] The realization of a counter-hegemonic cultural formation, then, will involve both the birth of new cultural "traditions and practices" and new ways of thinking about—of representing, to oneself and to the world—the relations of dominance and subordination that define the social order. Even when the culture and ideas of the ruling class are dominant, Williams attested, there are always alternative ways of being and modes of thought in a state of becoming, however embryonic. "New meanings and values, new practices, new relationships and kinds of relationship," Williams writes, "are continually being created."[21] Or formulated from the inverse perspective: "no mode of production and therefore no dominant social order and therefore no dominant culture ever in reality includes or exhausts all human practice, human energy, and human intention."[22]

Stuart Hall, in his essay "The Problem of Ideology—Marxism Without Guarantees," insisted, in rhythm with Williams, that we must not only address the "concepts and the language of practical thought which stabilize a particular form of power and domination . . . and which reconcile and accommodate the mass of the people to their subordinate place in the social formation"; we also need to attend, at the same time, to "the processes by which new forms of consciousness, new conceptions of the world, arise, which move the masses of the people into historical action against the prevailing system."[23] Marx was "surely correct," Hall argued, "to insist that no social practice or set of relations floats free of the determinate effects of the concrete relations in which they are located."[24] But even if, for example, terms such as "freedom" and "equality" derive their resonance in part from the common sense of market rationality—the freedom of labor and enterprise, the exchange of equivalents—these concepts are never fixed; they remain subject to redefinition and resignification outside and in opposition to the rule of capital. The determinacy of the economic, Hall observed, is in the first instance rather than the last. In the neoliberal present, the salience of that fact, and the urgency of the semantic struggles it implies, are acute. In its degraded neoliberal enunciation, "freedom" signifies the deregulation of markets, and the emancipation of the enterprises that reside therein, while "equality" functions as a descriptor of putatively universal market opportunity, or as one way of imagining the magical effects of the market's invisible hand. The need thus exists, as David Harvey and others have noted, for a radical reclamation of this vocabulary's more expansive discursive and material possibilities—"freedom" as another term for human flourishing beyond the logic of the market; "equality" as the outcome of socialistic redistribution.[25] This struggle will inevitably play out in the very ideological apparatuses—the media, the education system, think tanks, the religious sphere—that have facilitated the dissemination and entrenchment of neoliberalism. And it must, ultimately, be joined to movements that not only intervene in the contest over what the "repertoire of categories" that shape our social and economic life mean, but work toward the creation of new economic forms that will give rise to a new conceptual vocabulary.

The problem of ideology is closely joined to the question of the "spirit of capitalism"—the body of habits and ideas that, when assimilated and deployed by individual workers or entrepreneurs, justifies engagement in capitalism. Weber's investigation of this broad problematic focused on the supposed affinity between Calvinism and the will toward disciplined labor on the one hand and the perpetual accumulation of wealth on the other. *The Protestant Ethic and the Spirit of Capitalism* ([1905] 1958) is, among other things, an exemplary instance of a prominent historiographic and sociological tradition that seeks to explain "why Europe was first"—why capitalism evolved in the "Occident," to use Weber's terminology, before it was developed elsewhere. The myopia of this "diffusionist" reading of the political and economic origins of modernity is profound.[26] Capitalism, and the bourgeoisie whose "spirit" animated Weber's argument, were conditioned by colonial dispossession, by technologies of accumulation (slavery, resource extraction) that were paradigmatic in the space of the colony. Weber's emphasis on the "spirit" of capitalism disables understanding of the interrelation of core and periphery, the different sites and moments that comprise the capitalist mode of production. It is not simply the case, all this is to say, that capitalist ideology obscures the "real history" of capital. As I suggested above, in my brief reading of Althusser, theorizations of ideology and spirit often reproduce rather than counter the ahistoricity of the commodity form, precisely because they confine their analyses to those spaces/times wherein the "invisible threads" that secure capitalist social relations are robust and archetypal.

In the Introduction to *The Protestant Ethic*, Weber distinguishes the "very different form of capitalism" that prevails in the "Occident" from the capitalist modes that are paradigmatic elsewhere, or that have defined earlier epochs in modern economic history. He underlines, more specifically, the contrast between the "speculative and irrational character" of the "capitalist adventurer"— a globally common figure—and the "rational organization" and ascetic ethos displayed by the exponents of capitalism's Western development. Relatedly, Weber is keen to partition moments of accumulation marked by "acquisition by force, above all the acquisition of booty, whether directly in war or in the form of continuous fiscal booty by exploitation of subjects" from the "rational" system of "(formally) free labour," which is governed by the "spirit" of capitalism.[27] Like Marx, that is, Weber is invested in the distinction between primitive accumulation and expanded reproduction, crude violence and "formally free" modes of compulsion. Weber is also aligned with Marx when he writes that the "rational organization of free labour," which prevails in the Occident, is the truest, most fully realized capitalist form. Weber subtly resists the teleological implications of Marx's account—the suggestion that the moment of state violence gives way to the moment of "silent compulsion"—by acknowledging that "the capitalism especially concerned with exploiting wars" is extant, "even in modern Western countries." The system of free labor does not displace "war capitalism" (to borrow a phrase from Sven Beckert) but exists alongside it, "in addition to [it]."[28] Weber neglects, however, to extend this recognition of capitalism's concurrent—and spatially imbricated—moments into a consideration of the structural interconnections of primitive accumulation and expanded reproduction, state violence and ideology. Instead, he brackets the question of plunder—neglecting its enduring import—and turns to a sustained treatment of the "spirit" that makes possible the exclusively Occidental "rational capitalistic organization of labor."[29]

On the problem of ideology, Weber's revision of Marx has been well rehearsed. Most fundamentally, Weber argues that the "causal relation [between the economic base and ideological superstructure] is certainly the reverse of that suggested by the materialist standpoint." The spirit of capitalism is not an effect of capitalist relations and processes but their precondition: "[it] was present before the capitalistic order."[30] This idealistic hermeneutic has of course been subject to extensive critique. That basic materialist rejoinder, though, sometimes distracts from another telling point of divergence with the Marxist theorization of expanded reproduction and its ideological armature. Marx's consideration of expanded reproduction, recall, posed one two-part question: How are wage labor and capital (or the wage laborer and the capitalist) reproduced? His response to this question privileges the circuit of capital above that of wage labor. But Marx's framing of the problem does highlight the unique—if always of course conjoined—conditions, forces, and laws that compel the reproduction of labor power and capital, respectively. Weber, by contrast, imagines that the wage laborer and the capitalist are guided by the same rationality, the same spirit. Labor, first of all, "must be performed as if it were an absolute end in itself, a calling." The worker, Weber contends, must do more than calculate how the "customary wage" (the socially necessary wage) "may be earned with a maximum of comfort and a minimum of exertion." For capitalism to flourish—for the rational organization of free labor to take hold—the worker must additionally possess an "essential feeling of obligation to one's job . . . combined with a strict economy which calculates the possibility of high earnings, and a cool self-control and frugality which enormously increase performance."[31] The worker, that is, must regard and conduct themselves as an enterprise—not as a proletarian who aspires, individually or in concert with others, to reduce the rate of exploitation, but as an entrepreneur who seeks the expanded accumulation of "profit." (One can hear, in Weber's vocabulary, intimations of the ideology of *homo oeconomicus* that prevails in the neoliberal present.) Through the figure of the entrepreneur, Weber collapses the contradiction between wage labor and capital—or elides the labor–capital antinomy by identifying the entrepreneur as the symbolic subject of the capitalist mode of production.

Weber's focus on the figure of the entrepreneur as the paradigmatic exponent of the spirit of modern capitalism—the privileged repository of "that attitude which seeks profit rationally and systematically"—does not entirely reject the fact and consequence of class.[32] Indeed, Weber locates the purest form of the rational, profit-seeking attitude not in the "commercial aristocracy," but in the "rising strata of the lower industrial middle classes . . . the self-made parvenus of Manchester and Westphalia, who often rose from very modest circumstances."[33] If the spirit of capitalism pervades capitalist social relations—if it might be possessed by both the factory worker and the wealthy industrialist—it is most naturally resident in the striver of humble beginnings, who increases their stock through sober and concentrated labor and calculation. This thread in Weber's argument echoes the mythology of capitalism's genesis authored by liberal political economy, and critiqued by Marx in his reflections on "so-called primitive accumulation." To summon Marx's parodic paraphrasing of that origin story: "In times long gone-by, there were two sorts of people; one, the diligent, intelligent, and, above all, frugal elite; the other, lazy rascals, spending their substance, and more, in riotous living."[34] In the beginning, those who possessed the spirit of capitalism were able to differentiate themselves from those who did not. Weber's account simply applies this "nursery rhyme" to the moment not of primitive accumulation but of expanded reproduction.

Weber's *Protestant Ethic*, while a theorization of capitalist ideology, is itself an instance of capitalist ideology—one that neglects the enduring centrality of, even as it acknowledges, violent modes of accumulation, and one that obscures class contradiction. Weber's concept of "spirit," though, does possess a certain analytic force. If resonant in all epochs, the broad problem of the spirit of capitalism is especially urgent in times of capitalist crisis. In the moment of crisis, the voluntary consent and ideological investment of the "lower industrial middle classes" acquires an even greater importance to the reproduction of capitalist social relations broadly conceived. When that investment remains steadfast, even in the face of creeping insecurity and middle-class declension, reactionary political tendencies and movements are enabled, as the *petite bourgeoisie* articulates economic grievances through the vocabulary of race, nation, and culture—guarding rather than attempting to undo integral modes of social differentiation and inequity. But, as I will consider at greater length in Chapter 3, when economic crises instead provoke crises of consent among the middle classes the possibility of new class alignments and new anticapitalist formations comes into view.

Weber's notion of "spirit" has recently been revised and updated by the French sociologists Luc Boltanski and Eve Chiapello. Boltanski and Chiapello's *The New Spirit of Capitalism* (2005) focuses on the central importance of the *cadres*—a sort of managerial proletariat—to the legitimation and reproduction of post-Fordist capitalism in France. For Boltanski and Chiapello, the manager is the paradigmatic subject of the capitalist present—just as the entrepreneur of the "lower industrial middle classes" occupied a central place in Weber's account. But in contrast to Weber— who did not address at length the interrelation of the entrepreneur and other social classes or roles—Boltanski and Chiapello locate the manager, and the problem of spirit that figure clarifies, within a particular structure of dominance and exploitation. At the outset of their argument, they are careful to outline the distinction between the capitalist and the wage earner. In the most abstract terms, the capitalist is "anyone who possesses a surplus and invests it to make a profit that will increase the initial surplus." But more specifically, in Boltanski and Chiapello's definition, capitalists "make the requirement of profit maximization their own, and relay its constraints to the people and legal entities over whom they exercise controlling power."[35] The wage earner, meanwhile, possesses little or no capital, has no title to the means of production, and must sell her labor—the product of which is appropriated by the capitalist—in order to acquire the means of subsistence. Though the worker is compelled to work by the exigencies of survival, she is also nominally "free." Thus, the convergence of capital and labor "always involves a certain amount of voluntary subjection" on the part of the latter.[36]

The *cadres* occupy a liminal space within the capital–labor binary. Afforded a modest security by capital, they are tasked in exchange with convincing first themselves and then the workers they manage that "the prescribed way of making profit might be desirable, interesting, exciting, innovative or commendable."[37] Since the 1990s, the exigencies of "flexible" accumulation have corresponded to the innovation of a managerial lexicon that emphasizes the ideals of self-organization, creativity, and "intrinsic motivation." This spirit, Boltanski and Chiapello argue, is most purely distilled in management textbooks—prescriptive documents that render the large firm as a place of collective purpose and individual liberation, and that define the sphere of "enterprise" more broadly as a space of freedom, autonomy, and horizontal collaboration rather than drudgery, alienation, or repression. In one sense, the undoing of the Fordist archetype of the centralized hierarchical firm—and its displacement by the horizontal and spatially diffuse "network"—marks the redundancy of the managerial class to the reproduction of capitalist social relations. If workers are self-governed and self-mobilized, the *cadres* are a drain on the surplus rather than one of its key conditions. But in another sense, the "autonomous teams" of workers that replace the verticality of the firm represent not the disappearance of the managerial class but its universalization.[38] On the neoliberal shop floor, all workers are managers.

The genius of the new spirit of capitalism, then, is twofold: it generalizes managerial consciousness, instilling an illusory sense of power or agency not just in the actual middle manager but in the exploited and underemployed; and it mobilizes words such as "flexibility," "network," and "autonomy" to disguise the dissemination and deepening of precarity. Put slightly differently, the "new spirit of capitalism" is perfectly suited to the moment of capitalist crisis—as it presents the very symptoms of crisis (contingency, insecurity, etc.) as desirable, even liberatory. The "voluntary subjection" it names, moreover, refers not only to the passive consent of the worker—their submission to the wage relation or periodic state of "wageless life"—but to their capacities for more active practices of self-governance.[39]

The new spirit of capitalism is composed, in part, of the very language that guided anticapitalist critique in the postwar period—a critical vocabulary that counterposed the ideal of individual autonomy or liberation, and egalitarian social formations, to the rigidity and hierarchy of the bureaucratic organization. Over the past several decades, neoliberal capital has translated the demand for truer, more meaningful freedoms into the very rhetoric that supports and conceals new forms of unfreedom. Resisting the effects of this dissemblance will require rehabilitating the project of critique. Since the nineteenth century, Boltanski and Chiapello suggest, two vectors of critique have been formulated in response to capitalist alienation and inequity: the *artistic critique* "elaborates demands for liberation and authenticity," while the *social critique* "denounces poverty and exploitation."[40] Over the course of several decades in the middle of the twentieth century, the capitalist state incorporated some of the central ideas of the social critique—creating or expanding the social commons (welfare and public health insurance, for example) that protect society from the ravages of the market. In the neoliberal present, and in the wake of the communist world's disintegration, the capitalist state is rather less moved by the social critique, and has set about dismantling the public infrastructure it helped bring about. Neoliberal capital has focused, instead, on assimilating—and thereby diminishing the radical efficacy of—the artistic critique, the collective demand, voiced with a particular volume by the countercultural movements of the 1960s, for individual liberation. Capital, in other words, has conceded the ideal of individual freedom, but has insisted that the market is the privileged site and essential condition of that freedom rather than an obstacle to its realization.

Over the course of the past couple of decades, the social critique has begun to show signs of recovery. Increasing inequality, the generalization of economic insecurity, and recurring economic crises have amplified the critique of neoliberal technologies of financialized dispossession. As trade unions, once the core institutional source of the social critique, struggle to reverse their precipitous decline, adjacent sites and strategies of resistance have emerged—from the transnational networks of the World Social Forum, to the Occupy movement that spread across the world in 2011 and 2012, to the revival or innovation of leftist electoral platforms (embodied by social democratic politicians such as Bernie Sanders and Jeremy Corbyn) that explicitly reject the neoliberal consensus and advocate for a socialist reorganization of society. The material consequence of these and cognate movements and forces, which are at once disparate and connected, is yet to be determined. And their ultimate political success will almost certainly depend in some part on the revival of organized labor (whether or not workers acting in concert are able to win formal recognition in a juridical landscape increasingly hostile to union power); the potentiality of such a revival has recently been demonstrated, in the United States, by localized victories at several Starbucks stores and one Amazon warehouse in Staten Island, New York. The fate of the artistic critique—"the accusations formerly levelled at capitalism out of a desire for liberation, autonomy and authenticity"—is perhaps even less clear, precisely because that critique has been co-opted by the new spirit of capitalism.[41] Its resurgence will require developing a new critical vocabulary to address the distinctive anxieties that obtain in the late-neoliberal present—feelings of disenchantment and anomie that accompany the waning of desirable futures. This anomie is, specifically, an effect of the insecurity that has been generalized by neoliberal policies. And it is marked by the disappearance of "the purchase that people can have on their social environment, with a consequent fading of their belief in the future as a vanishing point which can orientate action and thus retrospectively confer meaning on the present."[42] In order to re-cover that purchase—the vitality of futurity—the former insecurity must be countered. In this way, the artistic critique and the social critique are necessarily bound up in one another.

Boltanski and Chiapello's examination of the "new spirit of capital-ism" describes the vocabulary and mechanisms through which individu-als justify and self-regulate their participation in capitalist processes. This fundamental concern, and their treatment of it, is closely concordant with Foucault's concept of "governmentality." Foucault delivered his reflections on governmentality in the 1970s, in two series of lectures at the Collège de France (in 1977–78 and 1978–79), which were later transcribed from audio recordings, translated, and published as *Security, Territory, Population* (2009) and *The Birth of Biopolitics* (2010). In these lectures, Foucault sketches a theory of government that critically revises his earlier inquiries into the juridical apparatuses of discipline and control. "Governmentality" signifies the "conduct of conduct"; it names a mode of state power that operates at a position of remove, not simply commanding and punishing—although those techniques of disciplinary power do not disappear even when they cease to be paradigmatic—but guiding, compelling the individual to regu-late themselves, thereby securing the integrity of the political community broadly conceived.[43] This shift from juridical and disciplinary power—which acts upon discrete bodies or subjects, and which is founded in some notion of right—to the governmental logic of security—which takes as its object the population at large, and which legitimates its policies via ap-peal to a fluid but normative set of outcomes rather than a stable sense of right—loosely corresponds, formally and historically, to the transition narrated by Marx between crude state violence and the "silent compulsion" of the market. And indeed, Foucault's theorization of "governmentality" encompasses his reflections on the phenomenon of "political economy." Like Marx, in other words, Foucault is interested in the technologies of governance that make possible the naturalization of capitalism as a mode of production and as a political rationality. He is particularly concerned, in his lectures at the Collège de France, with one distinct tradition of political economic thought—liberalism.[44]

"The fundamental question of liberalism," Foucault put it, is this: "What is the utility value of government and all actions of government in a society where exchange determines the true value of things?"[45] This problem could alternatively be posed in declarative terms: the utility of government, liberalism submits, is to encourage the pure realization of market mechanisms and the truth they disclose. Again in subtle agreement with Marx (among others), Foucault connects the liberal art of government not just to the maximization of market logics within any one bounded political space but to the expansionary imperatives of capital. The self-limitation of government is explicitly joined to the limitlessness of the market—and, by extension, to the project of European imperialism. Though careful to note the concurrence of globalist thought and militaristic nationalisms, Foucault's brief discussion of these planetary dynamics differs from the Marxist critique of imperialism in emphasizing the globalizing project as an enactment of the ideal of "collective and unlimited enrichment"—rather than as an expression of international competition for what remains of the noncapitalist world.[46] Foucault understands the basic contradiction that this liberal imperialist ethos both heightens and elides—the division between the accumulating and dispossessed parts of the world: "There will," he observes, "be Europe on one side, with Europeans as the players, and then the world on the other, which will be the stake. The game is in Europe, but the stake is the world."[47] This insight does not preface a treatment of the problem of primitive accumulation and its relationship to expanded reproduction, the structural interrelation between crude violence in the colonies and the ascent of liberal governmentality in the metropole. In reflecting upon the "global calculation" of European capital, however, Foucault tacitly encourages us to think about how liberalism, by positing the "truth" of exchange value and the market, obscures the actual origins of value in the exploitation of labor and in the depredation of the colonized world.

Central to Foucault's consideration of the global articulations of liberalism—the affinity between the liberal art of government and capitalist imperialism—is the concept of "freedom." The relationship between liberalism and freedom is paradoxical. "Liberalism," Foucault writes, "must produce freedom, but this very act entails the establishment of limitations, controls, forms of coercion, and obligations relying on threats."[48] On the

surface, this reads as a reprisal of the tension internal to liberalism, identified by John Locke and others, between liberty and security. Foucault's
consideration of this problem, though, implies a deeper dialectical fact:
it is not just the case that my freedom is conditioned by various checks
on that freedom, but that my freedom is made possible by the unfreedom
of others—just as the mutually enriching game of free enterprise within
Europe is enabled not just by the regulation of competition but by the dispossession of the colonized. Freedom is a technology of authority and not
merely something that exists in a zero-sum struggle with it. This reading
of freedom as a mode of power was further developed in Foucault's critical
meditations on *neo*liberalism.

Though tracing the intellectual genealogy of neoliberalism to the
counter-Keynesian thought of the Austrian School of economists—
including Friedrich Hayek and Ludwig von Mises—Foucault identifies
the political advent of neoliberalism in the postwar period, in the context
of German reconstruction. According to the liberalism of the eighteenth
century, the state delimits and legitimates the market. But in the aftermath
of the Second World War in Germany, when the state did not exist in any
stable sense, a new iteration of liberal policy and thought—often termed
"ordoliberalism"—emerged, which held that the market legitimates and
determines the state: "In other words, a state under the supervision of the
market rather than a market supervised by the state."[49] In this inversion,
Foucault contended, one can discern the fundament of neoliberal rationality. For the original neoliberals, moreover, the notion of the market—the
exchange and competition that unfolds therein—as a given, as something
that occurs spontaneously, is "naïve naturalism." Competition, in the neoliberal imagination, "is an historical objective of governmental art and not
a natural given that must be respected."[50]

If the neoliberal state must be "active, vigilant, and intervening," in order
to produce the formal conditions for free competition, one crucial component of this ambit is the conduct of individual behavior. This is where the
concept of a specifically neoliberal "governmentality" enters the analytic
foreground. "The *homo oeconomicus* sought after [in neoliberal society],"
Foucault notes, "is not the man of exchange or man the consumer; he is the
man of enterprise and production."[51] In the classical liberal imagination,

homo oeconomicus is the "subject or object of *laissez-faire*"—a person who, when properly left alone, pursues his own interest, which naturally coheres with the interests of others. In neoliberal thought—its American version in particular—by contrast, *homo oeconomicus* "appears precisely as someone manageable, someone who responds systematically to systematic modifications artificially introduced into the environment . . . someone who is eminently governable."[52] In this new formulation, the infrastructure and practice of individual freedom is not something to be respected, something to let be—but something that must be perpetually produced and policed. "Freedom" is not a right, to be enjoyed, but an injunction, to be heeded. Neoliberal governmentality, all this is to say, entrenches freedom as a technology of power and control. There are echoes here of the figure of "free labor" in the moment of primitive accumulation—the subject liberated from the feudal relation but also dispossessed of the means of subsistence, for whom "freedom" is a euphemism for the compulsion of the wage relation.

The Foucauldian critique of neoliberalism has been generatively developed, and brought to bear on the present, by Wendy Brown. In *Undoing the Demos* (2015), Brown describes how the neoliberal articulation of *homo oeconomicus* corresponds to the declension of democratic spaces and foreclosure of democratic possibilities. If in classical liberalism *homo oeconomicus* naturally resides in the economic sphere, in the neoliberal present the boundaries of his habitat encompass all spaces of public and private life. "Neoliberal rationality disseminates the model of the market to all domains and activities . . . and configures human beings exhaustively as market actors, always, only, and everywhere." As a result, Brown argues, the demos—the space of democratic imaginaries, formations, and subjectivities—is narrowed to the point of disappearance.[53]

In keeping with Foucault's intervention—and indeed with most theorizations of neoliberal ideology, spirit, or governmentality—Brown locates her account in advanced capitalist political economies. She recognizes, in accord with writers such as Naomi Klein, that the laboratory for neoliberal policy was the formerly colonized world, where "coups d'état and juntas, occupations, structural adjustments, and militarized disciplining of populations" continue to make possible the imperial imposition of neoliberal methods and ideas. And she identifies, too, one important lacuna in Foucault's account—his relative inattention to the fundament of "exploitation and domination" upon which "freedom in the realm of exchange sits."[54] But she focuses her inquiry on the manifestations of neoliberalism in the Global North—and in the sphere of consumption rather than production—where the "main instruments of implementation have been soft, rather than hard power."[55] "Boring in a capillary fashion" throughout the social sphere, neoliberalism has "taken deeper root in subjects and in language, in ordinary practices and in consciousness."[56]

One of Brown's central contributions is to expand upon Foucault's genealogy of *homo oeconomicus*, by counterposing this economic figure to the political being of *homo politicus*. Summoning Aristotle, Brown imagines *homo politicus* as the symbolic subject of a social order wherein popular and individual sovereignty are mutually securing, mutually constitutive. The figure of *homo politicus* embodies the ideal of a political community that is founded on and constructed to respect—socially, politically, legally—individual sovereignty, individual self-determination.[57] This appeal to the sanctity of the individual accords with the basic tenets of liberalism. The old Aristotelian notion of *homo politicus*, though, implies a "political exterior and subjective interior that is disharmonious with capitalism"—an idea, Brown notes, that is also found in the thought of both Weber and Marx. And it is precisely the ascendance of classical liberalism in the eighteenth century, and neoliberalism in the twentieth century, that occasioned the eclipse of *homo politicus* by *homo oeconomicus*—the subject of the demos by the subject of the market.[58] The hegemony of *homo oeconomicus* corresponds to two crucial "reorientations": "On the one hand," Brown writes, "it reorients the subject's relation to itself and its freedom. Rather than a creature of power and interest, the self becomes capital to be invested in, enhanced according to a specified criteria and norms as well as available inputs. On the other hand," she continues, "this conversion reorients the relationship of the state to the citizen. No longer are citizens most importantly constituent elements of sovereignty. . . . Rather, as human capital, they may contribute to or be a drag on economic growth; they may be invested in or divested from depending on their potential for

GDP enhancement."[59] These two epochal transformations have been cataclysmic for the conjoined ideals of freedom and democracy—hastening the radical declension of "public values, public goods, and popular participation in political life," and marking the supersession of the calculus of justice and equality (however ambivalently and unevenly those criteria have been pursued and realized in modern political orders) by metrics of credit-worthiness and profit potential.[60] Extending and revising Foucault's insights into the neoliberal articulation of the individual as enterprise, Brown suggests that when we all become self-managing capitals, accumulating our economic value for ourselves and for the state, our disposability is also maximized. When the individual becomes nothing more than a vehicle or repository for the appreciation of capital, the superfluity of human life is made plain.

Brown's critique of neoliberal reason, its utter saturation of human lifeworlds, does not culminate in a prescriptive meditation on potential routes of resistance. The ascendance of *homo oeconomicus*, she conveys, produces and is in turn enabled by an individual and collective sense of political impossibility. The dominant "structure of feeling" of the late-neoliberal present is depression—the common deference to the idea, enunciated by the guardians of capitalist order, that "there is no alternative." The triumph of the market may not be utopian (as its architects and acolytes once promised, in the earlier days of the "end of history"), but its ascendance does represent, we are instructed by the capitalist state, the only desirable or plausible future. The narrowing of the demos—and the eclipse of its proper subject, *homo politicus*—disables the critical imagination. However imperfectly realized, and however complicit in various structures of dominance, the liberal democratic vocabulary has historically animated various narratives of resistance to the violence of capital. But "when liberal democracy is fully transformed into market democracy," Brown observes, "what disappears is this capacity to limit, this platform of critique, and this source of radical democratic inspiration and aspiration."[61] Any anti-neoliberal politics will thus necessarily involve the reconstruction of the social and political commons and the forging of new democratic spaces, which might stage the construction of a new political and economic reality. The urgency of this twofold project of reclamation and creation was demonstrated by the Occupy movement of 2011. The encampments erected that fall in lower Manhattan, and then across the country and world, spoke to the possibility of and concretely enacted open and liberatory democratic forms—social and political hypotheses that promise a socialist transformation of economic life.

In *The Birth of Biopolitics*, Foucault argues that Marx's work lacks a theory of government. And that gap in Marxist thought explains, as Brown paraphrases Foucault, "the derivative and deeply impoverished political rationality in actually existing socialist states."[62] Whether or not we are as eager as Foucault to hold Marx responsible for the absence of "an autonomous socialist governmentality," this polemic does present a compelling provocation. It intimates that movements of resistance to contemporary capital must not simply deconstruct or denaturalize neoliberal reason, but must labor to formulate an alternative *political* rationality. And however skeptical Foucault might be about the prospects of a socialist theory of governmental reason, his genealogical methodology does remind us that the dominance of neoliberal rationality is not in fact historically inevitable, the product of a unitary and predetermined historical trajectory. It is, rather, the outcome of contingent processes of intellectual and ideological contestation, which are dialectically bound with economic relations and forces. Neoliberal reason insists that "there is no alternative"; but its own history—its radical displacement of social democratic culture and infrastructure—implies precisely the mutability of all political rationalities. In the current conjuncture as ever, Mark Fisher insisted, "emancipatory politics must always destroy the appearance of a 'natural order', must reveal what is presented as necessary and inevitable to be a mere contingency, just as it must make what was previously deemed to be impossible seem attainable."[63] One fundamental task of critique, this practice of denaturalization is also enacted, as I discuss below, in certain contemporary fictions of expanded reproduction.

Literature: Naturalization and Denaturalization

In *The Communist Manifesto*, Marx and Engels undertake a paean to the revolutionary powers of the bourgeoisie, that class which cannot exist without constantly revolutionising the instruments of production, and thereby the relations of production, and with them the whole relations of society. . . . Constant revolutionising of production, uninterrupted disturbance of all social conditions, everlasting uncertainty and agitation distinguish the bourgeois epoch from all earlier ones. All fixed, fast-frozen relations, with their train of ancient and venerable prejudices and opinions, are swept away, all new-formed ones become antiquated before they can ossify.

Subject to the transformative will of the bourgeoisie, "all that is solid melts into air."[64] One might thus expect the novel of expanded reproduction to be marked by a preoccupation with newness, with the perpetual flux of human social existence. "The new," Theodor Adorno wrote, "is the aesthetic seal of expanded reproduction, with its promise of undiminished plenitude." This is so, Adorno contended, because capital, "if it does not expand, if it does not—in its own language—offer something new, is eclipsed."[65] And certainly, if we focus on the formal innovations of modern*ism*—without attention to its narrative substance—this equation of expanded reproduction and the aesthetic of the new holds. But in one reading, the modern novel broadly conceived tends, in its quintessential bourgeois form, to accent not change but stasis and continuity, the mundane facts of quotidian existence. "Thus was the modern novel midwifed into existence around the world," Amitav Ghosh writes, "through the banishment of the improbable and the insertion of the everyday."[66] Franco Moretti, in *The Bourgeois: Between History and Literature*, makes a cognate point: "*regularity*, not disequilibrium, was the great narrative invention of bourgeois Europe. All that was solid, became more so."[67]

There is, in other words, a contradiction between the role of the bourgeoisie as a privileged agent of historical transformation, and the narrow, static narratives of many bourgeois novels—fictions that naturalize, by imagining the peaceful continuity of, capitalist social relations. Reflecting on this paradox, Moretti highlights the contrast, or transition, between the heroic narratives of the *ancien* aristocracy and, beginning in the nineteenth century, the self-effacing narratives of the bourgeoisie.[68] The former embellished the world-historical agency of its central protagonists and the latter erase it. This formal or generic evolution was occasioned, in part, by the establishment of expanded reproduction as the paradigmatic—symbolically if not materially ascendant—moment of capital, even as primitive accumulation proceeded apace. If once the ruling class marauded around the world brandishing its sword, now—in its bourgeois form—it was more at home in the back offices of the bank, diligently going over the accounting ledgers, or in the parlor, discussing world affairs over a brandy.

In Chapter 1, I invoked *Robinson Crusoe* as an archetypal novel of primitive accumulation. But *Robinson Crusoe* might also be read as a narrative of "conjuncture," which chronicles the transition between, or synchronic coexistence of, the moments of primitive accumulation and expanded reproduction. Though compelled toward a life of intemperate wealth-seeking, Crusoe constantly castigates himself for failing to heed his father's advice, that he should be happy occupying "the middle station" into which he was born. Crusoe's adventures do yield great wealth, which seems to affirm the virtues of a more restless imperial subjectivity. Crucially, however, Crusoe's stock expands most exponentially when he himself—stranded on his island—has been physically divorced from it. The plantation he established in Brazil produces, in his absence, an outcome that emphasizes the autonomous productivity of the market. Once established, via plunder or other forms of expropriation, capital, *Robinson Crusoe* suggests, grows of its own accord. It requires no heroic agent, only the most subtle clerical intervention. Defoe's novel, all this is to say, clarifies the distinction between two mythological paradigms: the mercantile adventurer, conjuring riches through derring-do, and the demure bourgeois, who defers to the market's beneficent and invisible hand. This distinction is likewise evident in Charlotte Brontë's *Jane Eyre*. Rochester accumulated his wealth in the West Indies, and returns to England wary of a more domestic—understood in the double sense of home and nation—existence. Jane's role, she determines, is to moderate Rochester's more worldly longings, and to soothe his psychological wounds—the costs of doing business in the colonies, of the violence of primitive accumulation. Rochester's transformation into a bourgeois subject, at peace with the quotidian pleasures of the manor, is thwarted by Bertha Mason, whose presence attests that the space of the colony, and the brutality that continues to unfold therein, will always haunt the metropole.

The specter of Bertha Mason, the specter of the "real history" of capital, points to another function of the bourgeois-realist novel, or another way of reading its critical efficacy. This latter hermeneutic approach examines how certain realist novels enact not the erasure or disavowal of the origins and contradictions of capital but their revelation. Lukács, in his essay "Realism in the Balance," argued that in realist fictions—the work of Balzac and Thomas Mann in particular—the relationship between appearance and essence, our consciousness of the world and its objective reality, is revealed with a singular clarity. The realist novel, in other words, is, in Lukács's account, an instance of mediation that itself illuminates the dynamics of mediation in society, the ways in which "the basic economic categories of capitalism are always reflected in the minds of men." When the machinery of expanded reproduction is operating "in a so-called normal manner," Lukács contended, "people living within capitalist society think and experience it as unitary," while "in moments of crisis . . . they experience it as disintegration." And realism, he insisted, is able to represent that experience of disintegration, and the heightened practices of cognitive mapping it makes possible, which might begin to apprehend the "underlying unity, the totality, all of whose parts are objectively interrelated" that "manifests most strikingly" in the time-space of crisis.[69]

I am keen to stress, in this book, that the three moments of capital constitute a concurrent interrelation rather than a succession of stages or epochs. But grounding this inquiry in the present, we are obliged to focus on the determining fact of crisis—not only on the cultural logics and narrative forms of "synthetic dispossession," which I will discuss in Chapter 3, but on those of expanded reproduction as well. What Robert Brenner has termed the "long downturn"—"the extraordinarily extended phase of reduced economic dynamism," beginning in the late 1960s and "persisting through the end of the old millennium and into the new"—is characterized by declining rates of profit and diminished productivity growth (in the advanced capitalist world most especially).[70] Thinkers that assimilate the "long downturn" thesis, such as the Endnotes collective, claim that neoliberal mechanisms of dispossession have restored the power of the capitalist class but have not solved the underlying crisis of profitability and the terminal decline it signals.[71] Other economic historians and theorists, among them David Harvey, note that the increasing mass of surplus value can act as a counterbalance, where and when rates of profit decline.[72] Declining rates of profit, moreover, do not mean that the movement of expanded reproduction has ceased, or will grind to a halt in the imminent future; profits continue to be made and reinvested. The threat and fact of decline, though, does shape the ambivalent structure of feeling that defines the moment of expanded reproduction, in the current conjuncture: the ideology and reality of growth is extant; but even spaces of security and belonging are today imbued with a sense of ennui and historical foreclosure.

The contemporary bourgeois novel captures this ambivalence. It betrays the crisis of capital's expanded reproduction—crises of governance and accumulation, and crises of futurity—while continuing to inhabit the moment of capital's perpetual growth and ideological hegemony. If, as Moretti submits, the bourgeois realism of the nineteenth century worked to solidify the fluid, and to reinforce the already solid, its twenty-first-century descendant confronts the outcome of that ideological trick—the pervasive sense, akin to a kind of mass depression, that this is the only or best possible world. The novels I consider below—Jennifer Egan's *A Visit from the Goon Squad*, Jonathan Franzen's *Freedom*, Benjamin Kunkel's *Indecision*, and Ben Lerner's *10:04*—depict that malaise, the paradigmatic lived experience of the moment of expanded reproduction, in the context of the neoliberal present; but they also begin, in varying and tentative ways, to imagine a way beyond it. All four texts make audible the market's silent compulsion, while reflecting on the possibility of reclaiming a more meaningful political subjectivity—one that conceives of "freedom" as something exercised within and upon history rather than outside of it or at its end, against the market rather than within it.

A Visit from the Goon Squad uses the culture industries—the music industry, specifically—as a lens onto the recent history of neoliberalism. In so doing, Egan's novel evinces the ideological process highlighted by Boltanski and Chiapello, the assimilation by capital of its own critique. The countercultures of the 1960s and '70s, enunciating one iteration of the "artistic critique," demanded deeper forms of individual and collective autonomy, beyond and in opposition to the stultifying institutions of the nuclear family, the mass market, the bureaucratic company, and the state. Capital in its neoliberal form, though, has been remarkably successful at integrating these demands into its own cultural logics—transmuting the appeal for greater liberation into vocabularies and narratives of "freedom" that conceal rather than challenge various apparatuses of repression, and that disable the possibility of meaningful liberation from the tyranny of the commodity form and machineries of reproduction.

Egan renders this story in especially stark terms by focusing on the music and politics of punk, and the diminishment or capture of that genre by neoliberal capital. *A Visit from the Goon Squad* integrates several narratives and characters, but it centers on the figure of Bennie Salazar—once, in his 1970s adolescence, the mediocre bass player in Bay Area punk band the Flaming Dildos; now the aging head of a corporate record label that he recently sold. His status as a sellout has compounded over time. And trading authenticity and meaning for money has resulted in not just spiritual but physical degradation. Bennie, for whom music and eros were always entwined, has taken to ingesting flakes of gold, in the hopes that this dietary supplement might reawaken his libidinal capacities. *A Visit from the Goon Squad* is more than just a chronicle of this somewhat conventional descent from youthful iconoclasm and verve to middle-age resignation. The novel is also, and more urgently, a sustained meditation on how the ascendance of neoliberal capital affects how we experience time, and how we locate ourselves in relation to its unfolding.

In the first of the novel's thirteen vignettes, which proceed in a nonlinear fashion, Bennie's young assistant Sasha expresses the paradox of contemporary bourgeois privilege—the acute feeling of being imprisoned by one's freedom, confined by the superfluity of choices and consumer objects in which one is immersed. Her apartment, she reflects, "which six years ago had seemed like a way station to some better place, had ended up solidifying around Sasha, gathering mass and weight, until she felt mired in it and lucky to have it."[73] In the eternal neoliberal present, the detritus of accumulation provides the illusion of warmth, and depression and contentment are almost indistinguishable affects. This depression, when it manifests in the novel, is a product of contemporary capitalism's conflicted temporal experience. On the one hand, "all that is solid melts into air"; capital's powers of creative destruction are constantly manufacturing new needs and desires, instilling the longing for an immediate gratification that is never actually realized, and preventing us from being fully present—socially, politically—in the present. On the other hand, "there is no alternative," no future beyond the permanent revolution of capital. We are both constantly hurtling toward the future—à la Walter Benjamin's Angel of History—and denied the possibility of futurity. For Bennie, the horizon of possibility lies not in the future but in the past. He listens to the music of his youth with a kind of crippling nostalgia, a longing for "muddiness, the sense of actual musicians playing actual music in an actual room." He yearns, in other words, for concreteness. (But this is a paradox of sorts, too, because the punk sound he tries to summon derived its power from its ephemerality and speed.) Today the quality of muddiness "was usually an effect of analogue signaling rather than bona fide tape." Indeed, "everything was an effect in the bloodless constructions Bennie and his peers were churning out . . . husks of music, lifeless and cold as the squares of office neon cutting the blue twilight." Bennie is producing a simulacrum of music, rather than the thing itself. And he himself, he realizes, has been made actually impotent by his complicity in the "aesthetic holocaust" of digitization. Hence the gold flakes, sprinkled in his coffee.[74]

The novel's toggling between present and past and, eventually, future, accents not contingency and chance—the paths not taken, the fact that things might have been, or might one day be, otherwise—but stasis and inevitability. Sasha's transition from radical independence to motherhood and domesticity is unremarkable, utterly mundane, as is Bennie's journey from punk dreamer to jaded record company executive. As Pankaj Mishra observes, "the incremental unfolding of [Sasha] and Bennie's life leaves us with a disturbing sense of their (and our) state of unfreedom: it shows us the full arc of their choiceless lives (within a society ideologically committed to the adventure of individualism and self-invention)."[75] This unfreedom, this choicelessness, is felt with a particular acuity by the novel's bourgeois characters. But it is embodied too by those to whom fate has been materially as well as spiritually unkind. The charismatic front man of the Flaming Dildos, Bennie's close teenage comrade Scotty, has traveled a more humble path and is working, in his middle age, as a janitor and litter collector. But he sees "what almost no one else seemed to grasp: that there was only an infinitesimal difference, a difference so small that it barely existed except as a figment of the human imagination, between working in a tall green glass building on Park Avenue and collecting litter in a park."[76] Egan's insight here, articulated in Scotty's voice, is that the one occupation possesses no more intrinsic meaning or worth than the other. This attention to the fictions of status, though, tends to obscure the contradictions of class. In *A Visit from the Goon Squad* and myriad other contemporary novels, the "artistic critique" of capital displaces the "social critique"—the material violence of poverty and exploitation is eclipsed by the existential problems of authenticity and liberation. And the absence of the "social critique" is related to the temporal disorientation that the novel makes vivid. The characters in *A Visit from the Goon Squad* feel lost within, or assaulted by, time precisely because they are indifferent to—make no attempt to locate themselves in relation to—the totality of capitalist social relations. The affect of wariness that they and the novel itself share, that is, is a symptom of the failure of cognitive mapping.

The novel's closing narratives point toward possible routes out of this individual and collective malaise. In the penultimate story, set in the novel's future and composed of a series of PowerPoint slides, Sasha's daughter Ally meditates on her parents' pasts and on her brother Lincoln's obsession with "pauses" in rock-and-roll songs—breaks in the music, both "quiet and busy," that contain multitudes, and that accentuate the sounds they interrupt. In one sense, then, the pauses that Lincoln meticulously reads and catalogs resonate with Walter Benjamin's "historical materialist," the figure who understands that "thinking involves not only the flow of thoughts, but their arrest," the figure who "blasts open the continuum of history" by pausing, so as to apprehend, the fissures and fractures produced and elided by "homogeneous empty time." Of course, the pauses that captivate Lincoln do not themselves elucidate "the constellation which his own era has formed with a definite earlier one," or the broader ensemble of relations within which he himself is situated. But they do signal the possibility of a "conception of the present as 'the time of the now,'" wherein the past becomes "citable in all its moments" and the future, the other world already immanent to this one, likewise comes into view.[77]

In the novel's final narrative, Scotty—last seen slapping a dead fish, caught that morning in the East River, on Bennie's desk—reappears, in the

2020s, as a redeemed artist. His "mournful vibrato" might be dire, but it resonates with the times: "two generations of war and surveillance had left people craving the embodiment of their own unease in the form of a lone, unsteady man on a slide guitar."[78] Scotty's music speaks to and channels the structure of feeling—the anxiety and depression and rage—that pervades the present (or near future), but it also evokes a more "pure" and "untouched" aesthetic and time.[79] Bennie himself, by this point, has exchanged his celebrity and power for an ostensibly purer—less corrupted and less lucrative—approach to the production of music. But he stages Scotty's comeback at least in part because he intuits that his music—the feelings it amplifies—will be salable. Scotty's redemption, then, represents not the transcendence of our unease but its commoditization.

This jadedness about the potentialities of radical politics and critique in the late-capitalist present is shared by Franzen's *Freedom*. *Freedom* is interested in the symbolic import, as well as the real lived experience, of the middle—middle America and the middle class. It foregrounds those spaces and subjects of our current social order whose identity is defined by its neither-here-nor-there-ness, its willfully inconspicuous nature. In this, *Freedom* exemplifies the contemporary iteration of the nineteenth-century bourgeois novels analyzed by Moretti, narrative worlds occupied by "un-marked and elusive" characters, protagonists distinguished not by their unique contributions to the movement of history—or their unique experience of that history—but by their sameness, as by the "methodical suppression of all sensuous traits."[80] Moretti describes the euphemistic transmutation of the "bourgeois" into the mythical figure of the "middle class," a process that allowed the bourgeoisie (qua the middle class) to "appear as a group that was itself partly subaltern, [who] couldn't really be held responsible for the way of the world."[81] This is the middle class to which Patty and Walter Berglund belong, though they maintain a conflicted relationship to it, aware of the structural inequities that their middleness buffers or conceals. They are the sort of people "who needed to forgive everybody so their own good fortune could be forgiven; who lacked the courage of their own privilege."[82] *Freedom* does depart from the archetypal bourgeois novel by venturing into the sphere of politics and implicating its protagonists, Walter especially, therein. But the politics that Walter espouses, if unusually audible, is precisely in keeping with the core function of the middle class, as imagined by the bourgeois philosophers of the nineteenth century—to combine a liberal sympathy for the oppressed classes with a fundamental belief in the legitimacy of class as such and of the ruling class in particular.

"By almost any standard," Patty Berglund reflects in her self-authored third-person narrative, "she led a luxurious life. She had all day every day to figure out some decent way to live, and yet all she ever seemed to get for all her choices and all her freedom was more miserable. The autobiographer is almost forced to the conclusion that she pitied herself for being so free."[83] Freedom, in *Freedom*, is figured as a kind of oppressive superfluity, a condition of bourgeois life in its post-materialist form that precludes purpose, that makes it more rather than less difficult to find some meaning in one's existence. "What she should have done," Patty acknowledges, "was find a job or go back to school or become a volunteer. But there always seemed to be something in the way," most significantly a "general freedom that she could see was killing her but she was nonetheless unable to let go of."[84] Patty is exhausted by her inability to act upon the world, to intervene in the unfolding of her own narrative and that of history at large. This is the fate of the bourgeois subject who, after denying or deemphasizing their own historical agency, has now convinced themselves that history itself is over. Instead of doing those things she should have done, Patty retreats to the realm of fiction, to Tolstoy and Conrad. Her most profound act of volition is that most commonplace subject of the bourgeois novel, infidelity. But the consummation of her long-harbored desire for Walter's best friend, Richard, fails to reanimate her life; it is another example of freedom's redundancy.

Walter, by contrast, *is* pressed into action when Richard, a musician, belatedly achieves a kind of rock stardom—the media account of which, in *Spin* and *Rolling Stone*, fails to note Walter's deep friendship and decades of emotional and intellectual support. Spurred on by this slight, as by simple envy and competitiveness, Walter resolves to enter public life in a more visible and impactful way. So he takes a job, in Washington, DC, as the manager of the Cerulean Mountain Trust—a project funded by the fossil fuel magnate Vin Haven that is committed to reconciling the protection of the endangered cerulean warbler with the capitalist exigencies of strip mining in West Virginia. Walter is drawn to the project out of concern for the bird and its habitat. But his interest is piqued because the objectives of the trust and its founder, he discerns, might align with his own pet political cause—the reversal of the population growth that will ultimately, he argues, make earth inhospitable to humans and animals alike. Walter, then, strikes a paradoxical figure; he is a paradigmatic bourgeois subject of the moment of expanded reproduction who is committed to arresting biological reproduction, the accumulation of people that enables the accumulation of capital.

A father of two, Walter is cognizant of the fact that his campaign against overpopulation might be met with the charge of hypocrisy: "you know, I did some breeding myself," he acknowledges. His apparent self-awareness, though, does not extend to a more global attention to the dynamic of uneven and combined development. He laments the stupid excessiveness of American society, and the ecological tragedy of its exurban form: "SUVs everywhere, snowmobiles everywhere, Jet Skis everywhere, ATVs everywhere. The goddamned green monospecific chemical-drenched lawns." But he reserves a special opprobrium for the litany of disasters unfolding in the developed world: "genocide and famine in Africa, the radicalized dead-end underclass in the Arab world . . . the Han Chinese overrunning Tibet, a hundred million poor people in nuclear Pakistan"—all of which, he suggests, could be "tremendously alleviated by having fewer people."[85] When Walter discovers that Vin Haven is simply using the trust—and Warbler Park—as cover, to disguise the expansion of his mining concerns across the state, he decides to act in a parallel way, using the specter of warbler extinction as a front for his crusade against humans having more babies. Walter's gambit, as Andrew Hoberek puts it, is that he can "bend Haven's self-interested motives in the service of enlightened public interest."[86] But the primitive accumulation that the trust furthers is the precise condition of possibility for the expanded reproduction that Walter hopes to slow down or reverse.

Though Walter persists in his delusion that this contradiction might be navigated if not transcended, Richard's astute skepticism cuts to the heart of the matter: "The real reason you can't get any traction with over-population," Richard counsels Walter, "is that talking about fewer babies means talking about limits to growth. . . . And growth isn't some side issue in free-market ideology. It's the entire essence."[87] Richard's insights point to the reactionary connotations of putatively progressive rhetoric such as "conservation" and "sustainability"—words that, while evoking the need to protect the environment from rapacious industry, also accord with a kind of conservatism, the possibility of preserving, in perpetuity, the hegemony of market forces (and the uneven social order to which they correspond). One cannot be, as Walter is, against growth but aligned with capital. Patty admires Walter's "indifference to money," his lack of interest in accumulating private wealth. But that indifference to capital, an effect and affect of bourgeois privilege, doubles as a kind of indifference to capitalism as such. Walter's foray into the public sphere, his assertion of political commitment, fails to confront the essential material and ideological fundament of the social order he hopes to transform—the capitalist market.

In the end, Walter retreats from the theater of politics to the family cabin in the woods of northern Minnesota, where he is reunited with Patty. There he trades the vast ambition of planetary population reversal for the modest scale and consequence of a private bird sanctuary. The symbolism of this denouement is manifold. It might be read as a parable of the inefficacy of liberal politics in the face of global capital; or as an allegory of the declension of the demos, and triumph of the private sphere, in the context of neoliberalism's ascendance; or as a broader commentary on the fading political agency of individuals and publics alike, in the context of history's assumed end. In another reading, though, Walter's withdrawal summons a truth that has long been expressed by the bourgeois novel: the world-historical consequence of the bourgeois and bourgeoisie is not expressed by concrete action on the global stage; simply doing nothing and being anonymous (it's notable that the Berglund's place of refuge is "Nameless Lake") as wealth compounds, as the stock of capital expands, as capitalist social relations are reproduced, is enough. This passive mode of conservation and sustainability is itself a profoundly impactful way of being in the world. Perhaps the ultimate "freedom" of the bourgeoisie is the ability to determine the course of history while apparently doing nothing at all.

However tactically and substantively misguided his political adventures might have been, Walter was attempting to reclaim the possibility of freedom, and of an authentic self, by working to redress, in one discrete context, the violence of capital's relentless expansion. Franzen's novel, in other words, conceives of the "social critique" of capital in instrumental terms. Walter's liberal politics promise, not the transcendence of social and economic injustice, but the redemption of bourgeois freedom and agency. Walter's retreat to Nameless Lake, at the narrative's close, signals the twofold redundancy of the "social critique"—the immense obstacles to progressive transformation in the current capitalist conjuncture, and the diminished possibilities for (active and not merely passive) bourgeois political agency. But despite its fatalism in this regard—and despite its narrowly bourgeois vision and concern—the novel does make plain the degraded resonance of freedom in its neoliberal articulation, and in so doing intimates, at least, that the "artistic critique" might be disentangled from its complicity with capital, and new imaginaries of freedom's possibilities might come into view.

This possibility is registered, too, by Kunkel's *Indecision*. Plagued by an ennui that resembles Patty Berglund's, the narrator-protagonist of *Indecision*, Dwight Wilmerding, is prone to meditating on the "Uses of Freedom." Faced with the prospect of a trip to Ecuador, in pursuit of an unrealized love, Dwight reflects that "I was trembling. After all here was a new place, therefore a new life, and hence an occasion for some quaking at the prospect of doing right away, if you want to, and can make up your mind, a wide variety of things in this world."[88] As in *Freedom*, the intimacy of freedom and anxiety is a symptom of the waning of historicity in the current capitalist conjuncture. Dwight's trip to Ecuador (of which more anon) is a sort of existential holiday from his New York life, where, as the "unambitious and flannel-wearing holder-down of a totally dead-end job," he embodies the various material and cultural clichés of perpetual late adolescence—a state of aimlessness and indecisiveness, marked by leisurely brunches, that reflects the apparent eternality of late capitalism.[89] Some-time after puberty, Dwight reflects, "I'd begun to proceed unsteadily from day to day as if I were on a bridge swaying in the wind while both sides of the canyon—I mean past and future—disappeared in foggy weather."[90] And there he remains. If the possibilities of doing "a wide varieties of things in this world" fill Dwight with disquiet, his job at Pfizer's "Problem Reso-lution Center" offers something of a respite. "It seemed to me," Dwight opines, "that the plight of the low-level corporate drone was unfairly ma-ligned by believers in social justice and human potential. It was true," he acknowledges, "that the pay was low, the benefits nonexistent, the question of upward mobility moot, and the institutional neglect of our hidden tal-ents almost complete. But what a tremendous, almost vegetal peacefulness there was in working for das Man!" Dwight's embrace of his own anony-mous mediocrity and neutrality, he surmises, will absolve him from any responsibility for "whatever happened to me or my country."[91]

Dwight, as he explains to his sister Alice, has a "resistance to events." "The Wall came down, whole world changed, now we're not going to die in a nuclear holocaust anymore. But it didn't really *feel* like anything hap-pening, not to me." Events, he concludes, "don't always seem to happen, even when they do."[92] Dwight's diagnosis betrays the obvious fact that the "end of history" is a question of ideology and affect rather than a concrete political-economic reality. And if a cognitive or psychological pathology, Dwight's condition might be corrected via pharmaceutical intervention. This, anyway, is the promise made by Dwight's roommate Dan, who sug-gests that Dwight's abulia—his absence of willpower, his allergic relation-ship to the "choices" that accompany his privileged subjectivity—might be cured by a new drug, currently in clinical trial, "Abulinix." Dwight takes the pill he is offered with uncharacteristic decisiveness, and he and Dan cel-ebrate by drinking some caffeinated malt liquor. While they are shopping for snacks (to pair with the alcohol) the drug's impact appears immediate, but Dan informs him that Abulinix takes a week or two to take. "A minute before," when he assumed the pill's influence, "all the commodities on the shelves had seemed to brim and gleam with imminent disclosures." But now, aware of its inefficacy, such items "were restored to being things that are only themselves."[93] It is significant that the drug's perceived first effect is not to help Dwight choose a snack, exactly, but to help him see where the snack comes from—its real history, its embeddedness in international structures of production and exchange. The implication is that Dwight's imprisonment in the perpetual present of capital, and the indecision that is the symptom of that confinement, is closely connected to the fetishism of the commodity. Liberating oneself from the end of history will require, *Indecision* insists, reckoning with history itself—the origins of the commodity, the reified social relations that it contains and conceals.

Heretofore, Dwight's vague knowledge of the commodity form was derived from his father, a commodities trader befallen by the downturn of 2000. "I knew," Dwight reflects, that "money had been invested at high risk, generating high returns, in gambles on foreign-exchange rates, actual commodities, interest rates, and so on. You took an average directional movement of this, and some strength indicators from that, and figured in some four-day average true ranges, and you fed this stuff to the computer until arrows came on screen telling you to get in or out."[94] Dwight has a firm grasp of the mystifying qualities of finance's lexicon and algorithmic complexity—but less of a grip on the material worlds that finance transforms, the contradictions it generates and exploits. His apprehension of those contradictions is deepened, though, by the aforementioned trip to Ecuador, where he meets and falls in love with a young Belgian socialist, and erstwhile anthropologist, Brigid. When Dwight, early in their relationship, asks Brigid, "so what's the scene here, like economically?" she replies with a "furious primer on underdevelopment." She explains, specifically, "how the oil companies spirited the crude out of Ecuador, leaving behind just a few dollars for pipeline builders and low-level managers; how the IMF made its new loans conditional on a screamingly high general sales tax; how local industry had hardly been allowed to develop, dooming the country to the mere export of unfinished goods *while a sedentary comprador class squatted atop their rentier wealth*" (emphasis in original).[95] At first, these pedagogical sessions have a purely cerebral effect on Dwight, and do not translate into manifest political commitment. More moved by the exoticism of his location, "high on benevolent novelty," Dwight resolves instead to "strew kindnesses throughout the world."[96]

But as the Abulinix begins to take effect, or as it seems to do so, the tenor of Dwight's enlightenment shifts—from philosophical meditations on the "uses of freedom" to political reflections on the urgency of socialism. His evolution is encouraged by Brigid, who insists that Dwight not simply register the realities of dispossession and inequality in Ecuador, but locate himself—his own privilege, the imperial subjectivity that is his birthright as a white, economically secure, American male—within global structures and processes of uneven and combined development. This exercise in rigorous self-critique, which doubles as a reckoning with the planetary aggregate of capitalist social relations, is, for Dwight, initially estranging. "Now that I thought of my particular American family, and the portion of lucky accident that seemed to have fallen onto our lives to get mistaken for grace, I became a little unreal to myself. Their luck had become my luck, and what did I do with my luck? It seemed like I just sat in it, waiting for more."[97] What is immediately alienating is not the fact of his privilege as such—the global asymmetries that it represents—but the smarting recognition that he has done so little with it, that he has passively waited for his stock of freedoms (and his inherited wealth) to accumulate, instead of exploiting the "uses" of those freedoms to some greater internal or external consequence. Which is another way of saying that Dwight's political self-becoming, even with the catalytic impacts of Abulinix and Brigid's intellectual and romantic charms, has not reached its narrative apotheosis.

In the meantime, before the novel's *bildung* trajectory does approach its denouement, Dwight has pangs of doubt about the need to really evolve at all. Perhaps, he reflects, "all along my mediocrity has been just what I needed to accept, to embrace, in order to have a healthy, happy [life]."[98] Brigid even seems to endorse this idea, and Dwight's earlier observation that he has a "resistance to events," when she notes that "nothing can happen to you. You are that type"—the anonymous, unremarkable, bourgeois, who acts upon the world and its historical movement, through passivity or otherwise, but is immune to being acted upon. Abulinix is not enough, it turns out; more potent drugs are required. Under the ecstatic influence of an "autochthonous hallucinogen," Dwight and Brigid consummate their union while enunciating the radical political possibilities their love would seem to prefigure. In the midst of their reverie, as they prepare to share a *tomate de arbol*, Brigid remarks, in the spirit of revolutionary speculation, that "when you eat from this fruit then whenever you put your hand on a product, a commodity, an article, then, at the moment of your touch, how this commodity came into your hands becomes plainly evident to you. Now," she imagines, "there is no more mystification of labor, no more of a world in which the object arrives by magic—scrubbed, clean, no past, all of its history washed away."[99] This vision recalls Dwight's ephemeral epiphany in the deli in New York, when—charged by the assumed effects of Abulinix—the curtains of commodity fetishism began to part and the snacks on the shelf hinted at their true origins and essence. Dwight decides, in Ecuador, to "sign up for justice." This resolution manifests, in the first instance, as an ideological embrace of democratic socialism; but it is expressed, too, by Dwight's avowed commitment to the imperative of cognitive mapping, the project of apprehending the totality of global social relations—crystallized in the commodity—and the complicity of oneself therein.

Back in the United States, with Brigid by his side, Dwight attends his high school reunion, at which he delivers an impassioned speech—on the urgency of democratic socialism, and on the need to exploit the freedoms afforded the privileged subjects of the advanced capitalist world in the service of freedom for everyone everywhere. "It seems to me," Dwight addresses his former classmates, "that we, in this room, for reasons of cruel and unusual socioeconomic conditions, have an especially big range of decisions we could make, and so there is a particular burden. . . . The weird thing about freedom to choose would seem to be that no one knows what do with it until they give it to others. . . . Only when other people have the same freedom that we have committed ourselves to squandering," he concludes, "only then will we finally know what we should have done with ours in the first place. So let us remain faithful to those privileged kids we were by seeking to honor and cancel our condition by making it general throughout the world."[100] Dwight makes good on this rhetoric by taking up a position in Bolivia, where he works on behalf of the local coca farmers, whose livelihood is threatened by national security forces acting as a proxy for the US government. Whether or not this political activism will contribute to a more equitable global distribution of freedom—and there is an evident affinity here between Dwight and Franzen's Walter, both of whom pursue political commitment in order to realize personal meaning—Dwight keeps close "the vision we combined to see in Ecuador, in which commodities disclose their history to the touch and in one huge epidemic of empathy we start repairing the world."[101] A consistently hilarious voice, it might be difficult to take Dwight seriously—but the formulation he arrives at here is earnest and urgent: any radical collective politics we create in the present will necessarily be prefaced and accompanied by a rigorous attempt to locate ourselves within the history that the de-fetishized commodity unveils.

The image of a commodity that reveals its own history is mirrored quite precisely in the early pages of Lerner's novel *10:04*. As "an unusually large cyclonic system with a warm core" approaches New York, the city was "becoming one organism, constituting itself in relation to a threat viewable from space."[102] This dialectical apparition of totality—a vision of collective possibility that is provoked by the planetary catastrophe of climate change—comes into focus when the narrator and his close friend Alex wander the nearly empty shelves of Whole Foods in Union Square, in the hopes of sourcing some emergency supplies. The imminence of the storm, the narrator reflects, "was estranging the routine of shopping just enough to make me viscerally aware of both the miracle and insanity of the mundane economy." Holding a can of instant coffee, the narrator grasps that "the seeds in the purple fruits of coffee plants had been harvested on Andean slopes and roasted and ground and soaked and then dehydrated at a factory in Medellin and vacuum-sealed and flown to JFK and then driven upstate in bulk to Pearl River for packaging and then transported back by the truck to the store where I now stood reading the label. It was as if," he observes, "the social relations that produced the object in my hand began to glow within it . . . the majesty and murderous stupidity of that organization of time and space and fuel and labor becoming visible in the commodity itself now that planes were grounded and the highways were starting to close."[103] Here the alteration of reality, and the global sight and orientation it enables, is conditioned not by drugs—although the narrator does feel "stoned"—but by climatological disturbance. The specter of ecological apocalypse makes visible the violence and inanity of the economic relations that produce surplus value, while simultaneously signaling the immanence of alternative ("good") forms of collectivity.

10:04 foregrounds the problem of reproduction—the possibility or impossibility of living on, and of creating newness, in a time in which the expansionary reproduction of capital disables the reproduction of life on earth. In the novel's opening scene, the narrator is celebrating the "strong six figure" advance for the book that we are reading with an "outrageously expensive" meal featuring baby octopuses that the chef had "literally massaged to death." This image of absurd consumption prompts a meditation on the immediacy of radical alterity, the other worlds within this one. Leaving the restaurant with his agent, the narrator reflects that "I felt subject to a succession of images, sensations, memories, and affects that did not, properly speaking, belong to me."[104] This intuition of otherness is echoed when the narrative transitions to the past, to a room in the pediatric wing of a hospital—adorned with "octopus and starfish and various gill-bearing craniate animals"—where the narrator is being diagnosed with the genetic disorder Marfan syndrome, a medical determination that prompts "the awareness that there was a statistically significant chance the largest artery in my body would rupture at any moment. . . . What I mean is that my parts were coming to possess a terrible neurological autonomy not only spatial but temporal, my future collapsing in upon me."[105] From this reflection on the acute and visceral experience of his own mortality—which dovetails with the specter of climate change, the mortality of the planet at large—the narrator moves to an anecdote about the possibility of biological reproduction. Alex desires a child, and he has agreed to contribute his sperm to the IUI process, fertility treatments that—in lieu of decent health insurance—his "strong six figure" advance will help pay for. In these opening pages, the novel's core themes are established—the possibility or impossibility of futurity, in a present defined by both the superfluity and scarcity of capital, as by the creeping catastrophe of a warming planet.

The narrator's interest in the possibility of becoming a father is heightened when he opens up his apartment to a participant in the Occupy Wall Street demonstration who is in need of a shower, and for whom he prepares a meal. This gesture of goodwill—a way of contributing to a radical event the narrator is sympathetic to but has not in any meaningful way joined—provokes an extended internal reflection on the politics of care and kinship. As it occurs to him that he almost never cooks for his friends, the narrator "was crushed to realize that nobody depended on *me* for this fundamental mode of care, of nurturing, nourishing . . . and for the first time I could remember I wanted a child, wanted one badly." But he then chastises himself for this selfish response to his self-reflexive attention to his own selfishness:

> You let a young man committed to anticapitalist struggle shower in the overpriced apartment you rent and . . . your thoughts lead inexorably to the desire to reproduce your own genetic material within some version of a bourgeois household. . . . Your gesture of briefly placing a tiny part of the domestic—your bathroom—into the commons leads you to redescribe the possibility of collective politics as the private drama of the family.

Instead, the narrator concludes, "what you need to do is harness the self-love you are hypostasizing as offspring, as the next generation of you, and let it branch out horizontally into the possibility of a transpersonal revolutionary subject in the present and coconstruct a world in which moments can be something other than the elements of profit."[106] The narrator is proposing a mode of love that resists, rather than works in complicity with, the expansionary reproduction of capital. This collective subject is at once urgently present and of the future, when the possibility of a community founded in opposition to the logics of the commodity form will acquire a more manifest form.

The Occupy encampment is one model of what that community might look like, "a proprioceptive flicker," to recite a phrase that reverberates throughout the novel, "in advance of the communal body."[107] But the narrator does not accompany the Occupy protestor on his return to Zuccotti Park, choosing instead to continue to an art installation uptown—Christian Marclay's *The Clock* (2010), a video work that is playing without interruption for seven days. In one sense, the narrator's bypassing of the Occupy encampment—an absence he promises will be redressed by subsequent visits to the People's Library—highlights the contrast between mere intellectualizing and concrete political action. The immediate transition to *The Clock*, though, suggests a less absolute moral. Art might itself hasten the construction of "a world in which moments can be something other than the elements of profit." *The Clock*, as the narrator summarizes it, is a twenty-four-hour montage of scenes from film and television "edited together so as to be shown in real time." The time on the screen—indicated by shots of a clock or watch—mirrors that in the "real" world of the theater in New York. Watching the film, the narrator "was experiencing time as such, not just having experiences through it as a medium. As I made and unmade a variety of overlapping narratives out of its found footage," the narrator reflects, "I felt acutely how many days could be built out of a day, felt more possibility than determinism, the utopian glimmer of fiction."[108] If the capitalist present, in Jameson's diagnosis, is drained of historicity, is defined by its *a*temporality, and if, we are told, "there is no alternative" to the eternal neoliberal present, the narrator's reading of *The Clock* points to a different way of thinking about and experiencing time in the current conjuncture: every instant contains myriad alternatives, the material and narrative fundament from which infinite other worlds might be constructed. The Occupy demonstration and the film are allied critical interventions—insisting on the multiplicity of possibilities that any given present, and thus the future, contains.

The narrator's decision to conceive a child with Alex is prefaced by and provokes sincere meditations on the prospects of biological reproduction in a time of deepening economic precarity and planetary mortality. Working through his anxieties about the process, and the future it implies, the narrator rehearses a conversation with his hypothetical daughter. "Why reproduce," she asks, "if you believe the world is ending?" The narrator replies: "Because the world is always ending for each of us and if one begins to withdraw from the possibilities of experience, then no one would take any of the risks involved with love. And love has to be harnessed by the political."[109] Here, then, the narrator slightly modifies his earlier self-admonition of the "self-love" that inspired his desire to reproduce. Reproduction, the act of bringing another person into the world and caring for them as they grow, is a creative practice, one that might contribute to rather than contradict the formation of a "transpersonal revolutionary subject" in the present. Giving voice to the narrator's own anxieties, though, his future child is unconvinced. "Can you imagine the world," she challenges, "when I'm twenty? Thirty? Forty?" The narrator concedes that he cannot.[110] But throughout the novel, the narrator glimpses, and is moved by, visions of what that future might look like, the other worlds that are immanent to this one, which will obviate the apocalypse or emerge in its wake. Looking across the water toward Manhattan, the narrator marvels at the thrill, the charge of possibility, produced by the "innumerable illuminated windows and the liquid sapphire and ruby of traffic on the FDR Drive . . . the human dimension of the windows tiny from such a distance combining but not dissolving into the larger architecture of the skyline that was the expression, the material signature of a collective person who didn't yet exist, a still uninhabited second-person plural." Only the built environment can provoke this frisson of the sublime, because "only then was the greatness beyond calculation the intuition of community. Bundled debt, trace amounts of antidepressants in the municipal water, the vast arterial networks of traffic, changing weather patterns of increasing severity— whenever I looked at lower Manhattan from Whitman's side of the river," the narrator reflects, "I resolved to become one of the artists who made bad forms of collectivity figures of its possibility."[111]

As his encounter with *The Clock* suggests, the narrator of *10:04* is occupied by the pursuit of aesthetic experiences that begin to undo the conjoined apparatuses of fetishism and reification. The "Institute for Totaled Art" curated by his friend Alena is one privileged source of inspiration. Housed in Alena's apartment, the Institute is a collection of artworks that have been cleansed of their exchange value, freed from their status as commodities, as a result of some minor, often imperceptible damage. "I was familiar," the narrator reflects, "with material things that seemed to have taken on a kind of magical power as a result of a monetizable signature"—such as a swoosh-adorned shoe, Picasso painting, or Louis Vuitton bag—"but it was incredibly rare to encounter an object liberated from that logic. . . . It was as if," he marvels, "I could register in my hands a subtle but momentous transfer of weight: the twenty-one grams of the market's soul had fled; it was no longer a commodity fetish; it was art before or after capital . . . an object for or from a future where there was some other regime of value than the tyranny of price."[112] The Institute recalls, in ways, the narrator's epiphanal experience in Whole Foods, when the estranging effects of the approaching storm suspend the powers of fetishism, endowing the can of coffee grounds with a transcendent aura that reveals the history of the commodity—the "majesty and murderous stupidity" of the social relations that produced the object and placed it in the narrator's hands. This dialectical phrase is later invoked in a passage that returns to the dinner scene of the novel's opening: "I swallowed and the majesty and murderous stupidity of it was all about me, coursing through me: the rhythm of artisanal Portuguese octopus fisheries coordinated with the rhythm of laborers' migration and the rise and fall of art commodities and tradable futures in the dark galleries outside the market and the mercury and radiation levels of the sashimi and the chests of the beautiful people in the restaurant—coordinated, or so it appeared, by money."[113] As Lerner has put it in an interview, "there is a sense in which community is already here . . . in the circuits of global capital (that moves a baby octopus from Portuguese waters to a Chelsea restaurant), and even if those are deeply perverted forms of interconnectedness they nevertheless have a utopian glimmer."[114]

As *10:04* demonstrates, the problem of ideology—the "representation of the imaginary relationship of individuals to their real conditions of existence"—is a problem of apprehending, or failing to apprehend, the contradictions that constitute, as Jameson has put it, "the ensemble of society's structures as a whole."[115] But it is also a problem of how the individual or collective subject locates within that ensemble, or those contradictions, the figment or outline of some alternative. The project of cognitive mapping contains a historical—and not merely spatial or structural—dimension. And that historical imperative bears upon the future as well as the past. Resisting the fetishism of the commodity will involve the illumination of the history of the object—the social relations that produced the surplus value it contains— *and* the revelation of a future wherein commodity rationality has lost its hold. The "totaled" commodity will disclose both the "murderous stupidity" of the totality of global capital, and the manifold majestic futures obscured by the mantra that "there is no alternative" to capital's eternal present.

Conclusion

If capital is founded through violence and primitive expropriation, how is it reproduced? In one sense, this question is technical. It refers, in Marx's account, to the distinction between simple and expanded reproduction—the mere consumption of the surplus or its reinvestment in fixed and variable capital. In another sense, though, this question concerns the social relations of capital—the "natural laws" of production that bind capital and labor, and the mechanisms of ideology, spirit, and governmentality that guide the capitalist's pursuit of profit and compel the worker to voluntarily sell their labor power for a wage. The "silent compulsion" of the market is especially pronounced in the current historical conjuncture, wherein the neoliberal idea that "there is no alternative"—a close rhetorical cousin of the notion that we live in the "end of history"—inhibits the cultural critique, and circumscribes the legislative redress, of deepening economic inequality and insecurity. Yet as the theorists of ideology—and, to a lesser extent, spirit and governmentality—remind us, what Gramsci described as the "war of position" between competing ways of imaginatively representing the world continues apace. And the contest between the forces of naturalization and the forces of denaturalization is enacted with unique clarity, I have argued, in the contemporary bourgeois-realist novel, the paradigmatic literary form of the moment of expanded reproduction. All of the novels I consider above depict the collective malaise that defines the lived experience of the "end of history," a time-space of putative triumph—the generalization of the conditions of perpetual growth—that is marked, in the advanced capitalist world, by the reality or feel of decline. But they also question the apparent fixity of capitalism, by exposing the fragility of its ideological armature. *Indecision* and *10:04*, in particular, herald, without themselves fully realizing, a narrative modality, or an emergent "structure of feeling"—a "cultural hypothesis"—that illuminates the history of the capitalist present and reclaims the possibility of its transformation or transcendence.

CHAPTER 3

Synthetic Dispossession

WITHIN THE CONTEMPORARY GLOBAL capitalist order, the emergency is the rule. Crises of democratic governance dovetail with economic crises and the planetary emergency of climate change. The generality of crisis is especially apparent in the moment of "synthetic dispossession." Therein, the deepening of insecurity and corresponding crisis of capitalist ideology provoke the resurgent importance of state violence. But the popular recognition of what Lauren Berlant terms "crisis ordinariness" gives rise to new vocabularies of political critique and cultural speculation, opening up the space for the emergence of alternative social and political formations.

The constancy of crisis in the current conjuncture is an effect, in large part, of synthetic methods of dispossession. Rosa Luxemburg observed, more than a century ago, that the perpetuation of capital requires "noncapitalist strata." She derived from this deduction a theoretical certainty in capitalism's mortality. When there is no longer an "outside" to assimilate—non-commoditized spaces or non-integrated markets—accumulation will cease.[1] The primitive accumulation and expansionary reproduction of capital is a finite process because the planet—its land, resources, and people—is finite. As David Harvey has described, though, capital strives to evade this apparently immutable contradiction by fabricating new outsides to capital—via the privatization of public goods and services, and the

120

deliberate devaluation of assets and labor (so as to enable their later seizure by currently idle or overaccumulated capital).[2] The synthesis and appropriation of new outsides to capital coincides, moreover, with the general ascent of financialization—the creation of money by money, without the necessary intermediation of the commodity (the speculative claim to a future surplus rather than direct investment in production, in the form, for example, of predatory credit or complex instruments of securitization).

When the bubbles created by liberated financial capital burst, the resultant crisis justifies the imposition of austerity and further rounds of privatization and devaluation. This regressive redistribution of wealth—which consolidates the power of the capitalist class, but which discourages meaningful economic growth—corresponds to the generalization of social and economic precariousness. The expansion of insecurity occasions a breakdown of consent, not simply within the working classes, but within the formerly secure middle classes as well. The consultants and managers who oversee the downsizing of the firm are still keen to invoke the virtues of efficiency and flexibility. And the newly adrift worker might maintain a compensatory belief, however threadbare, in the freedom and community promised by the "sharing economy." But growing insecurity inevitably gives rise to acute cultures of repression. In the advanced capitalist world, the increasing scarcity of secure employment and retrenchment of social protections have coincided with the militarization of public and private police, who occupy communities abandoned or razed by capital and further the project of mass incarceration. To again summon Stuart Hall, in the moment of crisis, "the masks of liberal consent and popular consensus slip to reveal the reserves of coercion and force on which the cohesion of the state and its legal authority depends."[3]

The activation of these reservoirs of force has provoked a renewed activist and scholarly interest in policing and other institutions of punitive state control. The paradigmatic economic and political forms of synthetic dispossession have also occasioned an intensive theoretical consideration of "precarity." In one simple definition, "precarity" names the "structure of affect," as Lauren Berlant has put it, of pervasive insecurity. Though the subjects and spaces of "precarity" are in theory myriad—encompassing both the migrant farmworker and the freelance graphic designer—its analytic currency is conditioned by the effects of synthetic dispossession (and neoliberal policies more broadly) upon formerly secure populations. It is continuous, Berlant has argued, with patterns of social and economic transformation that expose the bourgeoisie to "ordinary contingencies of material and fantasmatic life associated with proletarian labor-related subjectivity."[4] So if, in one sense, neoliberalism makes managers of us all—self-governing and self-surveilling—so too does it universalize the quotidian insecurities of working-class life. The theorists of precarity are interested in the political potentiality of this general insecurity—the recognition of our shared vulnerability and ethos of mutual care that it might provoke.

This politics of precarity has been elucidated by an expanding corpus of contemporary fiction, which is marked by the dialogue between two distinct "structures of feeling," two distinct ways of experiencing—and situating historically—the crisis of the capitalist present. Novels such as Dave Eggers's *A Hologram for the King* (2013) and Rafael Chirbes's *On the Edge* (2016) track the creeping boundaries of insecurity, and fading efficacy of ideology, within the ever-expanding time-space of crisis. The protagonists of these two texts—white men, in each case—are made anxious by their perceived loss of productive power, their redundancy as actors in the spheres of the market and history at large. The prevailing affect, here, is nostalgia—a longing for what has been lost, a bygone time or state of security and belonging. Eugene Lim's *Dear Cyborgs* (2017) and Barbara Browning's *The Gift* (2017), meanwhile, register the feeling and material fact of futurity, the new political horizons that come into view in the context of capital's diminished spirit—the flourishing of new cultures of solidarity, and the radical reconstruction of the social and political commons.

Crises of Accumulation, Crisis of Consent

Liberal political economy, and neoclassical economics, assume that the time of expanded reproduction is potentially interminable. If the laws of the market are respected and refined, the expansionary accumulation of capital can continue without interruption, as the factors of supply and demand will increase in equilibrial rhythm with one another. In this view, periodic crises are attributed to the excessive or imperfect regulation of the market, or simply explained as natural troughs in the business cycle, which ultimately trends toward perpetual growth. The Marxist critique of political economy argues instead that crises are not an aberration from the laws of capital but one sign of its essential contradictions and intrinsic limits.

Marx's writings on crisis are fragmented, and taken together they do not yield one internally coherent interpretation or theory. In different works, and in different passages therein, Marx focuses on the tendency of the rate of profit to fall; overproduction; underconsumption; and disproportionality (for example, a quantitative gulf between the production of raw materials and production of finished goods). One consistent point of focus in his provisional treatment of the problem of crisis, though, is the relationship between the destruction and accumulation of capital. The expansionary movement of capital, Marx observed in the *Grundrisse* ([1857–58] 1993), necessitates, or culminates in, the negation of both capital and wage labor (and the social relations that bind them). "The material and mental conditions of the negation of wage labour and of capital . . . are themselves results of its production process." In other words, the "highest development of productive power together with the greatest expansion of existing wealth will coincide with depreciation of capital, degradation of the labourer, and a most straitened exhaustion of his vital powers." But the process of annihilation/devaluation is, in the first instance, a means of survival—even if, over the course of history at large, it is a sign of capital's mortality. Capital's internal contradictions, especially its tendency toward overaccumulation, "lead to explosions, crises, in which momentary suspension of all labour and annihilation of a great part of the capital violently lead it back to the point where it is enabled [to go on] fully employing its productive powers without committing suicide."[5]

Marx highlighted in the *Grundrisse*, that is, "the violent destruction of capital not by relations external to it, but rather as a condition of its self-preservation."[6] He revisited and expanded upon these insights in *Theories of Surplus Value* ([1862–63] 2000), where he described how the destruction of exchange value provides an outlet for investment capital, which seizes upon and reintroduces into the sphere of circulation extant use values. "The *destruction of capital* through crises," Marx wrote,

> means the depreciation of *values* which prevents them from later renewing
> their reproduction process as capital on the same scale. This is the ruin-
> ous effect of the fall in the prices of commodities. It does not cause the
> destruction of any use-values. What one loses, the other gains. Values used
> as capital are prevented from acting again as *capital* in the hands of the same
> person. The old capitalists go bankrupt. ... A large part of the nominal capi-
> tal of the society, i.e., of the *exchange-value* of the existing capital, is once
> and for all destroyed, although this very destruction, since it does not affect
> the use-value, may very much expedite the new reproduction.[7]

The devaluation of assets and labor as a result of financial crises, and the utter destruction of commodities and fixed capital as a result of natural disasters and war, fuel the engines of profit generation. This is not a question of resuming the mechanisms of growth as such, but of synthesizing and exploiting circumstances conducive to dispossession. Capital strives to redress crises of overproduction in particular, Marx and Engels wrote in *The Communist Manifesto*, "on the one hand by enforced destruction of a mass of productive forces; on the other, by the conquest of new markets, and by the more thorough exploitation of the old ones. That is to say, by paving the way for more extensive and more destructive crises, and by diminishing the means whereby crises are prevented."[8] Capital may be able to defer the ultimate crisis in space and time, through the conquest of an extant outside, or through the creation of new "outsides" within already capitalized spaces—primitive accumulation and synthetic dispossession. But the immediate cure only deepens the underlying disease and accelerates its terminal trajectory.

Marx's reflections on capital's crisis tendencies were later elaborated by Rosa Luxemburg, as I've discussed, and by Rudolf Hilferding and V. I. Lenin—three thinkers who were writing at the heart of the modern imperialist era, and in the midst or aftermath of the cataclysms that shook the capitalist world around the turn of the century. In *The Accumulation of Capital* ([1913] 2003), Luxemburg chronicled the planetary dissemination of capital into the non-capitalist strata—the colonization of new markets and seizure of new resources. This attention to the imperative of primitive accumulation was accompanied, in *Reform or Revolution* (1899), by a sustained examination of two conjoined trends, which are pronounced in the moment of synthetic dispossession: the centralization of capital (in the form of cartels, trusts, or joint-stock companies), and the rise of financial capital. In the latter decades of the nineteenth century, the concentration of capital dramatically increased profits in certain industries, and appeared to mitigate the "anarchy" of competition. But in reality, the domestic power of cartels and trusts exacerbated the tensions between capital's national and international expressions—heightening the destructive confrontation of different capitalist states—and further encouraged the possibility of a truly global crisis. The stimulus provided by financial capital, meanwhile, alleviated economic crises in the immediate term but heightened the more protracted effects of overproduction. "If it is true," Luxemburg wrote, "that crises arise from the contradiction between the capacity, and tendency, of production to expand and the limited capacity of the market to absorb the products, then, in view of the above, credit is precisely the means whereby this contradiction is brought to a head as often as is possible. In particular," she continues, "it vastly increases the rate at which production expands, and it provides the inner driving force which constantly pushes production beyond the limits imposed by the market."[9] As Luxemburg considered at length in *The Accumulation of Capital*, imperialism becomes the means through which "the limits imposed by the market" are stretched—if never, of course, transcended. Eventually, Luxemburg avowed, the world market will encounter its own finitude. The expansionary drive of capital will be arrested by the limits of the earth itself. Like Marx and Engels, all this is to say, Luxemburg insisted, with equal parts anticipation and scientific rigor, that all of the ostensible correctives to capitalist crises—the concentration of capital, the interventions of finance, and the expansion of capital into the non-capitalist strata—actually increase the likelihood of a more planetary, and more catastrophic, crisis.

Key elements of Luxemburg's diagnosis—her attention to the antagonism between capitalist states, and her analysis of finance capital's destructive effects—were likewise central to the work of Lenin. Lenin focused on the connections between monopolization and imperialism—the progressive concentration of capital and its need to expand across space and

plunder its outside. His core argument was that the tendency toward monopoly in the industrialized world created crises of overaccumulation—
stores of capital with no profitable outlet—which compelled the export of
capital, in the form of finished products in search of new markets, and speculative capital in search of investment opportunities. As domestic rates of
profit decline, moreover, the vast—actual and potential—proletariat of the
underdeveloped world enabled capital to increase the rate of exploitation.
In simple terms, imperialism, for Lenin, is the political process through
which the essential relation of capital and labor is mirrored and magnified
by the uneven and combined development of the rich and poor nations or
regions of the world. It is the "highest stage" of capitalism for several reasons: it marks the transmutation of productive capital into finance capital
(financialization, Lenin insisted, is the final stage of capital's concentration,
the apotheosis of monopoly); it corresponds to the intensification of the
contest between different capitalist states, who compete, militarily and otherwise, for what's left of the non-capitalized world; and it generalizes the
proletarian condition—degrading labor in metropole and colony alike, and
thereby bringing into being a truly global revolutionary class. It should be
clear, by this point, that for both Luxemburg and Lenin the theorization
of crisis is closely joined to the prophecy of revolution. The inevitability
of crisis—indeed, of an ultimate crisis—is, in large part, what guarantees
the possibility of radical socialist transformation. There is, then, a way in
which the tone of the *Manifesto*—which conveys desire in the language of
certainty—creeps its way into the Marxist treatment of crisis.

In her reflections on finance capital, Luxemburg noted that credit "cuts
both ways":

> Having brought about overproduction (as a factor in the productive pro-
> cess), it then, in the subsequent crisis, assumes its character as a means
> of circulation and demolishes all the more thoroughly the very forces of
> production it helped to create. . . . Credit reproduces all the main contra-
> dictions of the capitalist world. It pushes them to the point of absurdity, it
> convicts capitalism of its own inadequacies, and it hastens the pace at which
> capitalism speeds towards its own destruction, the collapse.[10]

While credit facilitates growth, it also, in the moment of crisis, accelerates
and exacerbates the economic downturn. "At the first sign of a slump,"

Luxemburg concludes, "credit melts away. It abandons exchange just when it is most needed . . . and reduces the consumer market to a minimum."[11] Finance capital, though, does not merely give rise to the crisis and magnify its destructive effects; it exploits the very contraction it encourages, by betting on the declining price of, or seizing upon, devalued assets. Finance capital, that is, disrupts the imperatives of expanded reproduction, and demonstrates how new sources of profit might be found within or assembled from the ruins of crisis. In the context of crisis, synthetic "outsides" to capital are created, which capital then re-assimilates—deriving profits from the difference between an asset's new (devalued) and former (pre-crisis) price.

The recurring crises that mark the current capitalist conjuncture, in the wealthiest countries in particular, are a symptom of the increasing incongruence between the accumulation of claims on the future production of value and the actual quantity of value being produced. And the destabilizing implications of this disequilibrium are further intensified by the emergence and expansion of more "sophisticated" mechanisms of financialization—from the growth of "finance markets" (for example, mutual or monetary funds that allow the consumer to bypass the intermediary role of banking institutions) to the post–Bretton Woods liberalization of exchange rates (which encourages practices of risk arbitrage). Together, Cédric Durand observes, these transformations have led to "an explosion of new sectors of fictitious capital standing one degree further from production processes than the basic forms," from credit-default swaps to derivative contracts, which represent "a multiplication of the chains of organizing indebtedness."[12] The advent and proliferation of these new instruments of securitization—and the new spheres of financial exchange in which they operate—underlines again the ways in which speculation is not confined to periods of economic confidence; it also thrives within, even as it helps to provoke, acute crises. The crisis of 2008 did lead to a check on the growth of the more opaque or complex instruments of fictitious capital, such as collateralized debt obligations. But the elementary forms of "fictitious capital"—credit money, government bonds, and corporate shares—continue to occupy an outsized place in the economies of the core capitalist countries.[13] Finance can mask, for a time, the very contradiction of which it is symptomatic—the lack of symmetry, or indeed the profound disconnect, between the wealth that the economy actually produces and the claims upon that wealth. Just like the primitive accumulation of the fictitious commodities, the accumulation of fictitious capital is a method of overcoming or deferring crises that intensifies the contradictions that engender crises, and that is ultimately a sign of what Luxemburg diagnosed as capitalism's intrinsic limits.[14]

The concept of "fictitious capital" is closely joined to that of "creative destruction." Writing in the wake of the Great Depression, Joseph Schumpeter cast the process of "creative destruction" in a new and concentrated light. In *Capitalism, Socialism, and Democracy* (1942), Schumpeter defined capitalism as an "evolutionary" form. In this, he was self-consciously affirming—while extending and adapting—a central assumption of Marx's work, the idea that capitalism "is by nature a form or method of economic change and not only never is but never can be stationary."[15] Change is not a periodic effect of capitalist valorization but its most foundational imperative. Specifically, Schumpeter contended that the fundamental "impulse that sets and keeps the capitalist engine in motion comes from the new consumers' goods, the new methods of production or transportation, the new markets, the new forms of industrial organization that capitalist enterprise creates."[16] Schumpeter ascribed this dynamism to the figure of the entrepreneur and to the movement of "creative destruction" they inaugurate and facilitate. The maintenance and reproduction of capitalism is driven by a "process of industrial mutation . . . that incessantly revolutionizes the economic structure from within, incessantly destroying the old one, incessantly creating a new one. This process of Creative Destruction is the essential fact about capitalism. It is what capitalism consists in and what every capitalist concern has got to live in."[17]

Schumpeter composed his theory of creative destruction in the aftermath of the Great Depression. He insisted that the crisis of 1929 owed its severity to extra-economic factors. It was the consequence, specifically, of "anti-capitalist" policies that prevented the market from regulating itself, from correcting itself internally. If its autonomy had been respected, Schumpeter submitted, the market would have been able to maintain adequate levels of development and growth, to overcome, "of itself," cyclical downturns and obviate the possibility of mass poverty and insecurity. In this reading, the movement of "creative destruction" both demonstrates the generative potential of crises and actively works to prevent economic cataclysms. Karl Polanyi, by contrast, attributed the economic and political crises of the early twentieth century to the excesses of, rather than the external constraints upon, market freedom. "The origins of the cataclysm," he argued, "lay in the Utopian endeavor of economic liberalism to set up a self-regulating market system."[18] Polanyi's critique of that "utopian endeavor" takes a longue durée view. He focuses on the nineteenth-century transmutation of land and labor into commodities fully implicated in the sphere of market exchange, a process that coincided with the "disembedding" of the market from the "social system." Land, labor, and money, Polanyi contended, are "fictitious commodities." If the definition of a commodity is something "produced for sale on the market," land, labor, and money fit awkwardly into this category. Labor is first of all simply a human activity, land is nature (prior to its transformation into salable property), and money is something produced and regulated by governments (that is, not something whose value is primarily determined by the market). Treating these phenomena as commodities like any other has hugely destructive effects. It leads, in simple terms, to the violent deracination of people, despoliation of the environment, and—via cycles of inflation and deflation—social and economic instability and insecurity. If left unchecked, Polanyi observed, the complete subjection of human life and the natural world to the rationality of the commodity form, or the dictums of the market, will ultimately lead to the total annihilation of both people and nature. Capitalist history, though, is marked not just by the movement toward absolute commoditization, but by the counter-movement against the brutalities of the market: the rise of organized labor and advent of the welfare state, and the concomitant construction of various forms of "protectionism" that shielded, for example, farmers, the land itself, and monetary value from the shocks and ravages of the market. The high point of this second phase in capital's "double movement" (Polanyi's phrase) was the postwar period, when a tentative social democratic consensus took hold throughout much of the advanced capitalist world. But since the early 1970s, and with an increasing intensity over the past couple of decades, the capitalist elite has worked to erode social protections and market regulations, and to enable once again the unfettered colonization of the "fictitious commodities" of labor and land. The destructive consequence of this twofold transformation—the shrinking of the social commons and liberation of market forces—has been further aggravated by the deployment of various technologies of financial speculation. The ascent of "fictitious capital" today dovetails with the degradation by capital of people and nature.

Harvey uses the phrase "accumulation by dispossession" to describe the contemporary interrelation of fictitious commodities and fictitious capital. "Accumulation by dispossession," as Harvey defines it, comprises four primary phenomena: privatization and commoditization, financialization, the "management and manipulation" of crises, and the state redistribution of wealth. Through his elaboration of these four core means of accumulation, Harvey illustrates how neoliberal capitalism is premised on the regressive redistribution of wealth and income rather than on growth as such. His development of this basic argument summons, and engages, Luxemburg's insights into the "dual character" of capital accumulation—the creation of surplus value via the exploitation of labor, and the plunder of "noncapitalist strata." Harvey affirms Luxemburg's central contention—that capital requires something outside itself, to overcome or defer crises, and to sustain the expansionary creation of surplus value. Harvey's treatment of this inside-outside dialectic focuses on what he terms the "spatial fix" to crises of overaccumulation—the attempt, by capital, to resolve its intrinsic contradiction through geographic expansion or spatial restructuring.

Capital's "spatial fix" encompasses multiple phenomena, from the forging of new markets at home or abroad, to the external reinvestment of surplus capital, to the expansion of the proletariat and reserve army of labor. Harvey echoes Luxemburg's conviction that if spatial expansion can defer crises it also serves to intensify rather than finally resolve crisis tendency. Harvey helpfully extends Luxemburg's framework, though, by suggesting that capital "can either make use of some pre-existing outside (non-capitalist social formations or some sector within capitalism—such as education—that has not yet been proletarianized) or it can actively manufacture it."[19] For example, if the expanded reproduction of capital requires an increase in the labor force, this can be achieved in multiple ways: by seizing upon various extant "reserves" of labor, from peasant communities to colonized populations (an instance of primitive accumulation); or by deliberately inducing greater levels of unemployment, in order to put downward pressure on wages and create new investment opportunities for overaccumulated capital (an instance of synthetic dispossession).[20] The centrality of the latter devaluation of labor to the continuity of capital's expanded reproduction was highlighted by Marx. "Expansion," he wrote in *Capital*, "is impossible without disposable human material, without an increase in the number of workers, which must occur independently of the absolute growth of the population. This increase is effected by the simple process that constantly 'sets free' a part of the working class; by methods which lessen the number of workers employed in proportion to the increase in production. Modern industry's whole form of motion," he argued, "therefore depends on the constant transformation of a part of the working population into unemployed or semi-employed hands."[21] Both the external colonization and synthetic devaluation of the fictitious commodity of labor is made possible, moreover, by fictitious capital. And so too does fictitious capital drive the contemporary enclosure of common lands, or the private development of land historically held by small farmers. Land enclosure provides an outlet for surplus capital and catalyzes new rounds of real estate speculation. Over the past couple of decades, these and related processes of expropriation have played out with a particular intensity in the Global South. There, structural adjustment programs mandate that national economies institute policies of liberalization and privatization— relaxing the laws around land acquisition and providing tax incentives for foreign investors—in exchange for the right to increase the national debt (in the form of credit from the IMF or World Bank).

Harvey's concept of "accumulation by dispossession" clarifies the affinity between and structural interrelation of crude and synthetic forms of depredation. Marx, too, emphasized the connections between the former and the latter. His treatment of primitive accumulation not only addressed the enclosure of common lands and expropriation of bodies and resources; it also highlighted the fundamental contributions of "stock-exchange gambling and the modern bankocracy," as well as the "expropriation of the expropriators" (a phrase that nicely signifies the asset-stripping methods of contemporary private equity).[22] There are, though, important points of divergence between those modes of accumulation that involve the ex-propriation of an extant outside to capital, and those modes of accumulation that involve the *production*—and later seizure—of "external" entities or spaces. The distinction between primitive accumulation and synthetic dispossession is further evinced, as I have discussed, by the unique if allied forms of governance that prevail in either moment. Primitive accumulation is guaranteed by the threat or enactment of state violence. Synthetic dispossession, meanwhile, corresponds to the fluid combination of outright force and the waning but still pervasive effects of ideology.

Technologies of synthetic dispossession encourage the liberation of the market from its social constraints—the weakening of the welfare state and other forms of social protection, and the general declension of public and democratic spaces. And this transformation occasions the emergence of new paradigms of power and governance. In the advanced capitalist world, the privatization of the social commons has coincided with the militarization of public and private police and rise—in the United States in particular—of mass incarceration.[23] Foucault's prescient theorization of neoliberalism, composed in the late 1970s, highlights governmentality as the quintessential mode of neoliberal power. But in the decades since Foucault delivered his lectures, as the neoliberal rationality he diagnosed has strengthened its hold on social life and increased economic inequality, the ostensibly secondary technologies of discipline and control have reentered the governmental foreground. The declension of the welfare state is correlated to the deepening of the police state. And when crises of accumulation provoke crises of consent, the threat or enactment of state violence becomes yet more primary—not simply a "shield" for the ideological state apparatuses, as Althusser had it, but their dominant complement.

This shift was already registered, also in the late 1970s, by Stuart Hall and the other authors of *Policing the Crisis*. That trenchant work addressed the conditions of possibility for the popular panic, in the United Kingdom, surrounding "mugging" and the perceived rise of violent crime more generally. The trope of "mugging"—in cooperation with the adjacent figures of "*race, crime*, and *youth*"—acted, within the public imagination, as an "index of the disintegration of the social order," as a signifier of crisis that located the source of social insecurity in the specter of the young, Black criminal, rather than in the inequities of the broader political or economic order.[24] Though composed in the years immediately preceding the Thatcher government's violent imposition of neoliberal policies and ideas, *Policing the Crisis* indexed a crisis of political authority, as the hegemony of the postwar social democratic consensus was called into question by various embryonic social forces and the persistent realities of class contradiction. What defines the operations of governance in the moment of crisis, Hall et al. observe, is "the increased reliance on coercive mechanisms and apparatuses already available within the normal repertoire of state power, and the powerful orchestration, in support of this tilt of the balance towards the coercive pole, of an authoritarian consensus. In such moments," they argue, "the 'relative autonomy' of the state is no longer enough to secure the measures necessary for social cohesion or for the larger economic task which a failing and weakened capital requires. The forms of state intervention thus become more overt and more direct."[25] The enactment of the repressive state apparatuses, though, also serves an ideological function. The "reserves of coercion and force" are unevenly distributed. And it is precisely this uneven distribution that lends the ideological apparatuses of the capitalist state their distinctive, if less than universal, force. But as the compulsion of the market becomes yet less compelling and yet more audible, new political possibilities—the positive determination of a planetary rather than ethnically delimited and nationalistic precariat—might come into view.

The Politics of Precarity

The generalization of economic insecurity and waning efficacy of capitalist ideology have occasioned a significant theoretical reckoning with the problem of "precarity"—the affective registers and political consequence of precarious life. In *Cruel Optimism* (2011), Lauren Berlant explores what happens when the fantasies that guide our participation in political and economic systems—the idea, perhaps above all, that the "good life" might be ours—start to unravel, revealing the underlying realities of privation and depression, in a present defined by the "undoing of the demos" (to invoke Wendy Brown's phrasing) and creeping precariousness. *Cruel Optimism* tracks, in Berlant's own words, "the emergence of a precarious public sphere, an intimate public of subjects who circulate scenarios of economic and intimate contingency and trade paradigms for how best to live on, considering."[26] *Cruel Optimism* inhabits the space between one "structure of feeling" and another, a temporality of transition wherein tenuous attachments to redundant ways of imagining the world and our relationship to it begin to give way to new narratives and modes of being in ourselves and living together with others. Berlant uses the term "impasse" to capture this temporal aporia—"a stretch of time in which one moves around with a sense that the world is at once intensely present and enigmatic, such that the activity of living demands both a wandering absorptive awareness and a hypervigilance that collects material that might help to clarify things."[27]

The temporality of "impasse" is closely imbricated with, though not identical to, that of "crisis." On the one hand, the crisis is everyday, structural, and perpetual. But as a genre, "crisis" evokes the acute, the exceptional, the ephemeral.[28] The narrative disorientation that defines the time-space of crisis is, in one sense, an effect of this disconnect—which is also, paradoxically, something like a synthesis; the ubiquity and permanence of crisis is expressed by the quotidian experience of extraordinary forms of violence. And if exceptional violence works to obscure the structural constant of crisis, it is also symptomatic of it. We need, Berlant suggests, to situate our reading of the exceptional event—and its traumatic reverberations—within a broader assumption of "crisis ordinariness," a concept that more accurately describes how people encounter, and construct narratives in relation to, the degradations of contemporary capitalism. More concretely, Berlant writes,

> the current recession congeals decades of class bifurcation, downward mobility, and environmental, political, and social brittleness that have increased progressively since the Reagan era. The intensification of these processes, which reshapes conventions of racial, gendered, sexual, economic, and nation-based subordination, has also increased the probability that structural contingency will create manifest crisis situations in ordinary existence for more kinds of people.[29]

The instruments of synthetic dispossession intensify the conditions of insecurity and crisis, and broaden and pluralize spaces of immiseration and exclusion. The Mexican small farmer driven off her land by NAFTA migrates toward the maquiladoras of Juarez or the meatpacking plants, corporate fields, and service industries north of the border. The outsourced American worker, meanwhile, takes a job at Walmart, where she earns a fraction of her former wage selling the same commodities she used to produce. If these two subjects meet in the space and moment of synthetic dispossession, they are journeying, respectively, from the moments of primitive accumulation and expanded reproduction; and whatever language of affect or critique results from their convergence will also be informed by their disparate histories.

The crisis, and the insecurity it engenders, is general; but so too is it marked by difference and asymmetry. Social and economic vulnerability are unevenly distributed. There is, in other words, an analytic tension between the generality of crisis and, as Elizabeth Povinelli has put it, "the unequal distribution of life and death, of hope and harm, and of endurance and exhaustion."[30] In *Economies of Abandonment* (2011), Povinelli considers how that unequal distribution corresponds to the contemporary articulation of a series of binaries: biopolitics and necropolitics, governmentality and discipline/control, ideology and state violence. "Neoliberalism," Povinelli writes, "has not merely mimicked the move from *faire mourir ou laisser vivre* to *'faire' vivre et 'laisser' mourir*. It has resuscitated *faire mourir* into its topology of *faire vivre* and *laisser mourir*." According to neoliberal rationality, "any form of life that could not produce values according to market logic would not merely be allowed to die, but, in situations in which the security of the market (and since the market was now the raison d'être of the state, the state) seemed at stake, ferreted out and strangled."[31] But unlike the techniques of sovereign power theorized by Foucault, in *Discipline and Punish* and elsewhere, the contemporary act of making die is—with important exceptions, such as the "shock and awe" bombing of Baghdad—not designed as a spectacle, the terror of which would compel the submission of the public at large, but is rather carried out behind the scenes, or embedded in institutions and structures.

In this sense, Povinelli's understanding of the tense and temporality of crisis rhymes with that of Berlant. Both thinkers set out to describe an experience of suffering—and a struggle for survival—that cannot be apprehended through the vocabulary of the "event," but is quotidian, temporally diffuse. And like Berlant, Povinelli argues for the urgency of formulating a politics that illuminates and centers those lives that "drift across a series of quasi-events into a form of death that can be certified as due to the vagary of 'natural causes.'"[32] How, Povinelli asks, "does one construct an ethics in relation to this kind of dispersed suffering?" Such an ethics must begin by recognizing that my own "good life" is not just proximal to but conditioned by the suffering of others; it will require more than a gesture of empathetic recognition, but a reckoning with the dialectics of difference—the ways in which race, gender, sexuality, ability, and other modes of difference structure a social field wherein some lives flourish and others are consigned to premature death. Even as we observe the generalization of insecurity, and even as we posit the collective subject of the "precariat" to which that common vulnerability gives rise, we must attend to the longer—differentially experienced—history of insecurity and its uneven distribution in the present.

The late-neoliberal present is a temporality of both impasse and creativity wherein a "virtual space . . . opens up between the potentiality and actuality of an alternative social project." The practice of perseverance, of surviving, of living on, can generate new ideas and truths, and "new forms of life."[33] The "alternative social worlds" born of the time-space of precarity are themselves precarious, struggling for life—and against the "'wavering of death'"—even as they represent its endurance.[34] That vulnerability is determined by, or expressive of, the capitalist state's governance of difference. Povinelli outlines the distinction, or toggling, between modalities of state power that "call for the recognition of social difference" and those that "refuse not merely social difference but . . . reduce life to such a degree that that social difference cannot survive." In such indeterminate—yet overdetermined—contexts, "the point may well be to reshape habitudes ahead of recognition, to test something out rather than translate it, not to produce meanings that can be translated, or embodiments that can be recognized."[35] Just as the objective violence of perpetual and pervasive crisis is invisible, concealed by technologies of fetishism and reification, so too are the embryonic social worlds to which everyday suffering gives rise cloaked in "camouflage"—because the politics they signal are as yet "unthinkable," because they are rooted in marginal spaces and subjects, and because their

fragile newness has a better chance of survival if it can evade the apparatuses of surveillance.

Judith Butler's reflections on precarity pursue a subtly different route,
highlighting not the clandestine emergence of radical social formations but
their (para)-public and performative enunciations; not the citizen granted
or denied "recognition," but the body that enacts its rightlessness—and
its vulnerability—and thereby claims the right to have rights. Writing in
response to the early stages of the Arab Spring, and in seeming anticipation
of the Occupy movement, Butler meditates on the political possibilities
of "bodies in alliance" in the street: when "bodies congregate, they move
and speak together, and they lay claim to a certain space as public space."[36]
Butler does not only have in mind those spaces, such as the square, that
immediately signify the "public," or evoke the normative rituals of open
democratic contestation. If movements often depend "on the prior existence of pavement, street, and square," she asserts, "it is equally true that
the collective actions collect the space itself, gather the pavement, and animate and organize the architecture. . . . Bodies in their plurality lay claim
to the public," but also "find and produce the public through seizing and
reconfiguring the matter of material environments. . . . When crowds move
outside the square, to the side street or the back alley, to the neighborhoods where streets are not yet paved," Butler writes, "politics is no longer
defined as the exclusive business of a public sphere distinct from a private
one, but it crosses that line again and again, bringing attention to the way
that politics is already in the home, or on the street, or in the neighbor-
hood, or indeed in those virtual spaces that are unbound by the architecture of the public square."[37] Butler narrates, here, a politics that does not
totally leave behind—as in the autonomist tradition—the central sites and
institutions of established political and economic order, but rather forges
new forms of community, new strategies of persistence (of "living on," in
Berlant's phrasing) that act upon the "public" from within and without its
traditional boundaries.

In the face of a political and economic rationality that leaves some bodies to die slowly and kills others through more immediate technologies
of extermination, the collective that coalesces in the streets—as in other
common spaces, however provisional or ephemeral—embodies the fact

of mutual survival, the power of communal solidarity, and the speculative ideal of socialism. "As bodies," Butler writes, "we suffer and we resist and together . . . exemplify that form of the sustaining social bond that neo-liberal economics has almost destroyed."[38] From the Arab Spring, to the Indignados, Occupy, and Black Lives Matter movements, to the youth riots in London and Paris, the past fifteen years has witnessed an extraordinary profusion of public demonstration. The various documentary texts that have been produced about these unique and interconnected events index a variety of affects—from anger and exhaustion to exhilaration. One is struck, though, by how many participants in, for instance, a Black Lives Matter march in Memphis—an event responding to police brutality and marked, in the form of militarized riot police, by its immediate threat—describe the individual and collective feeling of the demonstration as something like happiness and joy.[39] This is precisely what the theorization of precarity, in the time-space of crisis, grasps: the paralyzing burden of neoliberal insecurity, and the collective volition to which the waning of "hope" might give way (if not give rise).

The attention of Butler and other theorists of precarity to enactments of radical politics within and beyond the square largely neglects one essential space of political contestation—the workplace. In the moment of synthetic dispossession, changing cultures of work shape the imagination and construction of alternative social and political worlds. The extraordinary growth of "care" work over the past several decades, for example, crystallizes the double resonance of precarity—as a state of insecurity, and as a foundation or marker of collectivity. In this era of public retrenchment, the material and emotional labor of security is increasingly outsourced by the state. The unpaid work of care or love in the domestic sphere—a instance of exploitation long the target of feminist critique—has thus acquired a more universal dimension, as the low-waged sectors of care and service grow in social and economic significance.[40] The expansion of care work corresponds to the retreat of the welfare state, as capital abandons any attempt to mitigate its destructive effects. The care worker tends to those whom the state has abandoned, even as they themselves occupy a position of social and economic insecurity. But if the relationship between the giver and recipient of care is entangled in the logics of accumulation (and its attendant inequities), it gestures toward non-reified social relations founded on the ethos of love.

Care work models one of the core contradictions that theories of neoliberal "affect" attempt to name—the concurrence of exhaustion or depression, on the one hand, and an effusion of love and utopian longing on the other. The capacities of the care worker to love, nurture, and heal are appropriated by capital. But one can imagine a social formation in which the reserves of "fellow feeling" that the care worker daily expends are channeled in other directions—toward the creation of "new social worlds"—or embodied by comradely love and political solidarity.[41] When the circuits of economic and social reproduction begin to break down, the labor of reproduction acquires, in the workplace as in the streets, a new political valence—one that indicates the fragility rather than virility of capitalist social relations, and one that promotes those cultures of giving and caring for human life that exist beyond and in explicit opposition to the biopolitical and necropolitical imperatives of the capitalist state.

Literature: Emergency and Emergence

In Chapter 2, in my historicization of the fiction of expanded reproduction, I outlined one common version of the bourgeois realist novel—familial dramas, or stories of individual becoming, wherein the interiors of mind and home displace the stage of public history. In rhythm with the "silent compulsion" of the market, such fictions work to naturalize capitalist social relations, the reproduction of which requires no heroic agent, indeed no intervention at all. My reading of *A Visit from the Goon Squad*, *Freedom*, *Indecision*, and *10:04*, though, indicated the emergence— or summoned the longer history—of another iteration of bourgeois realism. These novels reckon, in uneven ways, with the waning of historicity and agency in the late-capitalist present, and reflect on the possibility of reclaiming a more "productive" or determinative historical subjectivity (one that positions itself, in this case, in opposition to commodity rationality). In *The Financial Imaginary* (2017), Alison Shonkwiler argues that this concern with the "displacement of agency into disembodied market forces" was prefigured by—already central to—realist novels of the late nineteenth and early twentieth century.[42] Writers such as William Dean Howells, Henry James, and Theodore Dreiser, Shonkwiler observes, "all articulate ambivalences about the loss of material and tangible forms of industrial capital and the rise of new forms of abstraction."[43] Shonkwiler is referring in particular to the heightened importance of finance capital in the decades around 1900, and its mediation in novels such as James's *The American* (1877) and Dreiser's *The Financier* (1912). The eponymous protagonists of these works, Shonkwiler contends, fear both change and their diminished capacity to effect it. This ambivalence, Shonkwiler notes, was symptomatic not just of the "abstractions" of finance, but of the crises that both provoke and follow from financial processes—the profound inequalities of the Gilded Age, and the series of economic shocks and downturns that framed the turn of the twentieth century and demonstrated the dangers of monopoly capitalism. Howells's *A Hazard of New Fortunes* (1889), for example, depicts the concentrations of capital made possible by finance and the epochal struggle between capitalism and socialism. The change it represents, that is, is twofold: the disruptive consequences of financialization, and the threat posed to the bourgeoisie by a new collective subject of history—the proletariat.

If the specter of communism haunted the realist—and later modernist—fictions of the decades surrounding the turn of the twentieth century, this figment of another world is largely absent from one prominent strand of contemporary crisis fiction. The deepening middle-class anxiety made audible by Dave Eggers's *A Hologram for the King* and Rafael Chirbes's *On the Edge*—as well as several texts that I don't engage here, including Sam Lipsyte's *The Ask* (2010) and Jess Walter's *The Financial Lives of the Poets* (2009)—betrays a longing for the golden age of middle-class security, the avoidance of the proletarian condition rather than an embrace of the collective potentialities of the proletariat as an agent of historical transformation. These and cognate contemporary novels express what Leigh Claire La Berge, reading the financial forms of the 1980s, describes as "white masculine anxiety in the face of a newly global and permeable economy."[44] There is a through-line, in other words, between the financial fictions of the early twentieth century, the finance narratives of the 1980s, and the novelistic mediation of financialization in the wake of the 2008 crisis. In each instance, the deregulation of financial markets, innovation of complex financial instruments, and overaccumulation of fictitious capital is profoundly disorienting; the exemplary protagonists of these narratives, the current or erstwhile managers of money and men, struggle to make sense of the relationship between their own psychological unease and the pathologies of the economy itself.[45] In the novels I consider by Eggers and Chirbes, "cruel optimism" does not permit, or yield to, more radical political imaginaries or projects; nor does it have much of a part for the "part who have no part." This is not to say that the politics of these texts—the nostalgia they possess for more prosperous and less precarious times—is reactionary. The absence of any thematic of collective resistance or overcoming is not evidence of conservatism as such, but of the contemporary crisis of futurity, the naturalized assumption, the pervasive feeling, that "there is no alternative" to the perpetuity of neoliberal capitalism. The material potentiality of an alternative does begin to take shape, though, in an another constellation of texts that occupy the moment of synthetic dispossession. Barbara Browning's *The Gift* and Eugene Lim's *Dear Cyborgs* render the tentative creation, and speculate on the flourishing, of liberatory forms of social relation, from intimacy and love to socialistic community. *The Gift* and *Dear Cyborgs*, that is, register the ways in which the state of emergency is a state of emergence; the ascent of financial speculation, and the crises it engenders, provokes radical aesthetic and political speculation.[46] The dialogue between these two assemblages of contemporary fiction, and these two temporal experiences—one that chronicles the loss of something, the other what might take root and flourish in its place—recalls Antonio Gramsci's suggestion that "now is the time of monsters: the old world is dying, and the new world struggles to be born."

A Hologram for the King is a history of bourgeois loss and precarity, set against the backdrop of the Great Recession and the ascendance of post-Fordist cultures of accumulation. Freelance consultant Alan Clay is "virtually broke, nearly unemployed."[47] Having just missed out on a crucial deal to provide the blast-resistant glass to lower Manhattan's nascent Freedom Tower, Alan finds himself in pursuit of a hypothetical IT contract for a chimeric city in Saudi Arabia—a deal that would allow him to pay his daughter's college tuition and finance his dream of starting a small bicycle manufacture. He is brought to Saudi Arabia, in other words, by the nostalgic promise of industrial purpose and financial solvency.

Alan was once a bourgeois everyman, unmarked and indistinct, at ease in his position of happenstance privilege. "He looked like an average man. When shaved and dressed, he passed for legitimate."[48] But that anonymous security and belonging is now under threat. "Something had darkened under his brow." And on his neck, there is an undiagnosed lump the size of a golf ball, "something eating away at him, sapping him of vitality, squeezing away all acuity and purpose."[49] Once an archetype of white middle-class universalism—a figure of American prosperity, realized by his forefathers and inherited, with compounded interest, by each successive generation—Alan is now a symbol of American decline, a decline defined by the displacement of tangible production by abstract mechanisms of accumulation. "Born into manufacturing," he, like the country at large, "somewhere later got lost in worlds tangential to the making of things."[50] *A Hologram for the King*, then, is genealogically related to the early-twentieth-century fictions analyzed by Shonkwiler, texts that lamented the ascent of finance capital—its unmooring effects, in particular, on the industrial capitalist class. And it's notable that the subject of Eggers's recession novel is not the assembly-line worker whose job has been outsourced to the Global South—the proletarian who has become lumpen—but the manager cum management consultant whose client base is disappearing. After "a few decades with bikes, [Alan] had bounced around between a dozen or so other stints, consulting, helping companies compete through ruthless efficiency, robots, lean manufacturing, that kind of thing. And yet year by year, there was less work for a guy like him."[51] The irony, of course, is that Alan has been working to impose the same neoliberal forces—"efficiency," "leanness"—that now ensure his own redundancy. But his newly acquired precarity does not translate into a more robust identification with those who have long been subject to the whims of capital's creative destruction. Instead, he resolves to reenter the realm of security—and to do so by performing "an air of ownership, of belonging."[52]

On the plane to Saudi Arabia, the man in the seat neighboring Alan's—fueled by several gin and tonics and his own nostalgic attachment to the heyday of American manufacturing—reflects that "it should *matter* where something was made!"[53] Alan concurs. And he possesses an especial fidelity to the idea of "Made in the U.S.A." But this sensitivity to the origins of the things we consume is not indicative of a critical commitment to countering the effects of commodity fetishism. Substituting the abstract space of the nation for the concrete social cartography of the hidden abodes of production, "Made in America" obscures as much as it reveals about the actual history of the commodity. His nostalgia for the age of national industry, and international trade, is rather imbued with the neoclassical truisms of Microeconomics 101. "For a period," one of Alan's Saudi hosts recalls, in deference to Alan's career, "you had the Schwinns made in Chicago, the Raleighs made in England, the Italian bikes, the French. . . . For a time you had real international competition, where you were choosing between very different products with very different heritages, sensibilities, manufacturing techniques. . . . Alan remembered. Those were bright days."[54] In this vision of the market, the efficiencies of competition magically harmonize with the moral integrity of autochthonous industry. When he worked for Schwinn, Alan would journey from the factory floor to the dealership, where he'd see a kid "touching the bike like it was some holy thing. Alan knew, and the family knew, that that bike had been made by hand a few hundred miles north, by a dizzying array of workers, most of them immigrants. . . . Why did this matter?" Alan reflects. "Why did it matter that they had been made just up Highway 57?"[55] He lets the question hover, his mind occupied by other problems: "There had to be some reason Alan was here. Why he was in a tent a hundred miles from Jeddah . . . but also why he was alive on earth?"[56]

The fate of that dizzying array of workers, and of the working class in general, is displaced in the novel by the existential struggles of the managerial class. Alan's depression and underemployment find no cure in the Gulf, though, and the aimless, idle days he spends waiting for a promised meeting with King Abdullah prompt him to reflect: "This wasn't the freedom [he] sought. He wanted to be free to give his presentation, to get confirmation of the deal."[57] The freedom he imagines can only be realized through capitalist belonging—rather than in the transcendence of commodity rationality or capitalist social relations. For Alan, the silent compulsion of the market persists even when he himself has been cast into the growing ranks of the lumpen bourgeoisie. But the fragility of that nostalgic fidelity—both its subject and its object—is, in Eggers's novel, made perfectly plain. A casualty of economic transformation and economic crisis—the ascendance of "flexible" forms of production and the degradation of labor, processes that, again, he himself has helped administer—Alan is a paradigmatic subject of neoliberalism in the age of its perpetual twilight, a formerly secure member of the middle class who, to invoke Berlant's phrasing, is becoming exposed, however subtly, to the "ordinary contingencies of material and fantasmatic life associated with proletarian labor-related subjectivity." *A Hologram for the King* makes vivid, all this is to say, the generalization of insecurity in the moment of synthetic dispossession—even if its protagonist still enjoys the trappings of bourgeois luxury (the room service, the personal driver, the soothing dip in the hotel swimming pool). Regarding himself through the eyes of his coworkers, Alan sees a man who was "irrelevant, superfluous to the forward progress of the world."[58] This is not the trick of anonymity performed by certain protagonists of the nineteenth-century bourgeois novel—the denial of historical subjectivity that conceals the power of the ownership class, its *ruling* positionality. Discarded by the same forces of reproduction he once manipulated, Alan really is superfluous.

The people and things rendered superfluous by the creative depredations of capital are likewise at the center of Chirbes's novel *On the Edge*. An epic chronicle of the financial crisis in Spain, its social and cultural effects, *On the Edge* makes audible the silence of capital's arrest—the sense of absence and emptiness that pervades a moment wherein the machineries of production have been turned off, left idle "Five or six years ago . . . it seemed that not an inch of land would be left unpaved; now it looks rather like an abandoned battlefield, or a territory under armistice: sites overgrown with weeds, orange groves transformed into building lots; neglected, withered orchards; walls enclosing nothing at all."[59] Before, "the air was filled with the metallic sounds of vehicles carrying materials or dumpsters, dump trucks and trailers for transporting bulldozers and cement mixers." Now "everything seems quiet and deserted, not a single crane punctuates the horizon, no metallic noises trouble the air, no buzzing or hammering assails the ears."[60] In fact, the "no-man's land" of the quiet building site, a space of liminal or ambiguous possession, has not been deserted, exactly, but repurposed. Those pre-urban lots are now occupied by migrant laborers who "go marauding for metal, discarded household appliances, old furniture, copper, and whatever else they can find or steal," and who construct shacks out of and atop the rubble, "all within sight of the housing developments advertised on the huge roadside billboards as 'luxury estates.'"[61] As growth slows to the point of stasis, the detritus of accumulation is being mined for use value and exchange value by the expanding ranks of the precariat. But the privileged few who have retreated behind their gates pay the marauders little mind, as long as "the smell of putrefaction doesn't reach their private terrace."[62]

On the Edge is set in the near-inland village of Olba, the current malaise of which is owed to the deflation of the real estate bubble. The identikit developments recently thrown up along the coast—composed of cheap materials and financed by fictitious capital, now unoccupied or uncompleted—obscure the village's view of the sea. Such ruins, the skeletal built environment, signal the redundant vocation of the novel's narrator, Esteban. Dispossessed of his modest carpentry workshop after an ill-timed real estate investment, Esteban mourns the passing of a working life he had never embraced. He reflects:

> You discover the irritating calm of mornings with no alarm clock going off, the day like a meadow stretching out toward the horizon, limitless time, an unbounded landscape, no flocks graze in that infinite space, not a building to be seen, not even the silhouette of a tree. Just you walking in the void. Hell is a derelict warehouse, a silent hangar filled only with a terrible emptiness. In the end, the divine curse of earning our daily bread seems almost agreeable, the sound of alarm clocks, water gushing out of faucets or showers, the bubbling of the coffee pot, the hustle and bustle of morning traffic.[63]

Esteban shares this sense of emptiness with his former employees, whose resentment he feels acutely. "They hate me," he recognizes, "because I've smashed the milk jug they were carrying on their heads . . . but I'm not to blame for their dreams, I didn't encourage them. . . . I exchanged money for labor. . . . No dreams were in the contract."[64] Esteban highlights here the futility of his workers' investment in their labor. And he perceives, more

broadly, the declining efficacy of capitalist ideology in the current conjuncture. "A century ago," he reflects, "[business] signified action and progress,
but now it's a synonym of other words heavy with negative energy: exploitation, egotism, wastefulness."[65]

Esteban's sensitivity to the ebbing spirit of capital is bound up in his own
descent from security to insecurity. "What about *my* fragile state," he asks;
"does anyone care about that?"[66] In the new order brought about by the
crisis, there are two classes—one "proudly leave[s] the mall with bulging
shopping bags," while the other "[rummages] around in the dumpsters"[67]—
and Esteban increasingly feels a part of the latter. The crisis, he reflects,
"has made us all equal again, brought us all down to the same level, everyone on the floor."[68] The "us" here excludes the patrons of the mall. And
it includes the underemployed migrant worker (compelled toward Spain
by the consequences of primitive accumulation on the periphery), the exploited laborer, and the fallen members of the middle classes—the subjects
of capital's three moments. This shared insecurity, though, does not, in
On the Edge, translate into a politically effective solidarity. When Esteban
invokes the class struggle—a central element of his familial inheritance;
his father was a socialist radical who fought for the Republican side in
the Spanish Civil War—it is always with a question mark, and in the past
tense: "Wasn't it the determining factor that impregnated and marked everything? The engine of world history?"[69] If his father believes that "we're
still in the middle of a war and . . . the most interesting battle is still to
come," Esteban is rather more skeptical. He is resigned to his nightly card
game at the bar, and the constant litigation of how it all went wrong.

Though Esteban's exhaustion and cynicism discourage a more affirma-
tive political habitus, the experience of insecurity does sharpen his critical vision—his attention to the broader totality of capitalist contradictions
that the current crisis has exacerbated, and from which it has emerged. He
is sensitive, for example, to the endurance of the "dark days, which, one way
or another, are inevitable in what Marxists term 'primitive accumulation.'"
And he realizes that the denizens of capitalism's more privileged environs
cultivate a willful blindness to the violent conditions of their own practices
of consumption. "It has only taken a few years for us," the newly statured,
Esteban reflects, "to acquire . . . the illusion that we are all lords and ladies

of the manor, while in remotest factories, workers kill and skin and carve and package the animals we eat once they've become acceptably aseptic. . . . We force ourselves not to decipher the signs, so that the dismembered corpse doesn't shock us."[70] His apprehension of these murderous chains of production and consumption, and the ideology that conceals them, is not merely abstract, but includes a cartographic recognition of his own location within the global organization of capital. Nearby villages, "in what was the once fertile province of Valencia, now produce plastic packaging for fruit cultivated and picked eight or ten thousand miles away . . . [concentrating] the energies of all five continents." Savoring the taste of these snacks, Esteban "imagines the face of the pickers: almond eyes, olive skins burned by the sun, the intent gaze of the women shelling the nuts, which, at this precise moment, belong exclusively to me: I've bought their intent gaze, their quick movements, the bead of sweat rolling down between their breasts while they work in a zinc-roofed warehouse. With each nut, each seed, each fruit," Esteban reflects, "I'm eating the houses in which they live."[71] Esteban derives a kind of perverse pleasure from this sense of possession, the feeling of power that the act of consumption provokes; but in highlighting the objectification of people in the commodity, and in imagining the commodity's human history, he is exposing the apparatuses of fetishism and reification.

The potentialities of critique, and perhaps even manifest resistance, are enacted not just by these fragments of Esteban's cognitive mapping but by the novel's form. Esteban's testimony is occasionally interrupted by other voices, which join with rather than displace his own. As they accumulate, these solos acquire a kind of choral quality, even if the social realities they convey are defined by dissonance rather than harmony. A newly unemployed carpenter reflects that "I don't know exactly what I would be capable of doing to you—to you, who've got everything—but I do have a rifle at home." "Where are the Euros of yesteryear?" the fallen entrepreneur laments: "What became of those lovely purple notes? They fell as fast as dead leaves on a windy autumn day and rotted in the mud."[72] Another of Esteban's former employees recounts his earlier turn as a garbage collector, a job that afforded him a privileged insight into the "smell of the twenty-first century," the overflowing trash can, which mingles and melds with the fragrances of gasoline and lush, floral gardens. Just as these unique odors become "a single smell," the brief "I" interludes that intersect with Esteban's narrative constitute a differential unity that, while expressing (like the superfluity of waste) decay and decomposition, evokes as well the multiple vectors and dialects of contemporary anticapitalist critique. In Olba, this critique remains latent. The term "struggle" signifies, there, private suffering rather than collective rebellion. But as Esteban ruminates over his beer, the Indignados, in their multitudes, are occupying the squares of many Spanish cities—affirming the idea that the most interesting battle is still to come.[73]

The Indignados movement prefigured the Occupy Wall Street movement. In the years since it took shape, and as its guiding energy and ideas have found expression in other contexts, Occupy has been chronicled in fiction—for example, in Ben Lerner's *10:04*, as I discussed in Chapter 2, and in texts such as Barbara Browning's *The Gift* (2017) and Eugene Lim's *Dear Cyborgs* (2017). Though formally very distinct from one another, *The Gift* and *Dear Cyborgs* share a core concern with the alternative social formations that are born within, and in response to the psychological and material exigencies of, the time-space of crisis. These narratives pivot from Alan and Esteban's preoccupation with security and belonging, and begin to meditate on ways of inhabiting the world, collectively, that resist rather than conform to the dictums of the market.

The Gift joins a constellation of recent novels—from Karl Ove Knausgard's *My Struggle* series to Sheila Heti's *Motherhood* and Rachel Cusk's *Outline* trilogy—that fall under the heading of "autofiction," a term that describes fictions of the self, or works that combine elements of fiction and memoir. The term itself is not new—it originated in France in the 1970s—nor are the generic ambivalences that it captures. But the recent preponderance of autofictions, and the commercial success and critical attention with which they have been met, does feel eventful. And it prompts the question of their symptomaticity: Why these books, in this time? This surge of interest in the autofictional is, I think, an effect of the tension between two interlocking historical tendencies: the bourgeois desire to reclaim some sense of meaningful narrative subjectivity, in the context of the end of history (this desire guides, too, several of the novels I engaged in my treatment of expanded reproduction); and a new bourgeois sensitivity to the specter, if not the reality, of precarity. *My Struggle* dramatizes how our consciousness mediates the mundane activities that comprise the quotidian labor of human life. *Motherhood* is an intensive reflection on the problem of social and biological reproduction. In their obsessive inward focus, these texts exist on a continuum with realist forms that privilege the intricacies of the interior self. But many contemporary autofictions depart from that realist tradition, in crucial ways: if bourgeois realism imagines the domestic as a metaphor for the political or the public, or as its antithesis, recent autofictions insist that our daily existence—the creative ways we live and survive, in a time of manifold insecurity—is profoundly political, and perhaps even charged with a kind of epic significance.

The narrator of *The Gift*, Barbara Andersen, sends unsolicited ukulele cover tunes to friends and people she admires. Her hope is that in conveying "recordings of my uke covers as gifts, I could possibly help jumpstart a creative gift economy that would spill over into the larger sphere of exchange. The recent implosion of the global financial system made it evident that we needed to try something else."[74] As these words imply, Barbara is interested in thinking about how alternative, creative modes of interpersonal intimacy might serve as a laboratory for, or foundation of, alternative forms of human social existence. (There are echoes, here, of Ben Lerner's *10:04*, and the vision, articulated by that novel's narrator, of a personal love that will "branch out horizontally into the possibility of a transpersonal revolutionary subject in the present and coconstruct a world in which moments can be something other than the elements of profit."[75]) Barbara's commitment to the politics of the gift, and the act of giving, is an explicit counterpoint to the ideologies—and material reality—of scarcity and austerity, which are naturalized by the fact or specter of crisis. She cites Lewis Hyde: "In the world of gift, you not only can have your cake and eat it too, you can't have your cake *unless* you eat it. . . . Scarcity and abundance have as much to do with the form of exchange as with how much material wealth is at hand."[76] And in the realm of eros especially, "the more you give, the more you have."[77] "I didn't understand," she reflects, "why people couldn't have more than one lover the way parents can have more than one child or we all have more than one friend and it doesn't mean we love them less."[78]

The Gift chronicles Barbara's connection to several people in particular: her lover Olivia, a musician; her adolescent son; Sami, a German musician whose own ukulele compositions prompt an intimate but long-distance (virtual) friendship; and Tye, a performance artist in New York. Tye's performances are described in detail—not simply the substance of their composition, but the labor and financial investment that made possible their production. Tye prefaces one piece, in which he constructs a life-size replica of the Judson Church rose window, by indexing, for the audience, the costs associated with the installation: the U-Haul he rented, the wages extended to a friend who helped with the moving of materials, the wages he paid himself for carpentry work, and the time of the performance itself, which he is donating as a "community service."[79] While *The Gift* imagines a way of organizing human social life beyond the imperatives of austerity, it simultaneously brings into relief how the mundane facts of our extant money economy delimit spaces of creativity, and the effluence of love that Barbara imagines. That love is given more room to thrive in Zuccotti Park, where the Occupy movement began on September 17, 2011—six months, as Barbara notes, after Tye's performance. Though they don't join the encampment, Barbara and Olivia spend significant time in the park, hanging out, talking to people, and contributing books—including Barbara's own "postmodern novel"—to "The People's Library."

Barbara's ukulele covers perform the "creative gift economy" that she envisions. So too does the encampment at Zuccotti Park, whose critique of capital was at once diagnostic and prescriptive. The Occupy demonstrators called attention to the inequities of contemporary capitalism, its fundamental and acute contradictions. But they also modeled a utopian mode of social and economic organization, one inspired by the basic communist idea, "from each according to their ability, to each according to their need"—an understanding of giving and receiving that does not incorporate, and perhaps even transcends, the logics of debt and credit (logics, as Barbara puts it, citing David Graeber, that inform the "bourgeois politesse" of gratitude and supplication). This embryonic economy highlights the fact of our shared insecurity, while embodying at the same time, to summon Judith Butler's words, "that form of the sustaining social bond that neo-liberal economics has almost destroyed." Accessing a cognate idea, Barbara cites the young Marx: "To be sensuous is to suffer. . . . Man as an objective, sensuous being is therefore a suffering being, and because he feels his suffering, he is a passionate being."[80] We need the world to survive; but we also feel the world, its suffering and injustice. We are both objective and sensuous. If the rationality of the commodity form turns people into things, Marx, in the *Economic and Philosophic Manuscripts* (1844), proposes a counter-objectivity—one that recognizes our power to creatively remake the world, to animate the objects we encounter in the world, to the end of our own objective survival, as to the potentialities of creative human flourishing. These instances of "passion" might manifest in the realm of eros, where we embrace our radical vulnerability to arrive at a deeper sense of human being and reciprocity, or in the sphere of social and political life, where—speculatively—the objective fact of necessity will guide the formation of communities founded on mutual care and the freedom from want. Not necessity or freedom, as the liberal political imagination would have it, but freedom because of necessity.

Though merely a casual interloper in the encampment at Zuccotti Park, Barbara later contributes to the Occupy-affiliated "Free University," by leading a seminar on inappropriate intimacy, its aesthetic and political possibilities. One iteration of the university takes place on May Day, 2012, and the radical implications of the event are evidenced by the "disconcerting number of police officers standing around," as by the helicopters ominously circling overhead. The gathering is obviously peaceful, subdued even, but it is an attempt to lay claim to public space, and in so doing enact an alternative vision of what the public might be. Barbara shares with her two students her "optimistic reading of gifts and the notion that wealth might have some agency and want to move itself around."[81] One of her students notes that the concept of wealth possessed of agency and subjectivity, while interesting, is also compatible with the ideology of the free market, the assumption of the market's natural distributive efficiencies. Barbara concedes that that's a problem. At other times, she struggles with the antinomy, which might achieve a synthetic resolution, between ethics and politics. Lauren Berlant, an interlocutor of Barbara's, writes to her, in the novel, that "ethics to me feels like politics in denial, but that's not always true, because sometimes no matter how politically saturated a relation

is, it's just about one person showing up for another."[82] Perhaps, and this
is Barbara's faith, "one person showing up for another"—by sending them
a ukulele cover tune, by teaching a class at the Free University, by being
there emotionally and intellectually for a psychologically fragile friend in
Germany—is, to recall Ben Lerner's phrasing, "a proprioceptive flicker in
advance of the communal body." The ethos of the gift might signify—or at
least contribute to the theorization of—the performance of the communist
idea, *avant* its institutional realization.

When Barbara observes that the recent financial crisis compelled the
creation of new social imaginaries and forms, she betrays a subtle historical myopia. Her words imply, that is, that the crisis, and the political urgency it provokes, is historically specific, rather than a fundamental and
enduring feature of capitalist modernity. Like the theoretical turn toward
precarity, *The Gift* and other autofictions are conditioned, in part, by the
exposure of previously secure populations—the American middle class, for
example—to the specter and reality of insecurity. Barbara herself, a full
professor at New York University, is largely immune to both the recent
cataclysms of the market and its underlying inequities. But she is attuned
to the atmosphere of insecurity that *feels* newly general. In accord with
Butler's writings on precarity or vulnerability, or Berlant's theorization of
the affective structures of insecurity, Barbara is concerned less with the
history of the current crisis, and more with the futurity that is struggling
to emerge within it.

The futurity struggling to be born in the "impasse" of the present
is made vivid by speculative fictions, or fictions that reference and pursue the narrative openings forged by the speculative genres. Lim's *Dear
Cyborgs* belongs to the latter category. *Dear Cyborgs* begins with an address, in an epistolary voice that reappears, at the interstices of the narrative, throughout the novel: "Dear Cyborgs, Today's puzzler. Enforced
inescapable automatic insidious complicity. On the horizon no viable just
alternative and no path toward one. All proposals thus far fanciful, impossible, doomed. Sure, optimism of the will. But—either from the towers
or beyond the grid, in the trenches, amongst the ruins, or burb'd—what
to do?"[83] These lines of preface highlight the crisis of futurity that marks
the apparent perpetuity of capitalism. Yet the vocabulary of the narrator's

initial letter—its post-human addressee, the sites of struggle it invokes, and its subtle unfamiliarity—also evoke the immanence of other worlds, or other dimensions within this one.

Following this evocation of temporal indeterminacy and political urgency, the novel's narrative opening returns us to the narrator's childhood, "a time of my life so separated from what happened before and later that I think of it as a dream."[84] Eleven years old in a small town in Ohio, the narrator, the son of South Korean immigrants, befriends Vu, whose parents were refugees from Vietnam. The two boys are invisible, "such outcasts that our isolation hardly pained us, as we could barely conceive of an alternative."[85] The figment of an alternative that they can glimpse is derived from their immersion in comic books, first as readers—and consuming comics "was a sort of hedonistic, perhaps onanistic, act of defiance"—and later as co-creators of their own graphic narrative and universe.[86] Our introduction to Vu and the narrator is disrupted by parenthetical meditations on protests, reflections that resonate with the epistolary voice that framed the narrative, and that signal how the political and economic crises of the present are contiguous with, and heighten, longer histories of racialized exclusion and precarity.

From this story of two Asian American kids growing up in the Midwest, the narrative abruptly shifts to a different temporality and scale. Now the narrating "I" is an off-duty superhero, Frank Exit, at a karaoke bar with his Team Chaos colleagues, in a major American metropolis. Here protest is more than an object of philosophical rumination. It's the autumn of Occupy Wall Street, and the "People's Microphone" reverberates through lower Manhattan and indeed across the country and world, to South Korea, where Kim Jin-suk is staging a lone occupation of Crane Number 85, of Hanjin Heavy industries, in a shipyard in Busan—an act of protest that honors Kim Joo-ik, a shipyard worker who had, eight years prior, occupied a similar crane for 129 days, before ending his own life. Kim Jin-suk's message of solidarity to the Occupy demonstrators is relayed, to the narrator, by the holographic representation of the enigmatic character Ms. Mistleto—a wanted provocateur that the narrator, when on the superhero clock, pursues across the world. It's not precisely clear for whom the superhero crew is working—the government? Some other institutional guardian of the established order? But their critiques of that order, the inequity and insanity and malaise of late capital, are always astute. And when Ms. Mistleto details her impressions of Occupy, it is difficult to detect where her voice—her reading and translation of the world—displaces that of the narrator. She recalls merging with the crowds congregating at Zuccotti Park, all those people "who came to be near a moment that would exist only briefly, so that we could embody the flicker of their protest, a protest that seemed dangerous, that seemed real."[87] And Mistleto seems to be speaking in unison with so many others, too, when she reflects that the Occupy movement is inspired by the "knowledge that the entire social contract is contaminated, tainted, since it requires the hard labor of the unfortunate, as well as a violence to the earth and, importantly and even more subtly, an embedded faith in the eventual good of selfishness and greed."[88] What she grasps is that the Occupy movement is inspired not merely by the contradictions of capital in its neoliberal iteration, or by the insecurity that those contradictions magnify and generalize, but by a feeling of collective complicity or even guilt. And this recognition recalls the address that begins the novel, reinforcing the idea that the "structure of feeling" that marks the current crisis is becoming universal—or, as the figure of the "99 percent" suggests, nearly so. As the inequities of capital deepen, so too does the reservoir of resistors.

Mistleto's insights, though, depart from that "Dear Cyborgs" letter in one key way. Escaping the current state might in fact be "like willing the dead back to life," a sentiment with which the author of the "Dear Cyborgs" missive would agree; but if an "impossible wish," the "desire to transcend our limitations" is also "deeply human. . . . That's why it's important. It expresses an impossible desire as if it were not impossible. . . . I guess the crux of the matter," she concludes, "is whether this expression of the impossible can somehow lead to its possibility, that is, to it no longer being impossible."[89] The Occupy movement did not articulate a list of concrete demands to the Obama administration, or to the members of the Goldman Sachs board of directors. And its abstract appeal to the radical transformation of the current political and economic order was of course not immediately heeded by those in power. But the encampment at Zuccotti Park, and its sister assemblages across the world, as Mistelto intimates, constituted a cultural revolution, one that shifted the balance of possibility and impossibility in individual and collective consciousness. Mistleto's optimism of the intellect, though, is immediately contradicted by one of her companions. These protests, this unnamed interlocutor insists, are "just a way for excess and agitating energies to play themselves out, for these to be released in a harmless and managed way. There is almost a natural engineering," this voice continues, "where necessary and temporary aggregation of revolutionary forces occurs in order to bring about their elimination, either by actual destruction or, more effectively, by their co-optation into a toothless brand."[90] This is the debate, or the impasse, that *Dear Cyborgs* clarifies—the contest between our desire, and indeed our capacity, to imagine and create the rudiments of another world, and the will and capacity of capital to assimilate its own critique and reinforce the assumption that there is no alternative. *Dear Cyborgs* does not resolve this aporia, but we can hear Lim's voice in Mistleto's when the latter counters that "for the protestor, the protest makes a moral world in which she can abide."[91] The comic books read, composed, and inhabited by the narrator and Vu are another example of speculative worlds that feel like home—a space of belonging and of liberation. And as Hua Hsu has observed, *Dear Cyborgs* is "trying to do the same: to construct a world in which all of us might abide."[92]

This creative project dovetails, in the novel, with the critical diagnosis of the world that we inhabit now. Recalling another protest, in another city, Mistleto outlines the litany of "sins . . . bullet-pointed on homemade placards: climate disasters . . . ; the purchasing of politicians; war profiteering; carcinogens in our food; the overmilitarized police force; covert and overt racism; mass incarceration and disenfranchisement; the calculated intentional impoverishment of a working class; the nonstop production of sweet moral anesthesia for the consumer class; alienation; triumphalism; ugliness; etc." The demonstration was sparked when an environmental activist, who had been blocking the access road to a shale development site, was killed by a private army. And Mistleto feels an unusual energy in the gathering, as it continues to grow—a capacity for endurance, and for destruction. Usually averse to crowds, Mistleto finds herself being carried by its momentum; in the midst of this "anyonymous flow," she reflects, "I felt invisible, more a ghost. . . . For a long time I didn't care about the goal of the crowd, just that it was."[93] When the police intervene to break up the demonstration—with "flash bombs, rubber bullets and tear gas and then real bullets"—the crowd disperses but then reconvenes, and coordinated acts of riot culminate in the mass occupation of a central skyscraper. The police surround the building and cut off its links to the world beyond—power, internet, etc.—but the occupiers resolve to transmute this forced confinement into a space of freedom and newness. "We would," Mistleto recalls, "once again refashion the occupation, which the state had transformed into an incarceration, and make it into a utopian colony founded on principles of equality, collective decision making, cooperative labor, and shared property."[94] The occupation—its experiment in alternative ways of organizing human social life—lasts for years; and it ends when the police forces retreat (their presence has become too much of a drain on the coffers of the state), and the now-mobile occupiers themselves lose their will to continue the project. If ephemeral, though, the habitable world the protestors constructed has, perhaps, shifted the calculus of possibility and impossibility.

Mistleto is Frank's nemesis. His periodic pursuits of her, which take him to disparate corners of the world, always end in Mistleto's escape—evasions prefaced by her reflections on protest, and the adjacent questions of liberation and collectivity. But she is also mysteriously described, in a "Dear Cyborgs" letter that appears on Frank's desk, as his sister. And they do share a great deal. If Mistleto is occupied by the inequities of the present and the political forms that might enable their transcendence, Frank and his comrades spend much of their time meditating on the radical potentialities of art. All of the members of Team Chaos, beyond their occupational lives, and their after-hours karaoke dates, are artists, or have, at one time in their lives, aspired to make art. Dave, for example, is an art school dropout who destroyed his greatest work. "For some time," Dave reflects to his friends, "I'd been working on these drawings. At first they started out as one thing, and then they turned into something else, and then they turned closer to that first thing—but now with extra knowledge, if you know what I mean. It's often like that," he continues, "and I think the best work is when you don't have a plan, just a few rules."[95] Dave follows this reflection on the extemporaneous nature of creation—insights that might also apply to the construction of alternative social formations—with a story about an artist-friend of his, Ursula, who had achieved early commercial and critical success, before succumbing to an extremely painful and aggressive form of arthritis (a condition brought on by the intensity of her artistic practice). Unable to live with the pain, and the impossibility of returning to her work, Ursula takes her own life. Posthumously, critics who had dismissed the critical substance of her work—and her rejection of the art world's submission to the dictates of the commodity form—laud her "valiant defiance." On the surface, then, this is another parable of the ways in which capital is able to either destroy or assimilate—or, in this case, destroy and then assimilate—any modality of resistance to its ascendance. But Dave's story continues. After Ursula's passing, he begins drawing again, with a set of colored pencils he once received from her as a gift. The sketches he creates are inspired by memories of their friendship, and it feels, as he works, that the pencil was being moved by some external force, and that he "was trying to sketch the place Ursula had gone to, or, more accurately, the place she had become."[96] The point of the work, though, is less about the images that materialize on the paper and more about the process of their creation. Dave is determined to use the pencils to the point of their disappearance, and once he has done so, his own hands aching in an echo of Ursula's arthritis, he burns the scrolls of drawings. There is an analogy to be drawn here, perhaps, between the ephemerality of protest and the ephemerality of art; in either case, the means become an end in themselves, altering the horizon of political possibility (what ends can be imagined).

Muriel follows Dave's story with her own tale of art and self-sacrifice. As a girl, she had completed a series of paintings that felt fully realized; she had "captured in them something complex and savage from within."[97] The "strange and hollow" peace that follows this achievement compels her, that night, toward a bridge, from which she leaps, accepting the prospect of death but attaining instead only a broken back, and a slight limp that she still carries. Frank, for his part, has no anecdotes to contribute on the question of the political and aesthetic dialectics of creativity and destruction. But he does share his own struggles with writing. The author of a book of short stories, a "minor hit" in the genre of "moralistic science fiction," he later receives an advance to write a novel. "What was expected," he recounts, "was a slightly modified coming-of-age novel that traded on my Korean-American identity. Something not too obviously an assimilation tale—and above all clever—yet also something not too much a deviation from that sellable idea, so that the marketplace of culture could easily absorb my story without being too discomfited." His novel, as a second-generation immigrant story, would demonstrate that "I'm in on it, am injured by living in two worlds but yet whole and not broken, in fact, fortified and special in my elasticity, in the ability to be both of and other."[98] But he struggles to muster the "comic ability" required by such a narrative, and the novel is never written. *Dear Cyborgs* does resemble this unwritten text, in ways, while also deviating quite dramatically from its "sellable idea." Its "coming-of-age" trajectory is arrested after a few pages, and the singular narrating self—fractured or made whole by his double consciousness—is displaced by elusive and shifting narrative voices, as by a proliferation of generic modes and thematic concerns. Lim's text, though, *is* fundamentally interested in bringing Asian American history—specific articulations of cultural and political radicalism therein—to bear on the current crisis, and on the project of representing both its intractability and the possibility of its transcendence.

In certain chapters of the narrative, the "I" voice shifts, almost undetectably, from Frank Exit to the unnamed narrator of the book's opening pages, who is now grown up, and who has long moved on from the small Ohio town where he met and became close to Vu. In one such interlude, Vu returns to the narrator in a dream and recounts his experience working for the artist Sonny Rhee in Los Angeles. Sonny is known, in the art world, for her eccentric practice of only allowing twelve of her paintings to exist at one time. After creating a new work, she burns her oldest painting in the semipublic context of an intimate dinner party. And "even more diabolical," as Vu puts it: she insists that any buyer purchase all twelve of her paintings then in existence, and that they return the oldest painting as necessary, so it can be destroyed (in exchange for her newest work). When Vu asks about the significance of the number 12, Sonny invokes the work of Tehching Hsieh, a Taiwanese American performance artist who "was kind of a whisper; people talked about him, but he had barely an audience to speak of." All of his performances, as Sonny's twelve paintings reference, lasted for one year—"an important measure of time for humans, he says, because it's the largest single unit of time that occurs naturally."[99] In his most famous work, he punched a clock every hour, on the hour, for 365 days. *Time Clock Piece* (1980–1981) dramatized the tyranny of industrial time, our submission to the temporal imperatives of capital's pursuit of surplus value. Tehching Hsieh, Sonny reflects, "gave me an understanding about time and patience. But what he really gave me, the most important thing, was something else. He gave me a kind of realism about protest art. Tehching Hsieh says, *I don't think that art can change the world. But at least art can help us to unveil life*."[100] At the age of forty-nine, Tehching Hsieh stopped making art. His last performance, then, was a lesson in becoming invisible. And that invisibility, a recurring trope in Asian American literature, is double-edged: it signifies at once the marginality or exclusion of certain minority groups, and their hypervisibility in the eyes of the surveillance state.

An art that unveils life will, perhaps, make visible the structures of power that render some populations invisible (or marked for exclusion or exploitation or repression). And it will reveal the quotidian labor of survival. In the current conjuncture, that is, art that "unveils life" will necessarily be an art of precarity. At the karaoke bar, Frank expounds on the chimera of "American utopia and racial harmony": "the interlocking of all these communities, the painless and insidious assimilation, the flow of first to second to third and fourth generations, the seemingly unifying and seemingly ubiquitous materialist ambitions. And yet like the city itself the complex is unknowable, one's neighbors are so close yet so far away, we each find ourselves alone and apart."[101] But at other times, Frank concedes, "when I am going to the greengrocer for bell peppers and onion to make another basic bachelor's supper, when I stop to hear the busker's tambourine for just a minute before shyly dropping in a few coins . . . when I'm in line to buy Band-Aids and deodorant at the pharmacy—at these times I look around and see all my harried neighbors doing the same . . . it's then I do believe in some unity of purpose, despite the chaotic provenances of diaspora city."[102] There is a certain political potentiality, Frank concludes, in the vernacular cosmopolitanism of the metropolis, and in the everyday patterns of socially necessary consumption.

As the novel conveys elsewhere, though, this solidarity is not simply founded on a generic sameness, but on shared conditions of exclusion, repression, and struggle—conditions that summon extant histories of racialized dominance and resistance. Put slightly differently, the precarity unveiled by *Dear Cyborgs* grasps that the universal is found in the particular. The generalized structure of feeling that Lim so vividly captures—the insecurity and melancholy of our current political and economic predicament, the haziness of the horizon and the pressing question, as the opening "Dear Cyborgs" letter puts it, of "what to do?"—is historicized by the novel's grounding in immigrant histories and imaginaries, and by its invocation, most significantly, of late-twentieth-century Asian American cultural and political radicalisms.

On one social outing with Team Chaos—the superhero crew that, presumably, he and Vu created—the narrator reflects, to himself, but not to his friends, on the life of Richard Aoki, the Japanese American activist and leader, in the 1960s and 1970s, of the Third World Liberation Front. Aoki spent part of his childhood in an internment camp in Utah; he went on to become an important member of the Black Panther Party—famously providing the Panthers with firearms and training figures such as Bobby Seale and Huey P. Newton in their use—before it was discovered, in the aftermath of his death, that he had been an informant for the FBI. Though devastating, the narrator allows, this revelation did not negate Aoki's keen analysis of "how power operated, how class structures were created and maintained, and how racism was inextricable with that operation and structure."[103] And indeed, the narrator observes, "the analysis of race and power that became institutionally codified in the Ethnic Studies departments in California, and which has since spread to institutions nationally and worldwide, has had, to understate it, a great impact. In many ways," he suggests, "this ongoing analysis and study is the intellectual engine driving today's continuing battle for justice and civil rights."[104] The struggle for justice and liberation in the present, this observation implies, is rooted in the historical experience of those for whom precarity is not a new epiphany, and for whom crisis/emergency has long been the rule.

Frank's unwritten coming-of-age novel would have translated the particular (Korean American identity) into the universal (exchange value). Assimilated by the market, this artifact would have elucidated how both capital and the state incorporate, so as to exploit and manage, difference. *Dear Cyborgs* models a different articulation of the relationship between the particular and the universal, or of the movement—"transition," as Aimé Césaire put it—from the former to the latter. In Lim's novel, Asian American social, political, and cultural history acts as one particular from which an anticapitalist universal, a collective subject that will create another world within or beyond this one, might be constructed. This speculative abstraction counters the abstractions of capital—the manifold violence of primitive and synthetic dispossession in this time of monsters, the twilight of the neoliberal age.

Conclusion

In the moment of synthetic dispossession, the privatization of public services, and the deliberate devaluation of assets and labor, deepens the condition, and extends the sphere, of insecurity—while the liberation of finance capital both provokes and exploits crises, furthering the regressive redistribution of wealth. The intensification of insecurity, meanwhile, corresponds to the fading efficacy of capitalist ideology and heightened importance of crude state violence. The welfare state retreats in rhythm with the advance of the police state. In the moment of synthetic dispossession, the enduring fact that the emergency is the rule is made plain. This "crisis ordinariness" has occasioned a sustained theoretical reflection on the politics of "precarity." The theorists of precarity illuminate the distinctive ambivalence of the temporal experience of neoliberal crisis—on the one hand, the longing for something that no longer exists, the state of security or the dream of its realization; on the other hand, the speculative imagination, and quotidian creation, of alternative ways of organizing social and economic life, outside and in opposition to the logics of capital. These two "structures of feeling," and these two political routes, are likewise clarified by the four novels I considered above. *A Hologram for the King* and *On the Edge* depict the nostalgic attachment to the space and time of economic belonging. *The Gift* and *Dear Cyborgs*, meanwhile, limn one social and cultural hypothesis—the radical forms of intimacy and community that take root, and even begin to flourish, in the time-space of crisis.

CHAPTER 4

Interrelations

IN **THE HISTORY OF THE RUSSIAN** *Revolution* (1930), Leon Trotsky, expanding upon the historical insights of Marx and Engels, examined the simultaneity and geographic co-belonging of different modes of accumulation. The advent of capitalist rationality in non-capitalized societies, Trotsky observed, does not immediately lead to its total ascendance. In the colonized world and other peripheral or semi-peripheral places, non-capitalist forms exist alongside nascent capitalist relations.[1] Though focused on one national space, Trotsky's theory of "uneven and combined development" pointed to the concurrent combination of unique moments of capital within the broader world-system.

The problem of capital's essential unevenness was also engaged by some of Trotsky's contemporaries, notable among them Antonio Gramsci and José Carlos Mariátegui, who explored its implications for the potentiality of socialist revolution in Italy and Peru, respectively. In the middle and latter part of the twentieth century, meanwhile, a coterie of anticolonial and postcolonial intellectuals joined the premise of uneven development to the critique of empire and its afterlives. As elaborated by C. L. R. James, Aimé Césaire, Frantz Fanon, Walter Rodney, Stuart Hall, and many others—to cite just those thinkers who populate my own account—the anticolonial and postcolonial traditions are a vital resource for the contemporary project of theorizing the contradictions of global capital, the dialectical interrelation of distinct spaces, moments, and subjects within the capitalist world-system. The theoretical trajectories charted by anticolonial and postcolonial critics informed, for example, the innovation of world-systems theory—a body of thought whose diachronic and synchronic analysis of uneven and combined development is distinguished by a basic apprehension of capitalist modernity as colonial modernity.

The convergence of world-systems theory and postcolonial theory has guided contemporary inquiries into the relationship between global capital and world literature. Franco Moretti's influential essay "Conjectures on World Literature" (2000) defines world literature as a global system that mirrors and magnifies the world-system of capital. A more recent intervention, the Warwick Research Collective's *Combined and Uneven Development: Towards a New Theory of World Literature* (2015), analyzes how the literary forms of the periphery and semi-periphery register the "singularity . . . and internal heterogeneity"—the essential globality and inequality—of capitalist modernity. Guided by and expanding upon these and cognate contributions, I consider, in the latter part of this chapter, how three novels— Pitchaya Sudbanthad's *Bangkok Wakes to Rain* (2019), Neel Mukherjee's *The Lives of Others* (2014), and Rachel Kushner's *The Flamethrowers* (2013)— represent the unity and differential composition of global capital, the multiple moments that comprise the planetary political and economic order produced by colonial processes.

Uneven and Combined Development: Coloniality at Large

In *Capital*, there is an abiding tension between the teleology of development—the assumption that all societies, if asymmetrically advanced, are moving toward the same future of industrial production and universalized wage labor—and the fact of capital's intrinsic unevenness— the recognition that the development of the metropoles is enabled by the underdevelopment of the colonized periphery. Marx briefly addresses the fact of this unevenness in his reflections on primitive accumulation. The different instances of primitive accumulation—"the discovery of gold and silver in America, the extirpation, enslavement and entombment in mines of the aboriginal population, the beginning of the conquest and looting of the East Indies, the turning of Africa into a warren for the commercial hunting of black-skins"—arrive, he observes, "at a systematical combination, embracing the colonies, the national debt, the modern mode of taxation, and the protectionist system."[2] Marx's language here—his attention to different moments of capital in "systematical combination"—points to the possibility of a more synchronic apprehension of capital's uneven nature, the dialectical relationship between development and underdevelopment. Marx, though, placed greater emphasis, in *Capital*, on the linear progression from the moment of primitive accumulation to the moment of expanded reproduction—from the crude violence of capital's birth to the "silent compulsion" of capitalist social relations. Marx was keenly aware that "[this history] assumes different aspects in different countries, and runs through its various phases in different orders of succession, and at different historical epochs."[3] But his account of capitalism's emergence ultimately privileges the geographically (nationally) bounded sequence of stages, rather than their concurrent global articulation.

Later thinkers, both Marxist and non, did advance an understanding of primitive accumulation as not merely fundamental but perpetual. And this understanding necessarily grasped, in either implicit or explicit terms, how the multiple moments of capital do not correspond to discrete historical stages but are synchronously joined. Trotsky's theory of "uneven and combined development" was an attempt to capture that and other temporal interrelations—the simultaneity, for example, of urban industrialism and subsistence farming. Trotsky presented uneven and combined development as a law of history, the general condition of contingent historical change—the dialectical movement of contradiction and synthesis—across space and time, within, and perhaps beyond, the long history of capitalist modernity. The primary object of his inquiry, though, was Russia, and the history of the Russian Revolution. In Russia and other unevenly developed capitalist societies, Trotsky deduced, the revolution would necessarily be spearheaded by an alliance between the nascent industrial proletariat and the peasantry, which would preempt the political ascent of the bourgeoisie and seize control of the state and the means of production.

Writing at the same time as Trotsky, and addressing a related problematic, Antonio Gramsci delineated how the North–South divide within Italy compelled and delimited the prospects for communist revolution. More specifically—in "The Southern Question" (1926) and *Prison Notebooks* (1929–35)—Gramsci examined the interrelation of the modes of capitalist accumulation and governance that prevailed in either region, and the possible routes of solidarity between the northern proletariat and southern peasantry. In the North, the ideological hegemony of capital made possible the exploitation of wage labor in the factories. In the South, the economic expropriation and social marginalization of the peasantry was guaranteed by crude modes of police repression. The relationship between North and South, though, was defined not just by incommensurable difference but by structural entanglement. Gramsci described the South as an "exploitable colony" of the North. The extraction of natural and human resources in the South fueled processes of expanded reproduction in the North. The peasantry were driven off the land, and toward the FIAT assembly line, by mechanisms of enclosure and rapacious landlords. And the national banks that administered the dispossession of small agrarian producers in the South used the surplus value derived therein to catalyze the machineries of industrial accumulation in the North. The South's status as an internal colony also served an ideological function. The racialized image of "filthy" southerners helped to endow the proletariat of the North with a sense of their apartness from, and superiority to, the degraded agrarian masses in the South—a distortion of consciousness and cartography that heightened the "silent compulsion" of economic relations in the space of the factory. Gramsci's faith and contention was that these real and illusory fractures would be overcome by the political convergence of the proletariat and the peasantry, their articulation in a "historical bloc" that would transcend, on a national scale, the rule of capital and the bourgeoisie.[4]

Gramsci's reflections on the spatial and temporal asymmetry and internal contradictions of capitalist development within Italy—and indeed Trotsky's treatment of these same questions within Russia—resonated with the writings of another contemporary, José Carlos Mariátegui. Mariátegui's *Seven Interpretative Essays on Peruvian Reality* ([1928] 1988) chronicled how global relations of uneven development structured the combination of different moments of capital within Peru itself. The "new Peruvian economy," he argued, was "colonial to its roots." It was shaped, and continued to be defined, by the extraction of natural resources, as by the super-exploitation of indigenous labor in the mines and the fields.[5] Formerly, the means and outcome of these forms of depredation were the property of the settler-aristocracy. But the implication of Peru in global patterns of capitalist trade—the combination of extractive industry and international finance—had given rise to a domestic capitalist class that resembled a mature bourgeoisie (while retaining certain features of the old, feudal aristocracy). On the coast, this provisional capitalist class presided over industrialized cultures of agrarian production that incorporated a "system of free labor and wages." In the sierra of the interior, meanwhile, feudal forms of authority and accumulation continued to prevail:

> The free labor system has not developed there. The plantation owner does not care about the productivity of his land, only about the income he receives from it. He reduces the factors of production to just two: land and the Indian. Ownership of land permits him to exploit limitlessly the labor of the Indian. The usury practiced on this labor—translated into the Indian's misery—is added to the rent charged for the land, calculated at the usual rate. The hacendado reserves the best land for himself and distributes the least fertile among his Indian laborers, who are obliged to work the former without pay and to live off the produce of the latter.[6]

This internal unevenness was joined to the structural asymmetries of international systems of accumulation and trade. The markets of London and New York, Mariátegui wrote,

> regard Peru as a storehouse of raw materials and a customer for their manufactured goods. Peruvian agriculture, therefore, obtains credit and transport solely for the products that benefit the great markets. Foreign capital is one day interested in rubber, another in cotton, another in sugar. When London can obtain a commodity more cheaply and in sufficient quantity from India or Egypt, it immediately abandons its suppliers in Peru. Our latifundistas, our landholders, may think that they are independent, but they are actually only intermediaries or agents of foreign capital.[7]

Mariátegui derived from these insights an empirical and theoretical certainty in the necessity of communist revolution. Neither the bourgeoisie nor the exploited masses would be "liberated" by the progressive teleology of capitalist development. Like their counterparts in Russia, the Peruvian working class—at once agrarian-industrial and feudal, "free" and indentured—would outpace the revolutionary impetus of the bourgeoisie and spearhead the destruction of feudal relations, bypassing the stage of fully industrialized capitalism to arrive at the communist future.

The work of Gramsci, Mariátegui, and other Marxists writing from the (semi)-periphery, apprehended the capitalist world system—its constitutive unevenness—as structured by colonial relations and histories. Such thinkers impressed, in other words, the fundamental and abiding fact of a distinctly *colonial* capitalist modernity. Imperialism, they attested, is not a transient stage—the final stage, as Lenin had it—in the evolution of the capitalism mode of production, but an enduring mechanism of its perpetuation; just as the original act of primitive accumulation, as Luxemburg and others perceived, is, necessarily, constantly reprised.

The mutuality of colonial and metropolitan accumulation, and the interplay of repression and ideology therein, was theorized with a particular clarity by anticolonial thinkers in the middle decades of the twentieth century. Frantz Fanon, notably, observed in *The Wretched of the Earth* ([1961] 1963) that in the metropole,

> [t]he educational system, . . . the structure of moral reflexes handed down from father to son, the exemplary honesty of workers who are given a medal after fifty years of good and loyal service, . . . all these aesthetic expressions of respect for the established order serve to create around the exploited person an atmosphere of submission and of inhibition which lightens the task of policing considerably. . . . In the colonial countries, on the contrary, the policeman and the soldier, by their immediate presence and their frequent and direct action maintain contact with the native and advise him by means of rifle butts and napalm not to budge.[8]

Fanon accented the heightened importance, in the space of the colony, of crude state violence, and the concomitant insignificance of the ideological state apparatuses. But he was not simply drawing a contrast between the forms of governance that obtain in the metropole and the colony; he was also gesturing toward the fact that "the structure of moral reflexes" in the metropole is conditioned by, dialectically entangled with, the repressive violence of colonial relations.

This is true in multiple senses. The advent of Fordism in France—and the corresponding development of the ideological state apparatuses, including the welfare state—was enabled by the exploitation of labor and plunder of raw materials within the colonies, which also acted as a captive market for French goods. In Algeria—to keep with the specific settler-colonial context that shaped Fanon's work—the expropriation of arable land, and the exploitation of indigenous labor thereon, provided the textile mills of northern France with cheap supplies of cotton. The extraction of petroleum and natural gas, following its discovery in the Algerian Sahara in the 1950s, met and catalyzed a heightened demand for fossil fuels within the metropole. And the French settler population in Algeria, as well as the native bourgeoisie, was a major consumer market for French manufactures. For periods of the twentieth century, 50 percent of French exports were bound for Algeria. In the moment of decolonization, meanwhile, more than one million low-wage workers migrated to France from the west and north of Africa and from the Caribbean. By 1965, over 500,000 Algerians were living in France, many of them in *bidonvilles* that were subject to heightened levels of police repression. The intensive exploitation of colonial or postcolonial subjects within the metropole, in the construction and manufacturing sectors especially, fueled the accelerated economic development of the postwar decades, and contributed to the innovation and maturation of the social democratic state. Finally, the consent of the white working class in France was secured in part by the salve of superiority that colonial forms of racial thinking provided, during and in the aftermath of the imperial era. The sense of autonomy and belonging felt by the "free" white subject was made possible by the subjection of the colonized.[9]

The substance of this unevenness was likewise anatomized by the Guyanese historian Walter Rodney. In *How Europe Underdeveloped Africa* ([1973] 2017), Rodney laid out in lucid and meticulous terms the relationship between the primitive accumulation of capital in the colonies and the expansionary reproduction (or overdevelopment) of capital in the metropole. Underdevelopment, as Rodney defined it, expresses a particular relationship of exploitation: namely, the exploitation of one country by another. . . . And the underdevelopment with which the world is now preoccupied is a product of capitalist, imperialist and colonialist exploitation. African and Asian societies were developing independently until they were taken over directly or indirectly by the capitalist powers. When that happened, exploitation increased and the export of surplus ensued, depriving the societies of the benefit of their natural resources and labor.[10]

Rodney preferred "underdeveloped" to "developing," because the teleological implications of the latter word obscure how "many underdeveloped countries in Africa and elsewhere are becoming more underdeveloped in comparison with the world's great powers, because their exploitation by the metropoles is being intensified in new ways."[11] In the postcolonial period, these "new ways" include the uneven terms of international trade. Under the auspices of institutions such as the World Trade Organization (WTO), the nations of the Global North set the price for goods both exported from and imported to the Global South. And instruments of credit and direct investment result in the outflow of capital from the underdeveloped world, in the form of profits or debt obligations.

Though focused primarily on the colonial period, Rodney identified the genealogical connections between these new ("neocolonial") technologies of financial dispossession and the more primitive expropriation of the resources and labor of the colonized world. *How Europe Underdeveloped Africa*, that is, outlined the transition between two modes of capitalist governance—the crude violence of an occupying colonial power and the "more subtle and more dangerous" authority that inheres in the trade agreement or sovereign credit-debt relation. Importantly, though, these two technologies of power, and the moments of capital to which they correspond, are not merely successive but concurrent. And their interrelation, in the contemporary conjuncture, facilitates the intensification of older relations of exploitation. For example, foreign direct investment (FDI) in the national economies of the Global South might target extractive industries. And the "structural adjustment" programs imposed by the International Monetary Fund (IMF) likewise mandate, or compel, the sell-off of public goods (enabling their seizure by foreign or domestic corporations). Relatedly, the neoliberal ideology that greases the machineries of financial depredation necessarily dovetails with more overt, more explicitly violent forms of state control—as the insecurity produced or exacerbated by privatization, and by more primitive methods of plunder, provokes punitive technologies of policing (that equate precarity with criminality).

Rendering the dialectical interrelation of European development and African underdevelopment, Rodney also examined the concurrence of different modes of production within the colonized world. Specifically, he noted that workers in the colonies were compensated at less than the cost of their social reproduction. In order to meet the demands of their own survival, the colonized laborer was forced to supplement his degraded wage with subsistence forms of agriculture. "By any standards," Rodney wrote, "labour was cheap in Africa, and the amount of surplus extracted from the African labourer was great. The employer under colonialism paid an extremely small wage—a wage usually insufficient to keep the worker physically alive," and workers were thus forced to grow their own food.[12] Here and throughout the text, Rodney deploys a critical vantage—one earlier enacted by Mariátegui—that connects the uneven combination of different moments of accumulation *within* particular national geographies to the unevenness of the world-system at large.

Rodney's intervention also accentuated another modality of interrelation—the intersection of, or cooperation between, racist thinking and practice and economic exploitation. In certain passages, Rodney affirms deterministic historicizations of colonial power, which assume that the advent of empire was the consequence of economic imperatives rather than racial ideology: "it was economics," he asserted, "that determined that Europe should invest in Africa and control the continent's raw materials and labor." He was simultaneously attentive, though, to the fact that "pervasive and vicious racism was present in imperialism as a variant independent of the economic rationality." It was racism that "confirmed the decision that the form of control should be direct colonial rule."[13] And it was racism that made possible the severity of exploitation and ensured that the price of Black labor was less than the cost of its reproduction.

These dynamics—the combination of racial and economic rationality, in relation to the combination of different modes of accumulation, within the context of the colony—were later explored by Stuart Hall, in his essay "Race, Articulation, and Societies Structured in Dominance" (1980). Hall sought to avoid the reductivisms of both the "economic" and "sociological" explanations of race and racism. The "economic" approach, in Hall's phrasing, implies that "those social divisions which assume a distinctively racial or ethnic character can be attributed or explained principally with reference to economic structures and processes."[14] The "sociological" approach, meanwhile, assumes "the autonomy, the non-reductiveness, of race and ethnicity as social features."[15] Resisting the "mono-causal" hermeneutic of the economic vantage, and the abstract pluralism of the sociological perspective, Hall argued for the need to think about economic structures and social formations, class and race, as intrinsically bound up in one another. Bringing this core concern to bear on the history of racial capitalism in South Africa, Hall demonstrated how our attention to the intersection of different moments of accumulation is deepened when we attend, at the same time, to the intersection of different modes of social differentiation (for example, race, class, gender, sexuality)—and vice versa.

Hall adapted the term "articulation" from Althusser, for whom it named a joining that is not a synthesis, an interrelation wherein each element maintains its relative difference. Althusser used this concept to rescue the notion of "complex unity" from Marx's more "vulgar" materialist readers—and to impress how the myriad contradictions that comprise capitalist social order, which are not reducible to one another, combine in different ways in different spaces and times.[16] Hall's reflections on and deployment of the concept of "articulation," though, also summoned Marx's treatment of the structural combination of slavery and capitalism. Marx, Hall wrote, deduced that "slave plantation owners . . . participated in a general movement of the world capitalist system: but on the basis of an internal mode of production—slavery in its modern, plantation form—not itself 'capitalist' in character."[17] What Marx was identifying was the "articulation of different modes of production"—an essential feature of how capital operates, on the periphery of the world-system, and in the space of the colony, in particular.

In South Africa, Hall observed, "the reliance of the capitalist . . . on the non-capitalist sectors in the African areas for both cheap labour supply and subsistence reproduction enables capital to pay for labour-power below the cost of its reproduction, whilst having always available a plentiful labour supply whose costs of subsistence it does not fully bear."[18] And as Fanon outlined within a more global frame, the degradation of Black labor also helped secure the ideological enlistment of the white working class. As Hall put it, "racism is . . . one of the dominant means of ideological representation through which the white fractions of the class come to 'live' their relations to other fractions, and through them to capital itself."[19] Hall discerned that "where capitalism develops by means, in part, of its articulation with non-capitalist modes, the mode of political domination and the content of legitimating ideologies assume racial, ethnic and cultural forms."[20] This deduction models a way of thinking about race—its "social, political, and ideological levels"—that proceeds "not by deserting the level of analysis of economic relations (i.e. mode of production) but by posing it in its correct, necessarily complex, form."[21] Unique combinations of unique instances of accumulation correspond to unique articulations of race and class.

Distinguishing between the "economic" and "sociological" approaches to thinking about race and its autonomy or material basis, Hall foregrounded the problem of method. And he insisted, throughout the essay, on the need to arrive at more synthetic interpretative modes, which might resist narrow disciplinary conventions or methodological dogmas. Hall's essay on race and articulation, all this is to say, implied that the project of apprehending the interrelation of different spaces or moments of capital will require interdisciplinary—as well as intersectional—modes of inquiry. The imperative of inter- or trans-disciplinarity is shared by the project of world-systems theory. Reflecting on the origins of world-systems theory, Immanuel Wallerstein notes that the boundaries between the core social-scientific disciplines—anthropology, economics, political science, and sociology—are "barriers to further knowledge rather than stimuli to its creation."[22] World-systems theory set out to transcend, at once, the analytically confining frames of the nation-state and the scholarly disciplines. "The argument of world-systems analysis," he writes, "is straightforward":

> The three presumed arenas of collective human action—the economic, the
> political, and the social or sociocultural—are not autonomous arenas of

social action. They do not have separate "logics." More importantly, the intermeshing of constraints, options, decisions, norms, and "rationalities" is such that no useful research model can isolate "factors" according to the categories of economic, political, and social, and treat only one kind of variable, implicitly holding the others constant.[23]

This recognition of the non-autonomy of the various arenas of human social life—and the related attention to the "intermeshing" of distinctive logics and rationalities—is mirrored by the geographic lens of world-systems theory. Disavowing the utility of analytic approaches that regard individual states as autonomous entities, the world-systems approach highlights the historical interrelation of the nations or regions of the capitalist "core," "periphery," and "semi-periphery."

This conceptual framework owes a great deal to the insights of thinkers such as Gramsci, Mariátegui, Fanon, Rodney, and Hall into the uneven and combined development of capital, within national geographies and in the global context of colonial modernity. In his theorization of the interrelation of core, periphery, and semi-periphery, Wallerstein infers that the essential dynamic of the capital–labor antinomy—the exploitation of labor by capital—is mirrored, at the global level, by the "appropriation of the surplus of the whole world-economy by core areas."[24] And this economic unevenness, one expression of the colonial dynamic, corresponds to political asymmetry: "the strength of the state machinery in core areas is a function of the weakness of other state-machineries."[25] This dialectic might be framed in slightly different terms. The strength of the "state-machinery" in the core states manifests itself differently in different contexts. Domestically, the strength of the capitalist state is exhibited by the relative efficacy of capitalist ideology, and by the threat or actuality of police repression. Globally, meanwhile, the core capitalist states, while deploying the "soft power" of Nestlé and Disney, lean more heavily on crude militarism, what Fanon termed the "the language of pure force." And indeed, as I have argued, the effectiveness of capitalist ideology in the core is reinforced by the enactment of state violence in the periphery. The semi-periphery plays, in this framework, something like the role of the petite bourgeoisie in the Marxist analysis. The reproduction of the world-system depends on the ideological consensus of its "middle stratum," the semi-periphery that is exploited by (or dependent upon) the core but that exploits in turn more peripheral areas. (Think, for example, of Spain and Portugal in the sixteenth century, nascent empires that plundered the precious metals of the New World but used that wealth, primarily, to fund the purchase of finished manufactures from England or France.) The precise geographic organization of core, periphery, and semi-periphery is fluid, but the basic dynamic between these structural positions is, Wallerstein contends, continuous throughout the longue durée history of the modern capitalist world-system, from the fifteenth century to the present.

Wallerstein's reading of the capitalist world-system has been subtly but significantly revised by the work of Michael Hardt and Antonio Negri, who diagnose the redundancy of the geographic categories of core, periphery, and semi-periphery. Hardt and Negri's central thesis is that the binaries that ordered modern political order have dissolved. The supranational order of empire—a political-economic formation, marked, in their argument, by the global ascent of biopolitical production and global generalization of US constitutionalism—has transcended the modern antinomy of inside and outside, which formerly determined both the imagination and administration of difference and the relations and processes of capitalist accumulation. In place of the spatial entities and imaginaries that marked the era of modern imperialism, Hardt and Negri posit the disappearance of the outside and the advent of a "boundless universal space," the order of "Empire." Hardt and Negri's theory of Empire evokes Karl Kautsky's early-twentieth-century concept of "ultra-imperialism," which predicted the displacement of national economic interests by a globally unitary capital. Kautsky, though, imagined that the realization of the world market would occasion the dramatic diminishment of inter-state militarism, while the imperial order theorized by Hardt and Negri is defined by the generalization and permanence of war (which often takes the form of perpetual "police actions" rather than formally declared military interventions). They are sensitive, that is, to how the spatial order of empire is constituted by fissure, fracture, and contradiction. But their insistence on the transcendence of the geographic dynamics of modern imperialism approaches, at times, a dismissal of geography itself. Hardt and Negri affirmatively cite the analytic of uneven and combined development, without precisely detailing how it operates—spatially and temporally—within empire's planetary domain. "Through the decentralization of production and the consolidation of the world market," they write, "the international divisions and flows of labor and capital have fractured and multiplied so that it is no longer possible to demarcate large geographical zones as center and periphery, north and south. The geography of uneven development and the lines of division and hierarchy," they conclude, "will no longer be found along stable national or international boundaries, but in fluid infra- and supranational borders."[26] Hardt and Negri are eager to jettison the terms "core" and "periphery," "North" and "South," without introducing a new lexicon of spatial difference that might capture the "fluid borders" they invoke. The vocabulary of core and periphery and North and South might, however, be profitably retained. And it could, following Hardt and Negri's own insight, be applied to overlapping geographic scales, from city, to nation, to region and world. There are peripheries in the core; there are souths in the North. The precise dynamics of these extant asymmetries, within and across various spatial scales, are clarified, I submit, when the fact and consequence of capital's multiple moments is afforded analytic prominence.

Moments of Critique and Resistance

In certain passages of *Capital*, Marx outlines a definite historical path— from indentured or enslaved labor to wage labor; from the moment of primitive accumulation to the moment of expanded reproduction; from crude state violence to the "silent compulsion" of economic relations. When we highlight these passages of *Capital*, we are tempted to look for evidence of capital's "progressive" tendencies—the assumption that all societies, if unevenly developed, are moving toward the same historical end of free labor, large-scale industry, and abundant consumption. Elsewhere in his argument, though, Marx gestured toward the synchronic interrelation of different modes of governance and accumulation. The institution of chattel slavery, he discerned, was not a vestigial obstacle to the universal flourishing of capitalist rationality; unfree labor and free labor were (and are) complementary rather than contradictory forms. As Massimiliano

Tomba has more recently put it, "the crack of the whip of the slave-driver, then just as now, is synchronised with the rhythm of the world-market."[27] The accumulation of "relative surplus-value" (for example, by increasing the rate of exploitation) is always joined, Tomba notes, by the accumulation of "absolute surplus value," via crude or synthetic modes of dispossession.

In the contemporary capitalist conjuncture, the synchronous combination of the multiple moments of capital is elucidated by the "gig economy," which integrates primitive accumulation and synthetic dispossession with extant relations of industrial exploitation. "Start-ups" such as Uber garner massive amounts of venture capital funding, speculative investment that allows the company to withstand large quarterly losses as it ostensibly moves toward future profitability. Uber's investors are banking on the assumption that the company, by setting its fares artificially low, will draw consumers from and dramatically weaken both public transit and traditional taxi services. The goal, in other words, is to create a privatized transportation monopoly. Once its dominance is established, Uber will raise its fares and achieve a belated profitability. This integration of tech and finance is a paradigmatic instance of synthetic dispossession. Uber, enabled by the apparatuses of financialization, is opening up a new space for the creation of surplus value by deliberately devaluing the cost of the service it will later offer at an elevated price, once the landscape has been cleared of significant competitors. Its financial strategy, moreover, is premised on depressing the wages of the people who use their own automobiles to transport Uber customers (in advance of the day when such drivers will be replaced by a fleet of self-driving cars). Uber's model is not founded on the objective of economic growth—again, the company loses money every quarter, as it undermines other factors of the transportation sector—but on dispossession. How, then, does this instance of synthetic dispossession intersect with the moments of primitive accumulation and expanded reproduction? Most fundamentally, Uber's technologies of production—the smartphones that its customers and drivers use to arrange each individual transaction, and the automobiles themselves—are assembled in factories (the paradigmatic site of value generation in the moment of expanded reproduction), by some combination of robot and wage worker, in Shenzhen and Detroit (and many other places). The components that make up your smartphone, meanwhile, were produced at disparate sites across the world. And many of these parts are composed of raw materials extracted from the earth in West and Central Africa. To cite just two examples: coltan, which is refined into tantalum, is used in the manufacturing of your phone's capacitor, and cobalt is used in the production of its lithium-ion battery. The primitive accumulation of minerals underlies the manufacture of the technological instruments that function as one essential means of production for synthetic mechanisms of dispossession.

The rise of applications such as Uber, which "disrupt" traditional industries or sectors, is one example of the general neoliberal tendency toward ever greater economic insecurity. Those who drive for Uber (or Lyft) full-time struggle to get by, while many of those who "contract" with the company—Uber has argued in legal contexts that its drivers are not employees but contractors, and are thus ineligible for unionization—very often do so on top of other, full- or part-time jobs. (The Uber driver, then, is a contemporary descendant of the wage worker remunerated below the cost of their reproduction in the colonies.) The vocabulary of "disruption" and the "sharing economy" provides a certain ideological veneer to this erosion of economic security. But that veneer is thinning and cracking. As the precarity occasioned by synthetic dispossession deepens, the ideological efficacy of capitalism is diminished. In the space of the factory or office, in the moment of expanded reproduction, meanwhile, the workings of spirit, ideology, and governmentality still prevail, if tenuously. The Foxconn assembly line worker in Shenzhen is motivated not just by immediate economic exigencies, but by the promise of greater consumer power, and perhaps even middle-class opportunity, in a growing economy. The young men mining coltan in Rwanda, finally, do so under the watch of punitive corporate overseers or rebel groups. Their labor of primitive accumulation is enforced by the barrel of a gun.

These disparate subjects themselves constitute a "unitary constellation," which mirrors that formed by the unique moments of capital. How to limn the shape of that constellation, the space that separates one point from one another, and the routes of affiliation that connect them? This is a question that has long guided the project of anticapitalist internationalism. In the decades around the turn of the twentieth century, the concept of "uneven and combined development"—as it was theorized by Trotsky and others—centered on the question of how to think about the disjuncture between and entanglement of the urban and the rural, the industrial and the agrarian, within one national space, and in relation to the possibility of communist revolution. The rise of anticolonial thought, though, compelled a more global frame of analysis—one attuned, moreover, to the distinctive operations, within capitalist modernity, of race and coloniality. This is the story of the uneven efforts of Marx and Marxism, and the succession of communist internationals, to assimilate, into their theories of revolution, the tradition of Black resistance to slavery and colonialism. Inversely, this is the story of how thinkers such as Du Bois, James, Césaire, and Fanon worked to critique and revise the Eurocentric premises of much Marxist thought, by adapting Marx's theorizations of capital and labor to the manifold projects of Black radicalism—from the struggle for meaningful economic and political emancipation in the United States, to the struggle against colonialism in Africa, the Caribbean, South Asia, and beyond.

In the standard historiographic reading, the central antagonism of the First International pitted Marx against Bakunin, socialism against anarchism, the politics of statist reform against the politics of direct economic struggle, the "red" international against the "black" international. Though a marker of political philosophy rather than racial identity, the "black International" did find its firmest foothold on the periphery or semi-periphery of the capitalist world-system—Turkey and Egypt, for example—and in spaces of intensive primitive accumulation. It heralded an internationalism that was "black" not in the anarchist sense but because it was centrally informed by the dialectic of domination and resistance in the colonized world, and because of its attention to the imbrication of ostensibly backward modes of production—slavery, most specifically—and advanced industrialism. This planetary, anticolonial vision was not realized by the Second International itself, during which many European socialist parties aligned with their nation's participation in the inter-imperialist First World War. It was tentatively pursued, though, in the Third International (otherwise known as the Communist International, or Comintern), which established anti-imperialism as a core political platform, a necessary component or adjunct of the objective of communism itself. At the Comintern's second congress, Karl Radek spoke of the need to "reconstruct mankind on a new basis of freedom, where there will not be people of different-coloured skins with different rights and duties, where all men share the same rights and duties."[28] The head of the Comintern, Grigory Zinoviev, avowed, in an accordant register, that the organization would "unite under its banners speakers of all the languages of the world. The Communist International is sure that under its flag will rally not only the proletarians of Europe but also the mighty mass of our reserves, our infantry—the hundreds of millions of peasants who live in Asia, our Near and Far East."[29] This gathering of the Comintern was held in Baku, Azerbaijan, a site whose symbolic significance was owed to its place on the margins of the Soviet Union, and to its extractive economy (its vast oil reserves, most especially). The Baku congress underlined the central importance of the time-space of primitive accumulation—peripheral and semi-peripheral sites of fossil fuel extraction, in particular—to the industrial modernity of the twentieth century, and to the project of communist internationalism. But if delegates to the Comintern's Baku congress enunciated a more sophisticated recognition of capital's spatial and temporal multiplicity, and a more capacious conception of the "workers of the world," this appeal toward the global tended to elide rather than center the problem of difference—the question, for example, of how the colonized, and the subjects of primitive accumulation broadly conceived, would not just join but alter the theoretical vocabulary and political program of the Communist International.

Later Comintern gatherings, however, amplified the voices of anticolonial activists and thinkers, such as M. N. Roy and Claude McKay, whose insights shed light upon the conditions of racialized accumulation in the colonized world and in the United States. At the 1922 Comintern congress, McKay read several "Draft Theses on the Negro Question," which reaffirmed the International's commitment to anticolonial and antiracist politics, and which invoked the ideal of a "united front" of Black and white workers. McKay and other Black radicals such as Otto Huiswoud, though, also spoke to the "special form" of racist thinking and practice in the New World, and the "special position" in the capitalist world-system of the Black worker.[30] They signaled the possibility of an internationalist politics that attended to difference as well as sameness—the complex articulations of race and class, and the structural combination of the multiple moments of capital. Such an approach would join extant concepts of "uneven and combined development" and "permanent revolution" to the theories of racial capitalism being authored by Black thinkers in Africa, the Americas, and beyond. The radical political determinations implied by these critical developments were foreclosed, first of all, by the Comintern's Stalinist turn, and later by the specter and reality of the Second World War, which once again heightened nationalist currents within domestic communist parties, and which muted, too, emergent anticolonial energies. Those energies would be revived by the Fourth International. But they also, of course, found manifold intellectual and political expressions beyond it.

In the 1930s, C. L. R. James, in close dialogue with Trotsky, and in rhythm with nascent liberatory movements in the colonized world, sought to revise our understanding of the historical and contemporary dialectics of global capitalism. James's account of Toussaint Louverture and the Haitian Revolution imagined the plantation as a quintessentially modern space, and the slave as a quintessentially modern subject. In accord with the work of historians such as Eric Williams, *The Black Jacobins* (1938) argued that the plantation economy—the primitive accumulation of wealth in the New World—was one fundamental condition of possibility for the "age of revolutions" within Europe, the economic rise and political emancipation of the bourgeoisie. Adapting the Hegelian idea that the universal is found in the particular, moreover, James contended that the humanistic universalisms articulated in the event of the French Revolution were most fully and radically realized by Haiti's slaves in revolt. In sum, *The Black Jacobins* testified to the world-historical import of the Haitian Revolution by locating that event within the world-system of capital. James insisted that the underdevelopment of the colonized world was evidence of its modernity rather than a sign of its absence. And he grasped, simultaneously, that the subject of primitive accumulation, because of their central place within and exceptional insight into the dialectics of enlightened modernity at large, would necessarily occupy a vanguard position within any properly global anticapitalist struggle. Both rigorously historical and profoundly speculative, *The Black Jacobins* sketched an alternative genealogy of human freedom that opened up new imaginaries of anticapitalist and anticolonial futurity.

James's synthesis of Marxism and anticolonialism anticipated the theoretical contributions of thinkers such as Césaire and Fanon. Césaire's *Discourse on Colonialism* (1950) clarified one of the core assumptions of the theory of uneven and combined development, that capital in its imperial form produces at once sameness and difference—the global generalization of capital and the heightening of its intrinsic contradictions. Césaire's engagement with this idea, though, underlined how the underdevelopment of the colonized world occasioned the spiritual and moral degradation of, even as it enriched, European civilization. He described the "choc en retour" of colonial violence to Europe—the routes of connection, most specifically, between technologies of racialized mass extermination innovated in the space of the colony, and intra-European genocide in the moment of the Holocaust; and the more general "boomerang return" of colonial modes of governance and accumulation to the space of the metropole. Césaire, that is, foresaw certain aspects of the contemporary conjuncture—the enactment, in the Global North, of mechanisms of dispossession, and apparatuses of militarized emergency governance, that have long been the norm in the colonized world. And just as Europe had been transformed—enriched and degraded—by its colonial projections, so too would its future emancipation, Césaire avowed, depend on the revolutionary struggle of the colonized themselves, who might, through their negation of the absolute negation of colonial power, realize a "humanism made to the measure of the world." Césaire concludes his *Discourse* with an appeal toward "the only class that still has a universal mission, because it suffers in its flesh from all the wrongs of history, from all the universal wrongs: the proletariat."[31] In one reading, this closing note, which privileges an historically Eurocentric political category—the proletariat—is off-key. In another interpretation, Césaire is simply recasting that real and symbolic subject in the spirit of C. L. R. James. He is imagining the revolutionary potential of a proletariat that is made to the measure of the world, because it is rooted not merely in the space of the factory but also the plantation and the mine.

Like James, Césaire was from the West Indies, and his critical appraisal of colonialism on a global scale was informed by the unique history of the Americas—the intersections of capital and race in the New World, which refined the political and economic rationalities of colonial modernity at large. This attention to the unique yet paradigmatic history of the New World is less explicit in the work of another West Indian, Fanon, whose theorization of colonialism was most immediately inspired by Algeria's struggle for independence from France. But Fanon did assimilate some of the key insights of the historical critique of colonialism in the Caribbean, and in the Americas broadly conceived—for example, the idea, highlighted by James and by Eric Williams, that the so-called periphery of the capitalist world-system is in fact central, the source not only of the wealth that catalyzed the industrial and bourgeois revolutions, but the truest and most radical realization of the Enlightenment ideal of human freedom. His work, in other words, resonated not just with the immediate settler-colonial predicament of Algeria—and the entanglement of Algeria and metropolitan France—but with the substance and shape of coloniality within a global frame.

In the opening chapters of *The Wretched of the Earth*, Fanon outlines the spatial, temporal, and ontological binaries that structure the colonial city. "The colonial world," he wrote, "is a world divided into compartments . . . a world cut in two."[32] Fanon was not just concerned, though, with the division between the zone of the colonizer and that of the colonized, within the colonial city. He was equally attuned to the modes of spatial or temporal differentiation that defined the colony at large—the discontinuity between, and entanglement of, for example, the city and the countryside, the sites and subjects of industrial exploitation and primitive accumulation. He addressed, too, with singular acuity, the liminal spaces between the city and the agrarian hinterland. In his depiction of the revolutionary situation in Algeria, Fanon afforded great importance to the space of the shantytown and its collective subject, the lumpenproletariat. It was in the shantytown, Fanon contended, where "the rebellion will find its urban spearhead."[33] Forced toward the city by colonial expropriation in the countryside, the inhabitants of *les bidonvilles* "circle tirelessly around the different towns, hoping that one day or another they will be allowed inside."[34] In the shantytown, the dispossessed farmer met his urban comrades, the exploited industrial workers and the wageless lumpen, and in them saw his potential fates. The colonial shantytown was a space wherein the subjects of capital's multiple spaces and moments intermingled. If an older Marxist tradition foregrounded the factory as the space of collective subjective formation, and if James—working in a historical frame—focused on the plantation, Fanon identified an alternative, more pluralistic site of revolutionary becoming. The shantytown, for Fanon, was a concrete space, which illuminated the dialectics of domination and resistance within the space of the colony—the apparatuses of colonial power and surveillance, and the quotidian and anticipatory cultures of anticolonial resistance. But we might also extrapolate from Fanon's engagement with the shantytown a broader metaphoric significance—an injunction to center, in our analysis, spaces or instances where the denizens of or emigrants from capital's multiple moments converge, synthesizing new languages and formations of resistance.

Thinkers such as Fanon and James understood that, as Hall later put it, "capital reproduces the class, including its internal contradictions, as a whole—structured by race." Race and other imaginaries of difference "defeat the attempts to construct alternative means of representation which could more adequately represent the class as a whole, or which are capable of effecting the unity of the class as a result: that is, those alternatives which would adequately represent the class as a whole—against capitalism, against racism."[35] In recent years, the urgency of naming the collective subject of capital—of "representing the class as a whole"—has provoked the enunciation of terms such as the "precariat" and the "multitude." This provisional vocabulary of collectivity is responding to the apparent redundancy of the twentieth-century figure of the "proletariat"—that paradigmatic subject of capital, and agent of its overcoming, whose political centrality and rhetorical resonance were conditioned by the concentration of industrial production in the capitalist core, and industrial workers in the common space of the factory. The adequacy of that figure, as I have discussed, and as anticolonial thinkers perceived with a distinctive cogency, was always challenged by the endurance of agrarian production, by the geographic unevenness of colonial modernity, and by the ideological and structural expressions of race and gender; and its rhetorical and political force is today further diminished by the primacy of more diffuse and "flexible" modes of accumulation. In their theorization of the "multitude," Hardt and Negri do maintain something of the old "labor metaphysic" (to invoke C. Wright Mills's phrase). What unites the "multitude" is the global generalization of "biopolitical production." The workers of the world, they write, create "not only material goods but also relationships and ultimately social life itself," and it is these—"immaterial, communicative"—forms of labor power that are today qualitatively hegemonic.[36] The "precariat," meanwhile, denotes a yet more capacious condition and field, one that encompasses waged and wageless life, the post-Fordist workplace and the myriad spaces of social and economic insecurity with which it's contiguous. Attempting to "represent the class as a whole," each of these figures places the accent on sameness rather than difference—acknowledging without exactly revealing the heterogeneity, or the "internal contradictions," that structure the collective subject of capital.

Those "internal contradictions," I have sought to demonstrate throughout this book, correspond to manifold vocabularies and practices of critique and resistance. In the moment of primitive accumulation, militant struggles against the theft or destruction of land and resources dovetail with juridical appeals for formal recognition. In the moment of expanded reproduction, various sites of ideological contestation interact with struggles over the rate of exploitation. And in the moment of synthetic dispossession, demands for the restoration of bygone social and economic security exist in tense proximity to radical articulations of socialist futurity. How to unite these and myriad other space, modes, and languages of resistance? The barriers to such a synthesis are profound. The very patterns of uneven and combined development that compel planetary modes of struggle militate against their realization. Perhaps we must begin where Marx does, with that form that crystallizes the logics of capital, the commodity. The subjects of primitive accumulation, expanded reproduction, and synthetic dispossession are joined—actually or potentially—in their resistance to the commoditization of everything, including the elements of life itself: water, air, land, and the body—those phenomena, in David Harvey's words, that "are not produced as commodities."[37] As Polanyi insisted, capital, if left to its own devices, will destroy the two primary sources of value in the world: land and people. Acknowledging this fact, the capitalist state, compelled by popular struggle, instituted—over the course of a few, fleeting decades in the twentieth century—various protections against the relentless ravages of commoditization. But in the neoliberal period, this "second movement" of capital has been arrested and reversed, as the social commons and other sites of security have been opened up to the mechanisms of dispossession. In one possible future, critiques that target the intrinsic violence of the commodity form—its assault on our psychological integrity, on our relationship with one another, and on the web of life that sustains our existence on this planet—will become paradigmatic, and might even model or found a politics of resistance that articulates the theft of indigenous resources with the exploitation of wage labor, struggles against the advent of capital and struggles that target the inequities and alienations of its reproduction and reinvention.

Literature: Forms of Articulation

The question of how literary texts represent the structural combination of capital's multiple moments is closely joined to the problem of "world literature"—the problem of how literature apprehends the world at large, or evinces the local experience or constitution of global histories. The critical theorization of world literature has a deep genealogy, which is often traced to the nineteenth century—to Goethe, who famously announced, in 1827, that the "epoch of world literature is now at hand," and to Marx's vision, in *The Communist Manifesto*, of a world literature that would be brought into being by the world market. Marx's engagement with the question of world literature highlighted the correspondence between global political and economic forces and global cultural forms, and the critical urgency of analyzing that relationship in distinct historical conjunctures. Over the past several decades, this inquiry has shifted from a concern with the cultural-political cartography of what Michael Denning has termed the "Age of Three Worlds" to, in the aftermath of the Cold War, a focus on "globalization."

The discursive ascendance of "globalization" has revitalized debates about "world literature." The term "globalization" signifies, alternatively, the "end of history" generalization of capitalist markets and the liberal state, or the planetary manifestations of neoliberal rapacity. Contemporary discussions of "world literature" hinge on this contradictory meaning. In certain literary-critical forums, or in the work of certain influential scholars, "world literature" operates as a kind of premature universalism, a triumphalist descriptor of a world made flat by the provincialization of Europe and achievement of multicultural conviviality—"a more or less free space," as the Warwick Research Collective (WReC) paraphrase this pervasive imaginary, wherein "texts from around the globe can circulate, intersect and converse with one another."[38] Within the latter discursive sphere, concrete inequalities are transmuted, by the universal equivalent of the novel, into mere difference (qua entertainment). Another critical tendency, though, stresses rather the unevenness of both world literature and the global capital. Moretti's essay "Conjectures on World Literature" (2000) borrows its analytic framework from the world-systems approach to economic history, "for which international capitalism is a system that is simultaneously *one*, and *unequal*." In this vein, Moretti contends, there is "one world literary system" that is itself "profoundly unequal."[39]

This world-systems approach to world literature has been generatively elaborated by WReC. In *Combined and Uneven Development*, WReC define world literature "as the literature of the world system—of the modern capitalist world system."[40] Echoing Moretti, and invoking Jameson's notion of a "singular modernity," WReC suggest that "the multiple forms of appearance of unevenness are to be understood as being connected, as being governed by a socio-historical logic of combination, rather than as being contingent and asystematic."[41] In accord with my own conceptual framework, WReC identify the simultaneity of different but entangled moments of capital. WReC, though, assimilate from early-twentieth-century theories of uneven and combined development—as authored by Trotsky and others—a specific concern with *tense*, the intimacy of the old and the new, past and present/future, the archaic and the modern. Just as Trotsky identified the persistence of "backward" economic forms in the shadow of the factory, WReC highlight how, within the world of the novel, "realist elements might be mixed with more experimental modes of narration, or older literary devices might be reactivated in juxtaposition with more contemporary frames, in order to register a bifurcated or ruptured sensorium."[42] The combination of old and new literary forms reflects the combination of old and new modalities of accumulation. But while WReC describe these juxtapositions as "asynchronous," I want to emphasize how the structural combination of capital's multiple moments is characterized, precisely, by synchrony. The multiple moments of capital do not represent discrete tenses. Primitive accumulation, expanded reproduction, and synthetic dispossession belong, equally, to modernity and to the present. To again invoke Tomba's phrasing: the diagnosis of a "plurality of historical times, where forms of peasant slavery exist alongside high-tech production in the superannuation of the dualism between centre and periphery . . . is obfuscatory. . . . The real problem is their combination by means of the world market's mechanisms of synchronisation."[43] This is not to deny the properly historical character of capital—or to elide the concrete historical movement, within specific geographies, from, for example, peasant to industrial modes of accumulation. It is to insist, though, that our diagnosis of the present, as well as our reading of the past and speculation of the future, is sharpened when we foreground the synchronous interrelation of the multiple moments of capital.

The project of "world literature," as I conceive it, does not merely reveal the entanglement of different spaces within the world-system—or the global implication of local geographies; it also enacts the synchronization of the ostensibly diachronic. The work of that synchronization is performed both by the practice of criticism—for example, as I attempted to model in Chapters 1–3, in the juxtaposition of novels (or assemblages of novels) that inhabit the different moments of contemporary capital—and in the narrative imaginations of particular texts. The three novels I engage below illustrate, or begin to grasp, the simultaneity of the three moments of capital, within three spatial scales—the city, the nation, and the world at large.[44] I begin with a consideration of Pitchaya Sudbanthad's *Bangkok Wakes to Rain* (2019), which examines how interlocking histories of empire and capital combine and converge in the uneven present and antediluvian future of one metropolis. Moving to the national scale, I turn to Neel Mukherjee's *The Lives of Others* (2014), which reckons with the Naxalite response to accumulation by dispossession in India, and which reflects, in its form, the strategies of bourgeois self-narration that labor to keep the origins of wealth—in the fields and in the factories—out of view. Finally, I undertake a reading of Rachel Kushner's *The Flamethrowers* (2013), a novel that inhabits a global frame. Set against the backdrop of neoliberalism's

1970s emergence, *The Flamethrowers* connects instances of synthetic dispossession in postindustrial Manhattan to crises of capitalist ideology in the Italian auto industry and the primitive accumulation of rubber in Brazil. Illuminating the three moments of contemporary capital, each of these novels renders as well aspects of their combination—the articulation of unique modes of power and accumulation, unique structures of feeling, and unique vocabularies of critique and resistance.

Bangkok Wakes to Rain opens with a dense moving image of the contemporary city, which evokes the multiple histories the metropolis contains. A woman walks through a market, the sensuous plenitude of which transports her to her own childhood, as to her own indeterminate future. "Her nose picks up the ashen smell always in the air. Somewhere, a garbage heap incinerates underneath a highway overpass; in temples, incense sticks release sweet smoke to the holy and the dead; flames curl blue in the open-air gas grills of shophouse food stalls. She is a child or a few thousand years old."[45] The layered pasts that comprise the present encourage a kind of temporal disorientation—not a breakdown of cognitive mapping, exactly, but its suspension or deferral. The novel interweaves multiple narratives, each of which corresponds to a different era in the past, present, or future of the metropolis. This formal shape indicates the interrelation of capital's multiple moments, without precisely elucidating their synchronous convergence.

The woman that wanders through the market—and into her secure apartment building, where she is greeted by the "chilled, purified air" of the lobby—is immersed in the city but unable to locate herself within it. She does discern, though, that there is an all-seeing eye that records her presence, that polices by surveilling the large and small spaces she passes through: the market, the lobby of her building, the city at large. There was, she observes, "scant escape from being watched. . . . Eyes are everywhere, pointing down from balconies and windows, through the iron fencing and palm thickets that separate the building's grounds from the unruly street. She can feel eyes on her skin."[46] The pervasiveness of the surveillance apparatus acts as a metaphor, here, for the pervasiveness of capital itself. In its travels between past, present, and future—from the nineteenth-century colonial past, to the neocolonial militarism of the Vietnam War, to the skyscraper modernity of the present, to a future where only such towers peek above the rising floodwaters—*Bangkok Wakes to Rain* tracks how the advent, dissemination, and intensification of capitalist culture is experienced, by the inhabitants of the city and the world, as a process of declension, the narrowing of non-alienated and non-commoditized space. But the novel affirms, at the same time, that sanctuary persists, as a quotidian reality and speculative possibility.

In one of the novel's recurring narratives, Phineas, a missionary physician from New England, reflects on the intransigence of the Siamese, their resistance to the virtues of civilization, the inexorable march of history as progress. "They are," he writes in a letter home, "a proud, even arrogant people, having yet to come under the domain of a more advanced nation."[47] Phineas is principally invested in the benefits of Christian spirituality and modern medicine. In other passages, though, he extols the more profane contributions of free trade—"the export of teak and silk to the West, and the import of European and American goods to Siam." The improving effects of such exchange—in which he will have a monetary stake—"may prove to become my true, lasting mark on this world, more than medicine or faith alone could hope to effect."[48] As the novel jumps forward to the more recent past, to the present, and ultimately to the future, it illuminates the profound consequence of this imperial zealotry, the fundamentalism of capital. In doing so, *Bangkok Wakes to Rain* ventures beyond the city of its title, gesturing toward more global histories of accumulation.

In another of the novel's narratives, the African American jazz pianist Clyde plays back-to-back sets for US servicemen in Bangkok who are on R&R from the killing fields of Vietnam. Shortly after we meet him, Clyde is enlisted for a different, more mysterious gig. He performs for an audience of one, in an ornate old colonial mansion—the luxury of which was made possible by the proceeds of the imperial processes Phineas imagined— that is haunted by "twenty or so spirits" who have taken residence in a wooden pillar, "weathered and knotted, with dark globs of sap bleeding at its base."[49] Clyde is there to exercise these spirits, which visit the dreams of the house's owners, Master Rai and Khun Pehn, by manipulating the keys of an antique piano. Master Rai, instructs Khun Pehn, "wants you to know the spirits here are very eager for you to perform. And if you'd like, you can invite some of your own."[50] Clyde does, summoning the memory of his former collaborator and lover Morris, but channeling too, through the mediums of jazz and the blues, a deeper tradition, born of the Middle Passage and the New World to which it led, of Black oppression and Black survival. What histories are made audible or visible when the ghosts that haunt Clyde—that guide his hands across the keys—mingle with the ghosts that haunt the abode and consciousness of Master Rai and Khun Pehn?

This house is the site where the manifold histories that constitute the present are archived. Years after her separation from Master Rai, Kuhn Pehn, now an old woman, sells the home to developers, who use it as the foundation for a high-rise apartment complex. The colonial nostalgia the house embodies is easily commoditized; but the precise histories it contains have been erased. "What survived even in memory of that glorious former capital . . . ? Most modern citizens of Krungthep had difficulty recalling events more than months past." And yet, among the residents of this now twenty-seven-story building, rumors circulate about its cursed history. "The empty old colonial style mansion at the base was said by locals to have been owned by a wealthy family whose members mysteriously disappeared, one by one, until none were left. There had been," additionally, "numerous construction mishaps, with one worker losing an arm and others their minds." Another worker had fallen to his death, a calamity that briefly inhabited the collective consciousness of the city before it too was overtaken by the forces of amnesia. The building had been painted white, a symbol of its effort to erase its own history, "but with the traffic always languishing just below, the industrious fires of the city's coal cookers, and the rains depositing what factories had breathed out, streaks of soot and grime ran soon where rainwater had poured off."[51] Marketing itself as a place apart, the building is in fact utterly bound up in—a fitting symbol of—the mechanisms of erasure and reproduction that define the capitalist city's past and present.

The smoothness of the complex's day-to-day operations is ensured by the office assistant Nee. Like the building and Bangkok at large, Nee is haunted by a hidden history of violence. As a young woman she and her partner Siriphong were centrally involved in university protests against the return to Thailand from Singapore of former military dictator Thanom

Kittikachorn ("the colonel," in the novel). Kittikachorn's return—after three years of a tentative and partial experiment with more democratic forms—was facilitated by the monarchy and the military, and was precipitated by the specter of communism, which had been heightened by the victory of North Vietnam. On October 6, 1976, military and paramilitary forces attacked a demonstration of several thousand students. In the novel, Siriphong is counted among the dozens of victims. Nee makes a narrow escape to the river, where she swims underwater to precarious safety. By the end of the day, with her ears full of water, "all sounds had disappeared. It was the quietest she had ever heard the campus, not one sparrow noisy over classroom roofs."[52] This silence prefigures the strategies of official and informal forgetting that consign memory of the event to the realms of the private and unspoken, and that disable meaningful collective reckoning with the massacre's continuing reverberation. And this silence is present, all these years later, in the apartment complex where Nee works, the "pristine noiselessness" of which overwhelms her.

One of the building's tenants is Khun Pehn. When she learns that Nee graduated from a famous university in the 1970s, she is returned to the images of student protests and the brutal force with which they were met—"the horrific photos of bodies burned and blackened, bashed and pummeled until their faces seemed like overripe fruits. The young lives extinguished in the grand thoroughfares where they'd gathered." She had been skeptical of the students, whose "fiery passions would upturn everything for the worse and maybe even destroy the society she'd cherished." The violence of the state seemed natural, then, and over the years, as "those killings became a thing that happened further and further from her," this sense of normality was reinforced by spatial and temporal distance.[53] But now, in her old age, and as the city and nation descend once again into crisis, she "couldn't help but remember"—and she joins that memory to a recognition of the continuity of state violence (in the service of capital) across space and time, the routes of connection between historical and contemporary enactments of US militarism, for example, and the murder of those Thai students so many year ago. "They'd died," she thought, "and the game of musical chairs kept going anyway." And looking out the window, she perceives, in the tableau of the city, "the grand dance still in motion."

This sense of immanent violence soon acquires a more palpable form. With Nee at her side, "Khun Pehn pointed to the window. It was dark out, but enough blue had lingered in the sky for Nee to make out smoke pluming in the distance."[54] The promise of the apartment complex is that that distance is great; here one is safe from the smoke on the horizon, and the fire from which it emanates. But now Khun Pehn perceives that distance as an illusion. She perceives, too, that that illusion is made possible by amnesia, the injunction—intrinsic to the logics of capital and the state—to forget. "Forgetting was the thing one was supposed to do after calamity—not realizing the danger of confusion when someday the living would come to feel like ghosts, and the long departed came back to life when they liked anyway."[55]

In *Bangkok Wakes to Rain*, the interrelation of capital's multiple moments is figured, most explicitly, as a question of return. Histories of colonial power haunt the grand residence of Master Rai and Khun Pehn. The massacre of student protestors, decades in the past, disrupts the mechanisms of spirit, governmentality, and ideology in the present. And the plumes of smoke in the distance are registered, in the first instance, as an echo of earlier iterations of state violence, rather than as but the latest signal of that violence's structural continuity. In moments, though, the novel does approach a more concrete recognition of temporal simultaneity. The young worker who fell to his death during the apartment complex's construction, Gai, had, along with his colleagues, labored "for six weeks without a break, with the promise of one to be given if enough floors had risen. Songkram was a few months away, and they couldn't bear the thought of having to stay behind in Krungthep that holiday week. . . . What prouder accomplishment could there be than to still be on the payroll and also able to return to one's home province as the new year's bearer of a ring for one's mother or a Walkman for siblings?"[56] Gai is compelled to the scaffolding by the promise of consumerist belonging; for him, it is the silent compulsion of the market, and not the overseer's rifle, that secures his waged labor. But his death, however accidental, and its subsequent erasure—"after adequate sums changed hands between the right parties"—pointed to the concurrence of other modes of capitalist power, technologies of governance premised not on consent but on domination. And there is a certain connection, the novel implies, between the disposability of workers such as

Gai and the state's violent suppression of any resistance to the hegemony of capital.

The novel's speculative forays into the future, though, introduce again the problem of tense—the presence, specifically, not only of what is past but of what is to come. Before epochal floods submerge the city, the appearance of snakes in unusual contexts—on higher ground—is a sign of rising waters. But just as the past is repressed, so too is evidence of the future pushed out of mind: "not too many took notice of news that the rivers flowing through Greater Krungthep were rising. It was another wet season, and who should be alarmed by small pools that had begun to form at drainage gutters?"[57] The historic rains are one expression of climate change; the rising seas that exacerbate their acute effects is another. And while the floodwaters do initially recede, in the more distant future they become a permanent feature of the metropolis. "Old Krungthep" is underwater. "Anything has a way of disappearing," the anonymous narrator of the novel's future interlude puts it.[58] That disappearance competes with the memory of "the old ones," who tell scarcely believed stories of long-drowned markets, temples, and thoroughfares. As the water rises, the city shrinks. But if that declension troubles the concept of growth, it does not displace the adjacent ideals of accumulation and profit. Wreckage is salvaged for scrap and marketed to tourists—"knickknacks and sea-shell encrusted furniture—the more water warped and stained, the more sought after." Capital clings precariously, in other words, to the possibility of continued rounds of crude and synthetic valorization. Public farms are good for government PR, "but almost all of [the city's] food is being imported from a consortium of corporations, with the city's debt rising every day."[59] This new regime is guaranteed by new technologies of repression and control. "Each week brings in new orders and codes." When the waters came some were forced to migrate; the even less fortunate, who could not afford to resettle, were left to die as the ocean overwhelmed their communities and homes. Those streets that remain, if only fleetingly when the tides ebb, are cleaned by an ever-growing population of prisoners.

These novel mechanisms of control, though, are contiguous with the forms of state power resisted by Nee and her comrades so many decades ago. So too do the floodwaters have a much more distant origin. To cite merely the local history: In the nineteenth century, Thailand was three-quarters forest. In the early decades of the twentieth century, the lumber industry began to expand. That expansion accelerated in the aftermath of the Second World War and today only 15 percent of the country is forested. The country's industrial development in the postwar period—its provisional membership in the sphere of global capital—also coincided with the expansion of offshore drilling. Such drilling continues apace. Since 2000, Chevron has doubled its oil production in the Gulf of Thailand. And these localized instances of extraction are, of course, a tiny representation of primitive accumulation's contribution to the planetary incidence of carbon. While the submergence of Bangkok is a speculative event, belonging to the future, the extractivism that makes it imaginable has a much longer global history—one that runs throughout the centuries spanned by *Bangkok Wakes to Rain*.

As "Old Krungthep" is erased by the swelling rivers and seas, the denizens of "New Krungthep," those who did not or could join the march inland, search for or fashion out of salvaged materials a scrap of land or structure in which to belong and survive—on the highest ground, and on the higher floors of buildings that might at any instant finally succumb to the will of the water. In this, their struggle is continuous with other traditions of individual and social resistance to the pervasion of capital, its colonization of all realms of human existence. This struggle, moreover, as the novel recognizes, is not just about claiming or constructing some space outside capital—or some non-alienated space of belonging and security within its proper domain—but about carving out or maintaining a perch from which one might be able to see it. Once we are all underwater, with no hope of finding an island, the fact that the seas are rising—the causes and consequence of that planetary transformation—will be more difficult to perceive.

Bangkok Wakes to Rain intimates the synchronous interrelation of multiple moments, but it devotes greater attention to the presence of past and future—the histories of colonial dispossession and state violence that haunt the present; the subtle signs of rising waters, the submerged future, that register only briefly in the consciousness of the contemporary city. In this formal and thematic emphasis, *Bangkok Wakes to Rain* is not unique. The trope of haunting, the ways in which various hidden histories of violence linger in and impact upon the present, is central to the postcolonial or global novel broadly conceived. Another strand of contemporary fiction, though, places a greater accent on the concurrent articulation of capital's multiple moments. The novel I turn to now, Mukherjee's *The Lives of Others*, represents that simultaneity within a specifically national frame.

Set in India in the late 1960s, *The Lives of Others* centers on the Ghosh family, the shifting fortunes and fractures of which act as a lens onto the social inequities and political transformations of Indian society at large. The family's wealth and status come from paper. Pioneers of the industry in late-colonial India, their business concerns, and riches, expanded in the aftermath of independence. In the novel's present, though, the family firm is in crisis. There is labor unrest in the mills, and "the botched modernization of technology at one of the factories, all that high-risk borrowing against capital" has left the company in a precarious financial state.[60]

The novel begins far beyond the walls of the factory or the boardroom—and far beyond, too, the family house in Calcutta that is the story's primary dramatic stage. The opening scene introduces instead a parallel narrative world—the peasant struggle against primitive and synthetic forms of dispossession in rural India. Nitai Das "has begged all morning outside the landlord's house for one cup of rice. His three children haven't eaten for five days. Their last meal has been a handful of hay stolen from the landlord's cowshed and boiled in the cloudy yellow water from the well. Even the well is running dry. For the past three years they have been eating once every five or six or seven days."[61] His entreaties this morning are met, as they often are, with a beating. But instead of skulking away in resigned defeat, Nitai has an epiphany; he "knows what to do now." When he returns home—to his wife, who "can hardly hold her head up," to his children, who "have become so listless even [their shadows seem] dwindled and slow"—he kills his family and then himself, "returning from the nothing in his life to nothing."[62]

These words, which pose the dialectic of domination and resistance in the countryside—the negation of a negation that does not, in this case, culminate in liberation or affirmation—preface our introduction to the Ghosh clan, the interpersonal tensions of their privileged domesticity, and the political and economic forces currently buffeting their bourgeois existence. Throughout the remainder of the novel, the narrative moves between these two worlds, these two moments of capitalist governance and accumulation. The link between them is Supratik, one of the youngest Ghosh generation who has rejected his class inheritance and become a Naxalite activist. The substance of his political enlightenment and radicalization, and the plot of his experience in the peasant movement, is conveyed in a series of letters he writes to his aunt Purba, with whom he is in love. The bourgeois realism that defines the novel's Calcutta interludes dovetails with the epistolary enunciations of Supratik's political commitment. The distinction between the narrative's two primary moments, in other words, is marked by a formal disjuncture.

Supratik's letters to Purba are didactic. His aim is to "give [Purba] the tiniest glimpse . . . [of] the world that is my concern"—the world beyond the walls of Calcutta's luxury neighborhoods and establishments. "Inside-outside," he instructs: "the world forever and always divides into those two categories." He asks Purba to imagine "a row of sleeping men curled up like fetuses," on the street outside a grand hotel. "Only ten feet separate them from the world of extreme wealth. . . . Inside, the amount of water used daily to keep the lawns and gardens so lush could provide drinking water to each of the men for the month. Outside, these men have to walk miles sometimes to get to a public hand pump."[63] Supratik begins with this image not only because it brings into relief the stark contradiction between inside and outside, but because it crystallizes the connections between the world he currently inhabits—the world of the rural poor—and the world of bourgeois comfort he left behind. The men sleeping outside the hotel "come from the suburbs, the villages, the mofussils, to look for work in the big city. The lucky among them will become rickshaw-pullers. . . . The less lucky will dig ditches, carry bricks, sand, cement. . . . Some will be reduced to begging. You may ask," Supratik continues, "why don't they go back to where they came from, if this is what the city holds for them? I will answer with another question: do you know what life holds for them back home? We don't see them, so we don't think about them. But I have seen their lives, I have lived with them. For a while. I will tell you about it."[64] Supratik is highlighting, in this opening letter, a crisis of representation, or of cognitive mapping. Purba is unable to locate herself in relation to the social whole, precisely because, Supratik suggests, the inhabitants of the disparate spaces or moments of capital are invisible to her. Supratik's objective, like that of the novel itself, is to correct that blindness, and to thereby shed light upon the entanglement of, for example, the bourgeois home and the peasant revolt.

The conditions of that blindness, meanwhile, are evidenced by the everyday drama of the novel's domestic narrative. The Ghosh family is occupied by manifold tensions and worries, such as the fading marriage prospects of lone daughter Chaya, whose dark complexion and advancing age have scared off numerous potential suitors. This particular thread combines with several others—intrafamilial rivalry, resentment, and cruelty—to weave a familiar tapestry of bourgeois alienation and repression. The inwardness of the broader household is mirrored and magnified by the narrative's focus on the psychological life of the family's individual members. This part of the novel's double interiority manifests, then, as a kind of bourgeois novel par excellence. But *The Lives of Others*—in specific passages and in its overall form—betrays its own critical awareness of how the excitations of everyday life, or the tumults of subjective consciousness, often obscure the political forces that are roiling the Ghosh family and nation alike. "Who could have known," the narrator asks at one point, after invoking trouble in the factories, "that behind the pleasant, reliable surface a different drama had been churning away? The soothing pictures of the past were slowly revealing themselves as optical tricks."[65] These lines could serve as a description of the novel itself, which renders the richly textured veneer of bourgeois life, only to cut through that veneer to expose the world it conceals—the extant history of exploitation and expropriation, in the mills as in the fields, that structures the unevenness of contemporary Indian society.

In one of his letters to Purba, Supratik reflects on the existence that drove Nitai to kill his family and himself. "Starving for days at a time, but having to work—back-breaking physical labor—double, three times his normal effort because whatever he earned, the rice that he harvested, say, belonged to the moneylender, who had secured it at a price below the market rate. I suppose his creditors gave him enough to keep him working:

what use was a dead laborer to anyone? What was it like, having the last drop of your blood (and your land) squeezed out of you and there was nothing you could do about it?"[66] As Supratik's questions convey, Nitai was degraded to the point of death by multiple forms of depredation—from the expropriation of land to punitive usury. His misery and subjection belong at once to the moments of primitive accumulation and synthetic dispossession. Supratik's questions are posed to Purba, imploring her to appreciate the violence of rural poverty, and the broader system of capital it underlies. But the provocation "what was it like" is also directed at himself; it is an injunction to inhabit and know, at the limits of empathy, the existence of Nitai. Working in rural villages as a Naxalite organizer, Supratik joins the peasant laborers in the fields. "When you worked in the fields from six in the morning to four in the afternoon the tiredness resulting from it stunned you into silence. You went from being a human, animated by a mind and spirit and consciousness, at the beginning of the day, to a machine without a soul at the end of those ten hours."[67] This regime of accumulation is premised not simply on the exploitation of living labor but on its total negation—a negation that is secured by "the state and its biggest instrument of control and repression, the police."[68] His education in the countryside—however incomplete, and however great the distance between Supratik and the masses of rural poor remains—is a journey toward appreciating that fact and its political implications: the movement of peasant revolt will necessarily be violent. If Supratik and his fellow organizers, other privileged young men from the city, spend their first evenings in the countryside rehearsing old debates about the "relative merits of economism versus militancy," they soon deduce that the lives of the peasants "would never be improved by the corrupt, slow process of parliamentary democracy and elections. . . . Their freedom could only come about through armed rebellions of the kind that were erupting everywhere around them."[69]

If Supratik and his comrades insinuate themselves in the world of the rural poor in order to learn something of their lives, and the broader relations of power within which their struggle for survival plays out, they are also there in a pedagogical capacity. They endeavor to impress on the consciousness of the masses what their bodies and minds already intuitively know—that the *jotedaars* must be punished, and the only language they understand, the language they themselves most naturally speak, is violence. But if Supratik anticipated that because the degradation of the peasants was so profound "they would be simmering with anger and all we needed to do was a bit of stoking and there would be a giant conflagration that would bring down the blood-suckers and burn them to cinders," he soon arrives at a different recognition; the "slow-burning flame of resentment and deprivation had burned them, not the perpetrators. The embers of anger we had thought of fanning had burned them down into the ashes of despair. They were already dead within their lives." The farmers had "no hope, no sense of future, just an endless playing out of this illness of the present tense."[70] The mission of Supratik and his comrades is to restore the possibility of the future—for the farmers, but also for themselves. This absence of futurity functions as a link between the two worlds through which Supratik travels: the bourgeois milieu of the Ghosh family in Calcutta, and the extreme poverty of the rural villages. Supratik is compelled toward the country by the malaise of that bourgeois existence, as much as by his keen sense of injustice. The gulf between Supratik's own alienation and the human estrangement he bears witness to in the countryside is profound. But this dissonance belies a certain affinity. The novel, that is, is attuned to the routes of connection between the different spaces and subjects of India's capitalist order. And these connections, again, are expressed not just by the systemic combination of unique moments of capitalist governance and accumulation, but by the convergence or synthesis of unique languages of critique or resistance.

The Lives of Others represents the synchronous articulation of capital's multiple moments. But the novel also possesses a more historical imagination. Like *Bangkok Wakes to Rain*, it is attentive to the presence of the past, and the continuity across time of particular techniques or relations of capitalist power. "All the so-called reforms brought in by the government in the twenty-one years of Independence . . . had not improved the condition of the [farmers] one whit. The actors had changed; the play remained the same. The great magnetism was still at work: power spoke to and connected only with power; the government and its laws were for the benefit of the landlords, the powerful and the wealthy."[71] Interwoven with the chronicle of the Ghosh family's contemporary dramas is a narrative of the clan's economic history—the story of where their wealth came from. This story begins in the aftermath of the First World War, when Prafulla Ghosh sensed an opportunity in India's floundering domestic paper manufactures. While imported paper dominated the industry, Prafulla devised a kind of proto import substitution model, pushing the native product onto the market at prices significantly lower than that purveyed by British firms. At this point, Prafulla's concern remained with the point of sale rather than the point of production. But he soon established himself within the sphere of manufacture, by facilitating the devaluation of certain firms, which he later purchased at greatly depreciated prices. The family's own expansionary reproduction, all this is to say, was made possible by a nicely timed act of synthetic dispossession. It was abetted, moreover, by an abiding willingness to do business with the British—to profit from rather than challenge the economic fundament of colonial power.

The family also capitalized on India's midcentury independence—by cleverly negotiating the geographic cataclysm of Partition—and in the decade that followed succeeded in consolidating their position at the top of the paper industry. The restless drive of Prafulla, though, has led, in the present tense, to crisis. Perceiving the need to update production technologies in the mills, in order to maintain the company's edge, Prafulla had coordinated the purchase of new machinery from abroad on significant credit. As the implementation of the new machinery—and with it production and revenue—stalled, the burden of the loan had become overwhelming, crippling the company and plunging the family into a collective depression. The current misfortune of the company and family acts as a parable of the underlying rationality, and ultimate pitfalls, of expanded reproduction. Prafulla's will toward perpetual expansion is compulsive. But this compulsion, *The Lives of Others* makes plain, inheres less in the subject than the object. The desire for relentless growth belongs to capital itself. The capitalist is simply one medium for, the agent of, a "spirit" that is intrinsic to money, or the commodity form broadly conceived. The Ghoshes, too, like the workers in their mills and the farmers that Supratik joins in the fields, are diminished by the effects of reification, the violence of capitalist abstraction, however complicit they may be in a system that is premised on theft, exploitation, and degradation.

Prafulla's children and grandchildren did not inherit his entrepreneurial spirit. A couple of his offspring remain vaguely committed to the business, and are happy to enjoy their inherited wealth, but also tend toward apathy and incompetence if not more outright disaffection. And the disconnection of the subsequent generation is yet more pronounced, as Supratik's radicalism indicates. The transition from one generation to the next accelerates the fading efficacy of ideology, in pace with the deepening crisis of expanded reproduction. The question of whether the crisis of spirit within the family is a cause or consequence of economic decline is not definitively resolved in the novel. But it is made clear that the fact of crisis has begun to counter, specifically, the amnesic effects of fetishism and reification, and to open up the space for a belated reckoning with the origins of the family's wealth—the history of expropriation that made possible its advent and catalyzed its growth, and that is embodied by the house itself (grand but beginning to crumble, and shot through with fracture and contradiction).

> From all the things [Supratik] has bothered to find out about the way the Ghoshes ran their businesses—planting lumpens within unions to spark off violence so that all the union workers could be sacked; an old story of buying off a business from a friend's widow, who did not know any better, for a fraction of its real value; using the Hindu-Muslim riots the year before Independence, the year before he was born, to shut down mills, regardless of how many workers were deprived of their livelihoods, and buying up factories in areas emptied by migration—all this immorality and opportunism, this was what characterized them, not altruism, as the stories they had spun would have you believe.[72]

Supratik recognizes that this history of violence was concealed by "self-mythologizing through anecdotes proliferating like a particularly virulent strain of virus"—stories that brought the family and capitalist class together in "one huge, collusive matrix."[73] These anecdotes echo and amplify the history-erasing technologies of the commodity form. So Supratik sets out to expose and deconstruct the auto-mythology of both capital and the Ghosh family—by composing an alternative narrative, which he delivers in his letters to Purba.

The substance of Supratik's Naxalite commitment, though, implicitly avows that what is required is not merely a narrative counterpoint to the mythology of capital—the displacement of capital's fictive memory with its real history—but the actual material destruction of the relations of dominance and exploitation that prevail in the fields and factories alike. The form and effects of that counter-violence are made vivid in Supratik's letters, when he describes in graphic detail the slow disemboweling of one Naxalite target, a local moneylender and pawnbroker. This act is not carried out by Supratik himself, but he does soon bloody his own hands. And in the novel's closing pages, he is plotting a different sort of action—not direct assassination, of one landlord or creditor, but a more general form of terror—the derailment of passenger trains. The innovation of this tactic is his enduring legacy within the movement; and the second and final of the novel's epilogues turns to the present tense of 2012, when a young Naxalite activist named Subita Kumari—who was radicalized after her sisters were raped and murdered because her family resisted the attempts of a moneylender to seize their land—is removing fishplates from the tracks, between two population centers. Her work done, she disappears, with her comrades, into the forest. "In three hours," the novel concludes, "well before dawn breaks, the Ajmer–Kolkata Express, carrying approximately 1,500 people, is going to hurtle down those tracks."[74]

The Lives of Others is not interested in casting moral judgment—in condemning or affirming the Naxalite response to the violence of primitive and synthetic dispossession. The novel is more concerned to represent the conditions that compel that response, and the ideological infrastructure that keeps those conditions out of view. The novel works, in other words, to annotate the relationship between two abstractions—the abstraction of fetishism and reification (the abstraction of the commodity form), which obfuscates the origins of surplus value; and the abstraction of Supratik's theoretic dogma, which mandates the enactment of counter-violence. But the novel also poses a third mode of abstraction, which might elude if not transcend the dialectic of capitalist and anticapitalist violence. Supratik's younger cousin Sona is a math prodigy. He inhabits a higher realm, "above it all in the world of numbers."[75] Awarded his doctorate from Stanford at the age of nineteen, after winning a scholarship to study in the United States, he goes on to become a professor at his alma mater. And his work on prime numbers—specifically his insights into the problem of the "twin primes conjecture"—is recognized with one of the most prestigious prizes in mathematics, the Fields Medal. On this occasion, his mentor at Stanford remarks to a reporter that "most mathematicians are creatures somewhat dissociated from the real world. The abstract matters to them much more than the concrete. [Sona] is a very pure example of that. There is an innocence about him which the world has not been able to touch."[76] The privileging of the abstract above the concrete is also a defining feature of the profane world of the market below. But Sona is committed to a practice of abstraction that illuminates rather than obscures, and that is autonomous rather than an effect of commodity rationality. Prime numbers, the announcement of Sona's Fields triumph suggests, "are considered by mathematicians and scientists to provide the underlying design of many things in nature."[77] Sona has tapped into a frequency that is at once deeper and higher. It's not a frequency that is available to us all; nor is it one that might be deployed to undo the abstractions of capital. Its existence, though, does hint at the presence of other worlds within this one, the immanence of an outside to the time-space of capital.

The possibility of that outside, and the complexities of the politics that might realize it, are likewise registered by Kushner's *The Flamethrowers*. The novel begins in the American West, where "Reno" is making her way across Nevada by motorcycle, bound for the salt flats where she will attempt to set a new land-speed record—a trial, she hopes, that will double as a work of art. The desert that Reno is passing through is defined by an apparent emptiness that elides the region's original, indigenous occupants. The landscape is also marked, though, by the infrastructure of accumulation set in motion by the continent's settler-colonization—"brothels and wrecking yards, the big puffing power plant and its cat's cradle of coils and springs and fencing, an occasional freight train."[78] At a truck stop, drivers idle away their break from the road playing racing video games, the juxtaposition of actual driving and its simulation intimating the transition from real to symbolic labor—from work that produces value to work that acquires rather a certain cultural currency, or that is fetishized as itself an object of consumption. In these opening scenes, the concurrence of capital's multiple moments enters the field of vision.

Reno intends to photograph the line that her motorcycle, moving at a kind of transcendent velocity, will draw across the flats. The image "would be nothing but a trace. A trace of a trace [that might capture] . . . the experience of speed."[79] In rhythm with the aesthetic politics of the land art movement, Reno's participation in the speed trials will evoke the ideal of ephemerality—an ontological mode that resists by evading the ascendance of the commodity form, and the confinement of art in the space of the commercial gallery (the sphere of exchange value). Her creation will be "useless" in the eyes of the market; but its refusal of commodity rationality might signal the reclamation of a certain aesthetic or political autonomy, through or from which new vocabularies of anticapitalist critique might be formulated.

Reno's time in Nevada is a departure from her current home, and the novel's central locale, New York City. There, Reno is immersed in a world where artists are struggling to confront recent evolutions in capitalist culture and process. The abandoned industrial spaces of lower Manhattan have been converted into lofts occupied by artists and those keen to derive economic or cultural capital from their work. The crew of artists and gallerists that Reno runs with all affect a vaguely anticapitalist air. Sandro Valera—estranged heir to an Italian tire and motorcycle empire, and Reno's lover—works in a minimalist idiom, constructing "large aluminum boxes, open on top, empty inside, so bright and gleaming their angles melted together."[80] The objects refer to the assembly line but also obscure it. The boxes were fabricated by hand at a boutique facility in Connecticut and their exchange value has nothing to do with the labor that was put into them or any practicable utility they might have. Another artist, Sammy, completes a heroic performance piece, presumably designed to impress the tyranny of industrial time, in which he punches a clock every hour on the hour for a year. Gordon Matta-Clark (the actual historical figure) re-enchants abandoned factories, warehouses, and piers by carving holes into their exteriors—transforming them into "cathedral[s] of water and light."[81] Most of these artists diagnose the violence of the commodity form from a position of self-conscious remove. "I don't make a *wage*," Reno's friend Ronnie puts it. "I'm an artist, I'm not part of the system."[82] None of them reckon with their complicity in the transformation of the cityscape—a process of synthetic dispossession, facilitated by financial elites and enabled by the city's bankruptcy in 1975, which pushed the underclasses to the margins of the metropolis. Nor do they meditate on the fate of those displaced or devalued by the city's deindustrialization. With one exception: Burdmoore, erstwhile member of the real late-1960s activist group the Motherfuckers, longs for the day "when the people of the Bronx wake up, the sisters and brothers out in Brooklyn," and reclaim their right to the city.[83]

When Reno travels to Italy with her lover Sandro, the peripheral and dispossessed enter the foreground. Uncomfortably caught up in the Valera world, Reno begins to learn more about the history and present of the company and its cultures of production. In the postwar decades, "'everyone [had] his own little auto, put-putting around, well enough paid at Valera to buy a Valera, and tires for it, and gas."[84] As this Fordist idyll fades, its ideological armature is also diminished. Sandro's brother Roberto has instituted particularly draconian shop-floor policies. The workers live in squalor; and "their wives and children put together Moto Valera ignition sets at the kitchen table, working all night because they were paid by the piece, whole families contracted under piecework, which was practically slave labor."[85] Though many of the factories remain open, the post-Fordist paradigm—spatially and temporally diffuse systems of production, devalued labor—is taking hold. In response, the workers are in revolt—halting the assembly line and joining leftist youths in the streets.

The piecework performed in the home—"practically slave labor"—resembles the debt peonage of the Indians in Brazil who have long harvested the rubber for Valera tires. The Tappers run "from tree to tree, coated in sweat and jungle damp, zigzagging until . . . you are ready to collapse, feeling like your head is in a cloud of ammonia, dizzy, confused, pain shooting up your spine, muscles twisted into torn rags."[86] This brutal regime of labor—overseen by a patrão whose tools are "the cheap muzzleloader, mock drownings with water poured over a facecloth"[87]—helped fuel the "postwar miracle" in Italy and furnished the Brazilian government with enough money to construct from nothing the "all-inclusive concrete utopia" of Brasilia.[88] While Fordism gives way to post-Fordism in Italy and across the advanced capitalist world, the primitive accumulation of rubber in the Amazon proceeds apace, and the ranks of the tappers continue to grow, as the conditions of indenture are passed from one generation to the next. The patrão has a monopoly on the instruments of violence—"by the laws of harmony, you cannot both have guns"—so the only route of resistance available to the tapper is escape: "The green tree ferns pound into and out of view, branches scrape you, your feet are numb. You trip, you fall, you get up, you keep running."[89]

The tappers themselves are not represented in the 1977 movement in Italy. But the subjects of primitive accumulation, and the methods of resistance available to them, are. Italy's northern bourgeoisie, Gramsci observed in the 1920s, reduced the South to a colony, "enslaved to the banks and the parasitic industrialism of the North."[90] The Valera workers both within the factory and beyond it—on the assembly line and at the kitchen table—are migrants from the agrarian South, compelled toward the industries of the North by extractive forms of land rent. In the movement, industrial laborers—displaced by primitive accumulation, exploited by expanded reproduction, and increasingly degraded by synthetic dispossession—are joined by a diversity of contingents: the university students ("bespectacled and grave"), and ragtag bands of youth from peripheral slums—kids who "have no part in bourgeois life." In keeping with the Autonomist tradition, members of the movement set their own prices for commodities and services—"their own rent, their own bus fare"—and occupy spaces abandoned by capital. The factory workers carry their tire irons to the barricades, using the tools of their trade to resist the creeping redundancy of their trade. The ragged youth paint their faces and chant ironic slogans: "We want nothing! More work, less pay! Down with the people, up with the bosses!"[91]

Finding herself entangled in the movement in Rome—after taking flight from the unfaithful Sandro—Reno is struck by "the 'we' of it," the adhesive intimacy of the disparate bodies that converge in the square. She is sensitive to the different demands invoked and different tactics deployed by the different "sections" that compose the demonstration: some are more open to violence than others ("The gun was a tool like the screwdriver was a tool, and they all carried them")[92]; some desire the bourgeois security that has been promised them, and others work—in spiritual accord with the fleeing tapper in Brazil—to evade and abjure any capitalist rationality. But the ultimate feeling is of togetherness, of common humanity and common purpose—a "communal body" that derives its integrity and strength from the unique parts that make it up, that assembles a common vision of the future from different experiences of the present. The unity and difference of the demonstrators both reflect the singularity and heterogeneity of global capital and gesture toward the power of a collectivity that understands and embodies the idea that the universal is found in the articulation (joining) of manifold particulars.

Conclusion

Trotsky's theorization of uneven and combined development was an attempt to capture the differential unity of the capitalist mode of production, within discrete national spaces and in the context of the world-system. His insights countered more deterministic and more linear renderings of the laws of historical transformation within the epoch of capitalist modernity. His treatment of the simultaneity of putatively successive "stages" of development prefigured the conceptualization of capital's multiple moments that I have essayed in this book, while identifying the necessarily heterogeneous composition of the collective subject of anticapitalist resistance. The dynamics of uneven and combined development were also elaborated by two of Trotsky's contemporaries, and two other denizens of the semi-periphery, Gramsci and Mariátegui. The latter thinkers discerned that the patterns of unevenness within Italy and Peru, respectively, were connected to—an expression of—the dialectics of development and underdevelopment within a global frame. Mariátegui in particular anticipated the contributions of anticolonial and postcolonial thinkers in subsequent decades, who grasped that the unity and heterogeneity of global capital could not be explained without a sophisticated theory of imperialism—its economic logics, and its paradigmatic forms of governance and technologies of racial thought and practice. The anticolonial and postcolonial intellectuals whose work I examined above—James, Césaire, Fanon, Rodney, and Hall—demonstrated how the racial depredation of labor, land, and resources in the formerly colonized world continues to enable the expansionary reproduction, and ideological ascendance, of capital in the metropole.

The insights of anticolonial and postcolonial thought into the "complex unity" of global capital—the *articulation* of different modalities, spaces, or moments of accumulation—not only informed the development of world-systems theory, which possesses a basic understanding of capitalist modernity as colonial modernity; the critique of colonial history and rationality has also shaped the field of "world literature," its production and its literary-critical mediation. As a critical project, world literature is fundamentally concerned with those forms and strategies of representation that crystallize the planetary generality and essential unevenness of the capitalist world-system brought into being by colonial histories. This book has sought to further this urgent hermeneutic task, by delineating and juxtaposing distinct strands of global theory and fiction, and by engaging, in this final chapter, critical and literary works that reveal something of the concurrent interrelation of the three moments of capital—the combination or commingling of different modes of political and economic power, different patterns of thought and feeling, and different vocabularies of resistance.

CONCLUSION

World Theory, World Literature

THIS BOOK HAS ARGUED THAT CONTEMPORARY capital is composed of three synchronous moments: primitive accumulation, expanded reproduction, and "synthetic dispossession." These moments are defined by unique forms of governance and accumulation, and they correspond to unique trajectories of critique and unique strands of world literature. One key task of contemporary theory and criticism, I have contended, and the arc of this book has expressed, is to both delineate the multiple moments of capital and examine the dynamics of their concurrent interrelation.

In his reflections on primitive accumulation, Marx chronicled the violence of capital's birth—the enclosure of common lands in Europe, the extraction of natural wealth in the New World and beyond, and the traffic in African slaves. Capital, Marx wrote, enters the world "*dripping* from head to foot, from every pore, with *blood* and dirt."[1] Luxemburg and others later observed that the moment of primitive accumulation is not merely originary but ongoing. In order to survive, capital, backed by crude instruments of state violence, must constantly seize upon non-commoditized land, resources, and labor. Contemporary theories of primitive accumulation highlight that constancy—the fact of that repetition, and the reverberation, in the present, of longer histories of deracination, conquest, plunder, and bondage. This twofold attention to the history of the present and the presence of history is likewise exemplified by the contemporary novel of primitive accumulation—works such as Amitav Ghosh's *Sea of Poppies* and Michael Ondaatje's *In the Skin of a Lion*, which bring into view the genealogic and analogic connections between original and latter-day histories of expropriation, and which represent the experience of history as repetition.

In the moment of expanded reproduction, the basic mechanisms of economic growth—the transmutation of wage labor into surplus value, and the reinvestment of that surplus in the fixed and variable machineries of production—are conditioned less by outright force than by the "silent compulsion" of the market. The "invisible threads" that bind the worker to the wage relation, and the capitalist to the pursuit of profit, have prompted, over the past century or so, the parallel theorizations of ideology, spirit, and governmentality. Of these three ways of conceptualizing the technologies of consent—Marxist, Weberian, and Foucauldian, respectively—the critique of ideology, as it was elaborated by Raymond Williams and others, encourages a more dialectical understanding of the confrontation between the ideas of the ruling class and those strategies of representation that work to expose and undo the apparent naturalism of capital. The contemporary novel of expanded reproduction, the self-reflexive descendant of the bourgeois fictions of the nineteenth century, stages precisely this "war of position"—the interplay of the forces of naturalization and denaturalization. Texts such as Ben Lerner's *10:04* and Benjamin Kunkel's *Indecision* register the individual and collective malaise, one symptom of the "end of history," which defines the paradigmatic "structure of feeling" in the moment of expanded reproduction—in the context of the neoliberal present, wherein the enduring fact of growth is countered by the specter or reality of political and economic decline. In these novels, the workings of capitalist ideology are made visible; and so too do the histories concealed—and futures foreclosed—by that ideology begin to come into view.

The urgency of both witness and futurity is especially pronounced in the moment of synthetic dispossession. Therein, the insecurity engendered by financialization and privatization corresponds to the fading efficacy of ideology and amplification of "law and order"—the increasing centrality and intensity of police violence. In recent years, the generalization of insecurity, and enactment of the repressive state apparatuses, has provoked new vocabularies of critique—the theorization, notably, of "precarity" and its politics. In the work of Lauren Berlant, Judith Butler, and others, precarity signifies at once our common—if profoundly uneven—vulnerability to the exigencies of material scarcity, and the radical politics of mutual care that might emerge in the wake of capital's assault on the social commons. The novel of synthetic dispossession captures the aporia of crisis, the ambivalence of its temporal experience and affect: certain texts, such as Rafael Chirbes's *On the Edge*, depict the longing for a bygone state and subjectivity (economic security, belonging, and agency), while novels such as Eugene Lim's *Dear Cyborgs* work, in a speculative idiom, to limn the social formations and "cultural hypotheses" that begin to take root in, and imagine a way beyond, the impasse of the present.

My theorization of the three moments of capital joins a vital line of inquiry—one gestured toward by Marx and Engels, and one subsequently developed by Marxist thinkers on the (semi)-periphery, including Trotsky, Mariátegui, and Gramsci—into the uneven and combined development of capital, both within distinct national spaces and in the context of the broader world-system. The conceptual and methodological tools for apprehending global capital—its historical formation; its planetary generality and essential unevenness—were forged and sharpened by theorists of empire and its afterlives. C. L. R. James and Eric Williams accented how capitalist modernity was constituted on the margins of the world-system. In allied analytic terms, Walter Rodney anatomized the dialectics of growth, the ways in which the depredation of the colonies made possible the expansion of capital in the metropole. Relatedly, all of these interventions were attuned to the synchronous combination, rather than linear succession, of different modes of accumulation and governance—primitive accumulation and expanded reproduction; crude state violence and ideology. Thinkers such as Césaire and Fanon, moreover, grasped that colonialism disfigured the colonizer and colonized alike; and the global project of decolonization would necessarily join the revolutionary movement of *les damnés de la terre* to the liberation, within Europe, of the proletariat—that paradigmatic collective subject of capital, whose putatively universal character would finally be "made to the measure of the world," as Césaire put it, by the transcendence not just of capitalist social relations but all vestiges of racial thought and practice.

That phrase "made to the measure of the world" rhymes with my central objective in this book. I have sought to outline a new conceptual framework—based on the distinction between and interrelation of the three moments of capital—that might deepen our understanding of global capital, and its theoretical and literary mediation. I have worked, in other words, toward what we might call a new "world theory." And I have been guided, in this endeavor, not just by the entwined—defined by tension as well as affiliation—traditions of Marxist and anti- or postcolonial thought, but by the producers and critics of "world literature." In one sense, "world literature" signifies texts that represent global forces and histories—capital and empire, most especially—as well as texts that render the local experience or manifestation of those same forces and histories. These two categories of world literature encompass many of the novels that I have engaged—from Marlon James's *The Book of Night Women*, which reveals the thematic of domination and resistance in the space of the slave plantation, to Neel Mukherjee's *The Lives of Others*, which dramatizes the interrelations of distinctive moments of capital in postcolonial India. World literature, though, is a way of reading as well as a category of writing. And as it bears upon the moment of criticism, "world literature" implies the imperative of comparative methodologies; it signals the possibility, specifically, of dialogic encounters, between particular texts, that elucidate something of the shape and substance of capitalist modernity at large. Often or usually, the categories of nation, region, or language guide such comparative approaches. Foregrounding rather the different moments of capital, my own comparative modality has sought to map the unity and internal heterogeneity of both contemporary world literature and global capital itself. The novels of, for example, the moment of expanded reproduction do not always exhibit—in their geographic focus and thematic concerns—the more planetary, or more historical, consciousness that we often associate with world literature. But when juxtaposed with fictions of the moments of primitive accumulation and synthetic dispossession, their global implication comes into view. It is precisely the stark differences of form and content between, say, Jonathan Franzen's *Freedom* and Fiston Mwanza Mujila's *Tram 83* that betrays their co-belonging within the capitalist world system—the entanglement of freedom and unfreedom, ideology and violence, overdevelopment and underdevelopment.

The argument I've composed over the preceding chapters has relied heavily on the work of others, theorists and critics whose interventions illuminate the discrete moments of capital, and the discrete traditions of thought to which those moments have given rise. One thinker whose work I have returned to often is Stuart Hall. In my consideration of expanded reproduction, I invoked Hall's meditation on "The Problem of Ideology," and his attention, specifically, to the contest between dominant and emergent cultures of imaginative representation, within a discursive sphere that is determined in the first instance, but not the last, by the relations and logics of capital. In my treatment of synthetic dispossession, meanwhile, I summoned *Policing the Crisis*, a work coauthored by Hall that brings into relief the crisis of ideology, and resurgent importance of crude state repression, which accompany the pervasive insecurity engendered by neoliberal policies. Finally, my analysis of the *interrelation* of the three moments of capital deployed Hall's conceptualization, in his essay "Race, Articulation, and Societies Structured in Dominance," of "articulation"—a term that captures the "complex unity" of global capital, the concurrent combination of different modes of accumulation and governance, and the concomitant intersections of race and class. There is one other intervention of Hall's that I've not yet cited, but which likewise speaks to some of the core premises and deductions of this book: the essay "When Was 'The Post-Colonial'? Thinking at the Limit."

In that piece, Hall reckons with several abiding criticisms of postcolonial thought: the charge, advanced by Anne McClintock and others, that postcolonial theory reinforces a linear conception of time's unfolding, which obscures the persistence of colonial rationality in the moment of its supposed negation; Ella Shohat's argument that postcolonial theory, with its emphasis on hybridity, disavows the essential contradiction between the colonizer and colonized and thereby "posits no clear domination and calls for no clear opposition"; Arif Dirlik's contention that postcolonial theory displaces the material with the discursive, and neglects, specifically, "capitalism's structuring of the modern world"; and the assumption, shared by these and adjacent critiques, that the concept of "the postcolonial," its universalizing pretensions, elides the divergent historical trajectories of colonial power in particular national or regional geographies.[2] Hall's countering of these interlocking criticisms was characteristically deft. He suggested, notably, that the history of colonialism evoked by the term "postcolonial" "was no local or marginal sub-plot in some larger story (for example, the transition from feudalism to capitalism in western Europe, the latter developing 'organically' in the womb of the former)." It signifies, rather, the epoch of colonial modernity, within which we still live: "the whole process of expansion, exploration, conquest, colonisation and imperial hegemonisation which constituted the 'outer face,' the constitutive outside, of European and then Western capitalist modernity after 1492." The postcolonial "re-narrativisation" of colonial history

> displaces the "story" of capitalist modernity from its European centering to its dispersed global "peripheries"; from peaceful evolution to imposed violence; from the transition from feudalism to capitalism (which played such a talismanic role in, for example, Western Marxism) to the formation of the world market . . . ; or rather to new ways of conceptualising the relationship between these different "events"—the permeable inside/outside borders of emergent "global" capitalist modernity.[3]

This reconceptualization of the enduring history of "global capitalist modernity" has enabled, Hall insisted, a more extensive understanding of those spaces of encounter and synthesis produced by empire—spaces of *différance* that evince the unity and heterogeneity of both global capital and its collective subject of resistance. Colonialism was a global condition; so too is "the postcolonial" marked by its fundamental globality. Nigeria and the United States might not be postcolonial in the same way, Hall noted, but that does not mean that they are not postcolonial in any way.[4] They belong, commonly, to the capitalist modernity shaped by the history of empire and its afterlives—even if they occupy different coordinates within it. My hope is that the theory of capital's three moments I have essayed in this book might help us account for that sameness and that difference.

Notes

Introduction

1. Karl Marx and Friedrich Engels, *The Communist Manifesto* (1848), accessed at https://www.marxists.org/archive/marx/works/1848/communist-manifesto/.

2. Marx and Engels, *The Communist Manifesto*.

3. Though the historiographic literature tends to locate the political origins of neoliberalism in the 1970s, Michel Foucault, in his 1978–79 lectures at the Collège de France, notably highlighted the proto-neoliberal significance of the ordoliberals in postwar Germany, who imagined the market and its rationality as the foundation for the reconstituted German state. The intellectual history of neoliberalism, meanwhile, has even deeper origins. In the 1930s, economists and philosophers such as Friedrich Hayek and Ludwig von Mises formulated a critique of Keynesianism that associated the latter with "totalitarian" forms of collectivism such as Nazism and communism. Government planning, these "Austrian School" thinkers avowed, ultimately led to the negation of individual freedom. The realization of that freedom, Hayek, von Mises, and the other attendees of the famous 1947 Mont Pèlerin meeting insisted, required the liberation and generalization of market forces. While the Keynesian consensus prevailed in the immediate postwar period, neoliberal thinking took root in and spread throughout think tanks and other ideological state apparatuses; when the postwar political-economic order was thrown into crisis in the early 1970s, the already insidious ideology of neoliberalism found concrete political expression. For a bracing account of this intellectual history, see Quinn Slobodian, *Globalists: The End of Empire and the Birth of Neoliberalism* (Cambridge, MA: Harvard University Press, 2018).

4. See Leon Trotsky, *History of the Russian Revolution*, trans. Max Eastman (Chicago: Haymarket Books, [1932] 2008).

5. Michael Inwood, *A Hegel Dictionary* (Hoboken, NJ: Wiley-Blackwell, 1992), 311.

6. For a discussion of the relationship between the analytic of temporality and the practice of comparison, see Harry Harootunian, "Some Thoughts on Comparability and the Space-Time Problem," *boundary 2* 32, no. 2 (2005): 25–32; and Rey Chow, "The Old/New Question of Comparison in Literary Studies," *ELH* 71, no. 2 (2004): 289–311.

7. Raymond Williams, *Marxism and Literature* (Oxford: Oxford University Press, 1978), 132, 133.

8. Hannah Arendt, *The Origins of Totalitarianism* (New York: Harcourt Brace Jovanovich, [1951] 1973), 148.

9. Luc Boltanski and Eve Chiapello, *The New Spirit of Capitalism*, trans. Gregory Elliott (London: Verso, 2005), 8.

10. See Raymond Williams, "Ideology," in *Marxism and Literature* (Oxford: Oxford University Press, 1978); and Antonio Gramsci, *Prison Notebooks*, vol. 1, trans. Joseph A. Buttigieg and Antonio Callari (New York: Columbia University Press, [1929–35] 2011).

11. For two accounts of Marx's engagement with the question of world literature, see: Aijaz Ahmad, "The Communist Manifesto and 'World Literature,'" *Social Scientist* 28, no. 7/8 (2000): 3–30; and Martin Puchner, "Readers of the World Unite," *Aeon* (September 20, 2017), accessed at https://aeon.co/essays/world-literature-is-both-a-market-reality-and-a-global-ideal.

12. Louis Althusser, "Ideology and Ideological State Apparatuses," in *Lenin and Philosophy and Other Essays*, trans. Ben Brewster (New York: Monthly Review Press, 2001), 150.

13. Robert Brenner, *The Economics of Global Turbulence: The Advanced Capitalist Economies from Long Boom to Long Downturn, 1945–2005* (London: Verso, 2006).

14. Stuart Hall, Chas Critcher, Tony Jefferson, John Clarke, and Brian Roberts, *Policing the Crisis: Mugging, the State, and Law and Order* (London: Macmillan Press, 1978), 217.

15. See Anna Kornbluh, *Realizing Capital: Financial and Psychic Economies in Victorian Form* (New York: Fordham University Press, 2014); Leigh Claire La Berge, *Scandals and Abstraction: Financial Fiction of the Long 1980s* (Oxford: Oxford University Press, 2014); Annie McClanahan, *Dead Pledges: Debt, Crisis, and Twenty-First Century Culture* (Stanford: Stanford University Press, 2016); Elizabeth Holt, *Fictitious Capital: Silk, Cotton, and the Rise of the Arabic Novel* (New York: Fordham University Press, 2017); Alison Shonkwiler, *The Financial Imaginary: Economic Mystification and the Limits of Realism* (Minneapolis: University of Minnesota Press, 2017); and Arne De Boever, *Finance Fictions: Realism and Psychosis in a Time of Economic Crisis* (New York: Fordham University Press, 2018).

16. I have privileged here works of criticism that are concerned primarily or in part with the relationship between fiction and fictitious capital. An adjacent and equally vital critical conversation, though, centers on the conjunction of

contemporary poetry and contemporary capital. Christopher Nealon's *The Matter of Capital: Poetry and Crisis in the American Century* (2011), for example, locates poetic responses to the financial crisis of 2008 within a longer genealogy of American poetry's mediation of capitalist processes and forms. Joshua Clover's essay "Autumn of the System: Poetry and Financial Capital" (2011), meanwhile, argues that the movement of financialization—captured by the formula M-M', a revision of Marx's classic M-C-M'—occasions or is defined by the "conversion of the temporal to the spatial" (43), or the synchronization of the diachronic. The capitalist present, Clover submits, is characterized in part by the foreclosure or redundancy of narrative; and works of contemporary poetry such as Kevin Davies's *The Golden Age of Paraphernalia* (2008) "preserve" time "as an absence, as what it lost," while, perhaps, illuminating "a place where all moments are present" (45, 43). Joshua Clover, "Autumn of the System: Poetry and Financial Capital," *Journal of Narrative Theory* 41, no. 1 (2011): 34–52.

17. La Berge, *Scandals and Abstraction*, 4.

18. Stuart Hall, "Race, Articulation, and Societies Structured in Dominance," *Sociological Theories: Race and Colonialism* (Paris: UNESCO, 1980), 306, 341.

19. Frantz Fanon, *The Wretched of the Earth*, trans. Constance Farrington (New York: Grove Press, [1961] 1963), 38.

20. This prose in this paragraph first appeared, in different form, in the following article: Eli Jelly-Schapiro, "Historicizing Repression and Ideology," *Mediations* 30, no. 2 (2017).

21. Henri Lefebvre, *The Production of Space*, trans. Donald Nicholson Smith (Hoboken, NJ: Wiley-Blackwell, 1992), 385, 416.

22. Karl Marx, *Grundrisse: Foundations of the Critique of Political Economy*, trans. Martin Nicolaus (New York: Penguin, [1857–58] 1993), 524, 410.

23. See Ernst Bloch, *Heritage of Our Times*, trans. Neville Plaice and Stephen Plaice (New York: Polity, [1935] 2009).

24. Étienne Balibar, "On the Basic Concepts of Historical Materialism," in Louis Althusser, ed., *Reading Capital*, trans. Ben Brewster (London: Verso, 1997), 350.

25. Giovanni Arrighi, *The Long Twentieth Century: Money, Power, and the Origins of Our Times* (London: Verso, 1994), 6. For an intriguing reading/revision of Arrighi's argument, see Fredric Jameson, "Culture and Finance Capital," *Critical Inquiry* 24, no. 1 (1997). Jameson suggests that Arrighi's theorization of capital's systemic cycles implies the recurrence not of two phases but three: merchant, industrial, and financial; and the succession of these phases renders as historical narrative the Marxian dialectic of M-C-M'.

26. Massimiliano Tomba, "Historical Temporalities of Capital: An Anti-Historicist Perspective," *Historical Materialism* 17, no. 5 (2009): 56.

27. Massimiliano Tomba, *Marx's Temporalities* (Chicago: Haymarket Books, 2013), xiii.

28. Tomba, *Marx's Temporalities*, xiv.

29. Franco Moretti, "Conjectures on World Literature," *New Left Review*, no. 1 (January/February 2000).

30. The Warwick Research Collective (WReC), *Combined and Uneven Development: Towards a New Theory of World Literature* (Liverpool: Liverpool University Press, 2015), 14.

Chapter 1

1. Karl Marx, *Capital*, vol. 1, trans. Ben Fowkes (London: Penguin Books, [1867] 1990), 915.

2. Marx, *Capital*, 875.

3. Though Marx does not consider at length, in *Capital* itself, the constancy of primitive accumulation, he did undertake a sustained examination of this problem in the later years of his life, when he elaborated his insights into primitive modes of dispossession in a series of studies on the origins and evolution of capital in Russia, China, India, Southern Africa, and other semi-peripheral or peripheral societies. These reflections, it is assumed by many scholars, would have greatly informed his treatment of primitive accumulation in particular, and his critique of capitalism more broadly, in the unfinished second and third volumes of *Capital*. For a brief discussion of these late writings, see Peter Hudis, "Can Rosa Luxemburg Help Us Understand Racialized Capitalism?" (July 22, 2021), https://rosalux.nyc/can-rosa-luxemburg-help-us-understand-racialized-capitalism/.

4. Marx, *Capital*, 899.

5. Hannah Arendt, *Origins of Totalitarianism* (New York: Harcourt Brace Jovanovich, [1951] 1973), 148.

6. Marx, *Capital*, 165.

7. Marx, *Capital*, 874.

8. Marx, *Capital*, 895.

9. Marx, *Capital*, 896.

10. Marx, *Capital*, 899.

11. Marx, *Capital*, 917.

12. Marx, *Capital*, 918.

13. Marx, *Capital*, 925. Debates about whether the institution of chattel slavery is internal to the capitalist mode of production or one part of its constitutive outside remain central to the historiography of capitalism. In an earlier moment, historians such as Robin Blackburn, Rafael Marquese, Dale W. Tomich, and Michael Zeuske, in basic agreement with the insights of Eric Williams and C. L. R. James, chronicled the entanglements of New World slavery and global capitalism. In recent years, moreover, contemporary historians such as Walter Johnson, Seth Rockman, Caitlin C. Rosenthal, and Edward E. Baptist have illuminated the centrality of slavery to the development and mature form of American capitalism in particular.

14. Étienne Balibar, "On the Basic Concepts of Historical Materialism," in Louis Althusser, ed., *Reading Capital*, trans. Ben Brewster (London: Verso, 1997), 276.

15. Rosa Luxemburg, *The Accumulation of Capital*, trans. Agnes Schwarzschild (New York: Routledge Classics, [1913] 2003), 345. "Impelled to appropriate productive forces for purposes of exploitation," Luxemburg wrote, "[capital] ransacks the whole world, it procures its means of production from all corners of the earth,

seizing them, if necessary by force, from all levels of civilisation and from all forms of society" (338). The rhetoric here evokes Marx and Engels in *The Communist Manifesto*, and their rapt narration of the revolutionary powers of the bourgeoisie, that class that "tears asunder" non-capitalist modes of production and establishes in their place the basic technologies and social relations of "Modern Industry," creating a "world after its own image." But there is at least one key difference between Luxemburg on the one hand, and Marx and Engels on the other, in their respective characterizations of capitalism's planetary drive. Whereas Marx and Engels—in the *Manifesto*, anyway—attribute this globalizing desire to the bourgeoisie, and its insatiable longing for surplus value, Luxemburg implies instead that the imperialist agency (or pathology) inheres not in the capital*ist* but in capital itself. It is the logics of capital, and not the collective psychology of the bourgeoisie, that "impel" the perpetual movement into the non-capitalist strata.

16. Luxemburg, *Accumulation of Capital*, 343.

17. Luxemburg, *Accumulation of Capital*, 346.

18. Luxemburg, *Accumulation of Capital*, 397.

19. Luxemburg, *Accumulation of Capital*, 447.

20. Toward the end of his life, it's worth noting, Marx began to question these teleological assumptions; but his recognition of the synchronous combination of different modes of accumulation was never developed into a fully realized study.

21. Luxemburg, *Accumulation of Capital*, 434.

22. Glen Sean Coulthard, *Red Skin, White Masks: Rejecting the Colonial Politics of Recognition* (Minneapolis: University of Minnesota Press), 13.

23. Coulthard, *Red Skin, White Masks*, 9.

24. Coulthard, *Red Skin, White Masks*, 16.

25. David Scott, *Conscripts of Modernity: The Tragedy of Colonial Enlightenment* (Durham, NC: Duke University Press, 2004).

26. Antonio Negri, *Insurgencies: Constituent Power and the Modern State*, trans. Maurizia Boscagli (Minneapolis: University of Minnesota Press, 1999), 253.

27. Negri, *Insurgencies*, 253.

28. Negri, *Insurgencies*, 253.

29. Nikhil Pal Singh, "On Race, Violence, and So-Called Primitive Accumulation," *Social Text* 34, no. 3 (September 2016): 39.

30. Singh, "On Race, Violence, and So-Called Primitive Accumulation," 39. I am borrowing the phrase "the part who have no part" from Jacques Rancière (in Rancière's phrasing: "the part of those who have no part"). See Jacques Rancière, *Dissensus: On Politics and Aesthetics*, trans. Steven Corcoran (London: Bloomsbury, 2015), 150.

31. Singh, "On Race, Violence, and So-Called Primitive Accumulation," 43.

32. Silvia Federici, *Caliban and the Witch: Women, the Body and Primitive Accumulation* (New York: Autonomedia, 2004), 12.

33. Federici, *Caliban and the Witch*, 136.

34. Federici, *Caliban and the Witch*, 64.

35. Federici, *Caliban and the Witch*, 13.

36. Singh, "On Race, Violence, and So-Called Primitive Accumulation," 40.

37. Rob Nixon defines "slow violence" as "violence that occurs gradually and out of sight, a violence of delayed destruction that is deferred across time and space, an attritional violence that is typically not viewed as violence at all." Rob Nixon, *Slow Violence and the Environmentalism of the Poor* (Cambridge, MA: Harvard University Press, 2011), 2.

38. See Franco Moretti, *The Bourgeois: Between History and Literature* (London: Verso, 2014), 17–19.

39. Bashir Abu-Manneh, "Global Capitalism and the Novel" (2018), https://modernismmodernity.org/forums/posts/global-capitalism.

40. For a cogent reading of *The Book of Night Women*, and the dialectics of colonial enlightenment (and anticolonial resistance) therein, see Greg Forter, *Critique and Utopia in Postcolonial Historical Fiction: Atlantic and Other Worlds* (Oxford: Oxford University Press, 2019), 96–140.

41. Marlon James, *The Book of Night Women* (New York: Riverhead Books, 2010), 3.

42. James, *The Book of Night Women*, 26.

43. James, *The Book of Night Women*, 167–68.

44. C. L. R. James, *The Black Jacobins* (New York: Vintage, [1938; 1962] 1989), 11.

45. James, *The Book of Night Women*, 281.

46. James, *The Book of Night Women*, 304.

47. James, *The Book of Night Women*, 262.

48. This reading of the implication of the death of the Roget children—the ways in which it symbolizes the arresting of slaver's reproduction—is indebted to Greg Forter; see Forter, "Tragedy, Romace, Satire: The Genres of Anticolonial Resistance in J. G. Farrell's *The Siege of Krishnapur* and Marlon James's *The Book of Night Women*," in *Critique and Utopia in Postcolonial Historical Fiction*, 134–35.

49. James, *The Book of Night Women*, 17.

50. This account of the place of Obeah/Myal in the rebellion, and the function of the Yoruba deity Olokun in particular, draws from an article by Ana Ozuna, "Feminine Power: Women Contesting Plantocracy in *The Book of Night Women*," *Africology: The Journal of Pan-African Studies* 10, no. 3 (2017): 132–48.

51. James, *The Book of Night Women*, 408.

52. James, *The Book of Night Women*, 417.

53. Amitav Ghosh, *Sea of Poppies* (New York: Picador, 2008), 3.

54. Ghosh, *Sea of Poppies*, 28–29.

55. Ghosh, *Sea of Poppies*, 28.

56. Ghosh, *Sea of Poppies*, 92–93.

57. Ghosh, *Sea of Poppies*, 93.

58. Ghosh, *Sea of Poppies*, 78.

59. Ghosh, *Sea of Poppies*, 112.

60. Ghosh, *Sea of Poppies*, 394, 348.

61. Ghosh, *Sea of Poppies*, 394.

62. Ghosh, *Sea of Poppies*, 10.

63. Ghosh, *Sea of Poppies*, 439.

64. Ghosh, *Sea of Poppies*, 439.

65. Ghosh, *Sea of Poppies*, 438.

66. Hernan Diaz, *In the Distance* (Minneapolis: Coffee House Press, 2017), 21.

67. Diaz, *In the Distance*, 22.

68. Diaz, *In the Distance*, 35.

69. Håkan's captivity in Clangston, and his exposure therein to commodity fetishism, genders the commodity form as feminine. This interlude in the novel might be read, in other words, as an unsettling expression of a representational tendency diagnosed by Andreas Huyssen, Mary Louise Roberts, and Rita Felski, among others: the ways in which male writers and critics often depict commodity culture as a feminizing threat to men, thereby obscuring the commodity as a technology of alienation and reification. See, for example: Mary Louise Roberts, "Gender, Consumption, and Commodity Culture," *American Historical Review* 103, no. 3 (1998): 817–44; and Rita Felski, *The Gender of Modernity* (Cambridge, MA: Harvard University Press, 1995). In its entirety, though, *In the Distance* brings such alienation and objectification into stark relief and evinces, moreover, the intrinsic interrelation of commodity rationality and patriarchal violence.

70. Diaz, *In the Distance*, 61.

71. Diaz, *In the Distance*, 86, 89.

72. Leanne Simpson, "Interview by Naomi Klein," *Yes!*, March 5, 2013, https://www.yesmagazine.org/peace-justice/dancing-the-world-into-being-a-conversation-with-idle-no-more-leanne-simpson, cited in Imre Szeman, "On the Politics of Extraction," *Cultural Studies* 31, nos. 2–3 (2017): 442.

73. Diaz, *In the Distance*, 82.

74. Diaz, *In the Distance*, 95.

75. Diaz, *In the Distance*, 198.

76. Diaz, *In the Distance*, 233.

77. Diaz, *In the Distance*, 233.

78. Diaz, *In the Distance*, 239.

79. Diaz, *In the Distance*, 238.

80. Diaz, *In the Distance*, 240.

81. Diaz, *In the Distance*, 245.

82. Diaz, *In the Distance*, 250.

83. Diaz, *In the Distance*, 256.

84. Fiston Mwanza Mujila, *Tram 83*, trans. Roland Glasser (Dallas: Deep Vellum, 2015), 1–2.

85. Fiston Mwanza Mujila, "Interview by *Afrikult*," *Afrikult*, 2016, http://afrikult.com/interview-with-fiston-mwanza-mujila-on-his-novel-tram-83/.

86. For a deep theorization of the relationship between the superfluity of wealth and the superfluity of racialized bodies, in the time-space of extraction (specifically the "racial city" of Johannesburg), see Achille Mbembe, "Aesthetics of Superfluity," 375–80.

87. Mujila, *Tram 83*, 6–7.

88. *Tram 83*'s representation of women—and its depiction, more specifically, of sex workers in the space of the nightclub—has been met with trenchant criticism. Sharae Deckard, for example, observes that the novel "attempts to critique the pervasiveness of misogyny and sexual violence, including the epidemic of rape, which accompanies conflict mineral mining in the Congo, but because it cannot conceive of female agency outside of objectification, only replicates the virulence of sexist rhetoric and conditions." Sharae Deckard, "Trains, Stone, and Energetics: African Resource Culture and the Neoliberal World-Ecology," in Sharae Deckard and Stephen Shapiro, eds., *World Literature, Neoliberalism, and the Culture of Discontent* (London: Palgrave Macmillan, 2019), 254. Mujila has responded to similar lines of critique here (among other places): http://afrikult.com/interview-with-fiston-mwanza-mujila-on-his-novel-tram-83/. The Nigerian writer Otosirieze Obi-Young usefully summarizes the critical conversation surrounding the book in the African literary community in this piece: https://brittlepaper.com/2017/04/fiston-mujilas-tram-83-misogynist-poverty-porn-zukiswa-wanner-richard-oduko-lead-strong-reaction-pa-ikhides-damning-criticism/.

89. Mujila, *Tram 83*, 36–37.

90. Mujila, *Tram 83*, 42, 43.

91. Mujila, *Tram 83*, 47.

92. Mujila, *Tram 83*, 87.

93. Mujila, *Tram 83*, 96.

94. Mujila, *Tram 83*, 111.

95. Mujila, *Tram 83*, 1.

96. Mujila, *Tram 83*, 108.

97. Mujila, *Tram 83*, 116.

98. Mujila, *Tram 83*, 116, 124.

99. Mujila, *Tram 83*, 152–53, 155.

100. Fiston Mwanza Mujila, "Interview by Sofia Samatar," *Bomb*, September 16, 2015, https://bombmagazine.org/articles/fiston-mwanza-mujila-roland-glasser/.

101. Mujila has invoked Hugh Masekela's song "Stimela" ("Coal Train") as a source of inspiration for *Tram 83*. For an illuminating reading of that song—the dialectic of colonial domination and pan-African anticolonial resistance to which it gives voice—in relation to Mujila's novel, see Sharae Deckard, "Trains, Stone, and Energetics," 245–48.

102. Mujila, *Tram 83*, 180.

103. Mujila, *Tram 83*, 210.

104. The above readings of *In the Distance* and *Tram 83* first appeared in the following article: Eli Jelly-Schapiro, "Extractive Modernity at Large: The Contemporary Novel of Primitive Accumulation," *Interventions: International Journal of Postcolonial Studies* (published online December 2021; forthcoming in print); reprinted with permission: https://www.tandfonline.com/journals/riij20.

105. Michael Ondaatje, *In the Skin of a Lion* (New York: Vintage, 1997), 10.

106. Ondaatje, *In the Skin of a Lion*, 7, 8.
107. Ondaatje, *In the Skin of a Lion*, 34.
108. Ondaatje, *In the Skin of a Lion*, 105–6.
109. Ondaatje, *In the Skin of a Lion*, 17.
110. Ondaatje, *In the Skin of a Lion*, 107.
111. Ondaatje, *In the Skin of a Lion*, 109–10.
112. Ondaatje, *In the Skin of a Lion*, 42.
113. Ondaatje, *In the Skin of a Lion*, 115.
114. Ondaatje, *In the Skin of a Lion*, 116.
115. Ondaatje, *In the Skin of a Lion*, 122.
116. Ondaatje, *In the Skin of a Lion*, 124–25.
117. Ondaatje, *In the Skin of a Lion*, 124–25.
118. Ondaatje, *In the Skin of a Lion*, 143.
119. Ondaatje, *In the Skin of a Lion*, 145.
120. Ondaatje, *In the Skin of a Lion*, 145.
121. Ondaatje, *In the Skin of a Lion*, 149.
122. Ondaatje, *In the Skin of a Lion*, 172.

Chapter 2

1. Karl Marx, *Capital*, vol. 1, trans. Ben Fowkes (London: Penguin Books, [1867] 1990), 712.

2. Marx, *Capital*, 715.

3. Marx, *Capital*, vol. 2, trans. David Fernbach (London: Penguin Books, [1885] 1993), 159.

4. Marx, *Capital*, vol. 1, 717.

5. Marx, *Capital*, 717.

6. Marx, *Capital*, 717.

7. Marx, *Capital*, 719. Multiple scholars have noted the absence in *Capital* of a sustained theorization of the reproduction of labor power. In *The Limits to Capital*, for example, David Harvey writes that "Marx's rather surprising failure to undertake any systematic study of the processes governing the production and reproduction of labour power itself . . . [is] one of the most serious of all the gaps in Marx's own theory." David Harvey, *The Limits to Capital* (Chicago: University of Chicago Press, 1982), 163, cited in Michael Denning, "Wageless Life," *New Left Review*, no. 66 (November/December 2010). Had Marx further developed his treatment of this question, he might have complicated the "simple" duality of worker's consumption—the consumption of the means of production, on the one hand, and the means of subsistence, on the other—to incorporate the evolving needs and desires, beyond the imperatives of survival, of the working class. In pace with the growth of the economy at large, the worker develops new "needs and wants." The generation of such desires implies the latent consumerist power of a wage-laboring class that facilitates growth not only by consuming the means of production and means of subsistence, but by serving as a market for commodities that contain nonessential

use values. As the Fordist era clarified, the growth of working-class consumption serves a twofold purpose: it meets capital's need for an ever-expanding market, and it helps strengthen and tighten the ties that bind the worker to the wage relation. But despite its positive implications for the capitalist, the consumerist agency of the worker is most often not freely given (by the capitalist) but won through collective struggle. This is particularly true when the new wants and needs are not industrial commodities (a refrigerator or television, say) but "social goods"—from education to visual art and other forms of "cultural capital." What Marx described as the "worker's own need of development," one consequence of expanded reproduction, threatens the tenuous harmony of capital and wage labor, as the space and means of working-class self-development are realized through class struggle and might help cultivate heightened levels of class consciousness. For a discussion of Marx's provisional engagement with these questions—the political economy of labor power, and the social reproduction of wage labor—see Michael Lebowitz, *Beyond Capital: Marx's Political Economy of the Working Class* (New York: Palgrave, 2003). Also see Tithi Bhattacharya, "How Not to Skip Class: The Social Reproduction of Labor and the Global Working Class," *Viewpoint Magazine*, October 31, 2015, https://www.viewpointmag.com/2015/10/31/how-not-to-skip-class-social-reproduction-of-labor-and-the-global-working-class/#rf29-5148.

8. Marx, *Capital*, 719.

9. Marx, *Capital*, 899.

10. Amitav Ghosh, *The Great Derangement: Climate Change and the Unthinkable* (Chicago: University of Chicago Press, 2017), 17–19.

11. Karl Marx and Friedrich Engels, *The German Ideology* ([1845–46] 1932), trans. S. Ryazanskaya, in Robert C. Tucker, ed., *The Marx-Engels Reader* (New York: Norton, 1978), 149.

12. Marx and Engels, *The German Ideology*, 154.

13. Karl Marx, "The Eighteenth Brumaire of Louis Bonaparte" (1852), trans. Friedrich Engels, https://www.marxists.org/archive/marx/works/subject/hist-mat/18-brum/ch03.htm.

14. Marx and Engels, *The German Ideology*, 172–73.

15. Marx, "The Eighteenth Brumaire."

16. The abrupt rise in oil prices in 1974 exacerbated already declining rates of growth in France. The Keynesian attempt to stimulate demand failed to redress the crisis, and by the end of the 1970s stagflation had set in and wages were depressed.

17. In one suggestive passage, Althusser invokes the "explicit or tacit combinations" of ideology and repression that enable the reproduction of capitalist social relations. But this route of inquiry—which would compel a consideration of the historically contingent and spatially complex articulations of state violence and ideology, primitive accumulation and expanded reproduction—is only hinted at. Althusser, in other words, does not consider the global conditions of possibility for the development of the ideological state apparatuses in France—the processes of primitive accumulation in the colonies that fueled the growth of the postwar welfare state; and

the colonial forms of unfreedom and crude state violence that made possible the ideological ascent of the "free" French citizen. The intensive pursuit of these "explicit or tacit combinations" is foreclosed by the abiding ahistoricity of Althusser's account.

18. Louis Althusser, "Ideology and Ideological State Apparatuses," in *Lenin and Philosophy and Other Essays*, trans. Ben Brewster (New York: Monthly Review Press, 2001), 109, 116, 109.

19. Raymond Williams, *Marxism and Literature* (Oxford: Oxford University Press, 1978), 109.

20. Williams, *Marxism and Literature*, 108.

21. Williams, *Marxism and Literature*, 123.

22. Williams, *Marxism and Literature*, 125. There is an anticipatory echo here of Dipesh Chakrabarty's concept of "history 2s"—those cultural practices or forms that are coincident and spatially bound up with but escape capture by, and perhaps even disrupt, the logics of capital. See Dipesh Chakrabarty, *Provincializing Europe: Postcolonial Thought and Historical Difference* (Princeton, NJ: Princeton University Press, 2000), 47–71.

23. Stuart Hall, "The Problem of Ideology—Marxism without Guarantees," *Journal of Communications Inquiry* 10, no. 2 (1986): 29.

24. Hall, "The Problem of Ideology," 43.

25. See David Harvey, *A Brief History of Neoliberalism* (Oxford: Oxford University Press, 2005), 183–88.

26. For an examination of "diffusionist" representations of the history of capitalist modernity, see J. M. Blaut, *The Colonizer's Model of the World: Geographical Diffusionism and Eurocentric History* (New York: Guilford Press, 1993).

27. Max Weber, *The Protestant Ethic and the Spirit of Capitalism*, trans. Talcott Parsons (New York: Charles Scribner's Sons, [1905] 1958), 20–21.

28. Weber, *Protestant Ethic*, 21.

29. Weber, *Protestant Ethic*, 22.

30. Weber, *Protestant Ethic*, 56, 55.

31. Weber, *Protestant Ethic*, 63.

32. Weber, *Protestant Ethic*, 64.

33. Weber, *Protestant Ethic*, 65.

34. Marx, *Capital*, 873.

35. Luc Boltanski and Eve Chiapello, *The New Spirit of Capitalism*, trans. Gregory Elliott (London: Verso, 2005), 6.

36. Boltanski and Chiapello, *New Spirit of Capitalism*, 7.

37. Boltanski and Chiapello, *New Spirit of Capitalism*, 8, 58.

38. In keeping with this rhetorical shift, one common anti-union tactic of contemporary firms is to reclassify jobs as "managerial" so that they exist outside of the bargaining unit.

39. The problem of un- or under-employment is today coterminous with the problem of "automation"—the replacement of human labor power by machines. In some instances, as Aaron Beranav has observed, automation is "labor-augmenting"; extant forms of labor are joined to new technologies of production. In other instances,

the robot does not collaborate with but replaces the human worker. This "labor-substituting" expression of automation heralds a future in which the wage relation that has always defined the capitalist mode of production is utterly transformed, or indeed rendered obsolete. The new paradigm of production that automation promises—wherein surplus value is generated largely by machines, and claimed exclusively by the capitalists who own them—has been met, on the socialist left and libertarian right, with divergent visions of what the social relations of capital (or economic relations broadly conceived) will look like in the future. On the right, figures like Peter Thiel and Elon Musk have indicated that some form of universal basic income (UBI) might soon be required, to obviate the revolt of the wageless lumpen. On the left, the possibility of "fully automated luxury communism" (a world beyond both work and scarcity) is accompanied or countered by rigorous examinations of the actual effects of automation in the capitalist present. Jason Smith's *Smart Machines and Service Work* (2020), for example, considers how automation in one sector of the economy often increases the mass of labor power deployed by other sectors. The workers made redundant by automation in one industry form a reserve army of labor, which is then seized upon by other industries (who have determined that employing this precarious labor is cheaper than replacing it with machines). The assembly line worker displaced by automation gets a non-union job in the service sector, where their hourly wage is less than half of what it once was. This is one example of what I call "synthetic dispossession": the fabrication and subsequent re-assimilation of an outside to capital. An adjacent way of reading the fate of wage labor in the context of the capitalist present, exemplified by the Endnotes collective, contends that processes of deindustrialization (in conjunction with automation) are producing a global population of the unwaged that is "pure surplus," that cannot be reabsorbed by capital: "It exists now only to be managed: segregated into prisons, marginalized in ghettos and camps, disciplined by the police, and annihilated by war" (2010; 51). The creation of this "pure surplus," they argue, is basic to the expanded reproduction of capital, which constantly expels more labor than it absorbs. Another notable contribution to the contemporary discussion of automation has been made by Gavin Mueller, whose *Breaking Things at Work* (2021) tracks the history of collective struggles against automation and mechanization, from the Luddites through to the present. Mueller contends that the automation of production does not exactly or merely displace human labor but reconfigures it, altering its structure and experience; in response, workers across time have mounted organized forms of resistance to the advent and imposition of new technologies, which sought and seek to reclaim some control over the mechanisms of production, and the broader culture and meaning of human labor. See: Gavin Mueller, *Breaking Things at Work: The Luddites Are Right About Why You Hate Your Job* (London: Verso, 2021); Aaron Beranav, *Automation and the Future of Work* (London: Verso, 2020); Aaron Bastani, *Fully Automated Luxury Communism: A Manifesto* (London: Verso, 2020); *Endnotes 2: Misery and the Value Form* (2010).

40. Boltanski and Chiapello, *New Spirit of Capitalism*, 346.

41. Boltanski and Chiapello, *New Spirit of Capitalism*, 419.

42. Boltanski and Chiapello, *New Spirit of Capitalism*, 421.

43. Wendy Brown, *Undoing the Demos* (New York: Zone Books, 2015), 117.

44. Despite the subtle resonance between Marx's treatment of the transition from primitive accumulation to expanded reproduction (state violence to ideology) and Foucault's account of the shift from juridical/disciplinary to governmental technologies of power, their respective understandings of "political economy" also contain significant points of divergence. Marx's critique imagines political economy as an essentially discursive phenomenon, a mode of representation, which, at turns, both illuminates and obscures the true origins of value within capitalism. (Adam Smith and David Ricardo formulated a "labor theory of value," for example, but elided the fundamental importance of primitive accumulation). For Marx, that is, classical political economy is a narrative, the ideological substance of which justifies and naturalizes various forms of capitalist alienation and expropriation. This narrative, as Michael Perelman has observed, did inform the "terroristic laws" that conditioned processes of primitive accumulation and enforced labor discipline; but it does not, in Marx's writings, act as a signifier of a specific state form or specific mode of governance. See Michael Perelman, *The Invention of Capitalism* (Durham, NC: Duke University Press, 2000). Foucault, meanwhile, understands political economy less as an ideology and more as a *science*—not simply a way of representing the world but a form of knowledge about the world (a technology of "veridiction"), which evinces and enables the commonsense "nature" (qua "truth") of market processes, and which is instantiated by the liberal art of government.

45. Michel Foucault, *The Birth of Biopolitics: Lectures at the Collège de France, 1978–1979*, trans. Graham Burchell (New York: Picador, 2008), 46.

46. Foucault's characterization of this liberal imperialist ethos resembles, in ways, Hardt and Negri's theorization of "Empire," which I discuss in Chapter 4.

47. Foucault, *Birth of Biopolitics*, 55–56.

48. Foucault, *Birth of Biopolitics*, 64.

49. Foucault, *Birth of Biopolitics*, 116.

50. Foucault, *Birth of Biopolitics*, 120.

51. Foucault, *Birth of Biopolitics*, 147.

52. Foucault, *Birth of Biopolitics*, 270.

53. Brown, *Undoing the Demos*, 31, 35. Brown is especially interested in an analytic term that Foucault periodically invokes or reflects upon, in his later work, without theorizing at great length—the problem of *political rationality*. "Political rationality," as Brown paraphrases Foucault, "is not an instrument of governmental practice, but rather the condition of possibility and legitimacy of its instruments, the field of normative reason from which governing is forged." Brown is careful to stress that political rationality, this "field of normative reason," is not synonymous with governmentality; if governmentality originates in and emanates from the state, political rationality is more diffuse, and less precisely rooted, "although it circulates through the state, organizes it, and conditions its actions" (116, 118). In

Foucault's formulation, Brown summates, political rationality "[gives] new shape and orientation to the state, but also [governs] subjects themselves and every institution on the landscape: schools, hospitals, prisons, families, human rights organizations, nonprofits, social welfare agencies, youth culture, and more" (121). In this list, one can hear echoes of Althusser's treatment of the ideological state apparatuses. But the concept of political rationality also departs from the classic Marxist theory of ideology. Political rationality, in Foucault's usage, is not an epiphenomenon of capital (an expression of its essential logics) but rather a "field," "order," or "condition" that could "give capitalism itself a new form" (120).

54. Brown, *Undoing the Demos*, 79.

55. Brown, *Undoing the Demos*, 47.

56. Brown, *Undoing the Demos*, 35–36.

57. Brown, *Undoing the Demos*, 109.

58. The eclipse of *homo politicus* by *homo oeconomicus* corresponds, in ways, to the emergence of modern/biological racial thinking, and the displacement of the Aristotelian notion of political difference within history by biological difference outside of history. For an account of the latter transition, see Ivan Hannaford, *Race: The History of an Idea in the West* (Baltimore: Johns Hopkins University Press, 1995).

59. Brown, *Undoing the Demos*, 110–11.

60. Brown, *Undoing the Demos*, 110.

61. Brown, *Undoing the Demos*, 208.

62. Brown, *Undoing the Demos*, 74.

63. Mark Fisher, *Capitalist Realism: Is There No Alternative?* (London: Zero Books, 2009), 17.

64. Karl Marx and Friedrich Engels, *The Communist Manifesto*, trans. Samuel Moore ([1848] 1888), https://www.marxists.org/archive/marx/works/1848/communist-manifesto/.

65. Theodor Adorno, *Aesthetic Theory*, trans. Robert Hullot-Kentor (London: Bloomsbury Academic, [1970] 1997), 30.

66. Ghosh, *The Great Derangement*, 17. For a sharp review of Ghosh's book, which has informed my own engagement with it, see McKenzie Wark, "On the Obsolescence of the Bourgeois Novel in the Anthropocene," August 16, 2017, https://www.versobooks.com/blogs/3356-on-the-obsolescence-of-the-bourgeois-novel-in-the-anthropocene.

67. Franco Moretti, *The Bourgeois: Between History and Literature* (London: Verso, 2014), 15.

68. See Moretti, *The Bourgeois*, 1–23.

69. Georg Lukács, "Realism in the Balance," trans. Rodney Livingstone, in Lukács et al., *Aesthetics and Politics* (London: Verso, 1980), 32.

70. Robert Brenner, *The Economics of Global Turbulence: The Advanced Capitalist Economies from Long Boom to Long Downturn, 1945–2005* (London: Verso, 2006), xix.

71. See *Endnotes 2: Misery and the Value Form* (2010).

72. See David Harvey, "Rate and Mass," *New Left Review*, no. 130 (July/August 2021).

73. Jennifer Egan, *A Visit from the Goon Squad* (New York: Anchor, 2011), 14.

74. Egan, *A Visit from the Goon Squad*, 22, 36, 23.

75. Pankaj Mishra, "Modernity's Undoing," *London Review of Books* 33, no. 7 (March 31, 2011).

76. Egan, *A Visit from the Goon Squad*, 93–94.

77. Walter Benjamin, "Theses on the Philosophy of History,", trans. Harry Zohn, in *Illuminations: Essays and Reflections*, ed. Hannah Arendt (New York: Schocken, [1955] 2007), 262, 263, 254. For a reading of the resonance of punk music in Egan's novel, see Martin Moling, "'No Future': Time, Punk Rock, and Jennifer Egan's *A Visit from the Goon Squad*," Arizona Quarterly 72, no. 1 (Spring 2016).

78. Egan, *A Visit from the Goon Squad*, 336.

79. Egan, A Visit *from the Goon Squad*, 313.

80. Moretti, *The Bourgeois*, 17.

81. Moretti, *The Bourgeois*, 12.

82. Jonathan Franzen, *Freedom* (New York: Farrar, Straus & Giroux, 2010), 7.

83. Franzen, *Freedom*, 192.

84. Franzen, *Freedom*, 179.

85. Franzen, *Freedom*, 217, 220.

86. Andrew Hoberek, "Post-recession Realism," in Mitchum Huehls and Rachel Greenwald Smith, eds., *Neoliberalism and Contemporary Literary Culture* (Baltimore: Johns Hopkins University Press, 2017), 238.

87. Franzen, *Freedom*, 361.

88. Benjamin Kunkel, *Indecision* (New York: Random House, 2006), 10–11. For a reading of *Indecision* that thinks about the novel in relation to the problem of historicity in the capitalist present, see Emilio Sauri, "Cognitive Mapping, Then and Now: Postmodernism, *Indecision*, and American Literary Globalism," *Twentieth Century Literature* 57, no. 3/4 (Fall/Winter 2011): 472–91.

89. Kunkel, *Indecision*, 26.

90. Kunkel, *Indecision*, 19.

91. Kunkel, *Indecision*, 21.

92. Kunkel, *Indecision*, 140.

93. Kunkel, *Indecision*, 38.

94. Kunkel, *Indecision*, 78.

95. Kunkel, *Indecision*, 104–105.

96. Kunkel, *Indecision*, 119.

97. Kunkel, *Indecision*, 156.

98. Kunkel, *Indecision*, 174.

99. Kunkel, *Indecision*, 216.

100. Kunkel, *Indecision*, 234.

101. Kunkel, *Indecision*, 236.

102. Ben Lerner, *10:04* (New York: Farrar, Straus & Giroux, 2014), 16, 17.

103. Lerner, *10:04*, 19.

104. Lerner, *10:04*, 3.

105. Lerner, *10:04*, 5, 7.

106. Lerner, *10:04*, 47.

107. Lerner, *10:04*, 28.

108. Lerner, *10:04*, 52, 54.

109. Lerner, *10:04*, 94.

110. Lerner, *10:04*, 94.

111. Lerner, *10:04*, 108–109. Lerner has engaged this idea elsewhere, in his poem "Plume," which reckons with the Deepwater Horizon oil spill and the politics of our collective response (or nonresponse) to it. There too Lerner suggests that "built space has an emotional power for me natural space does not"—precisely because built space, even the violent infrastructure of oil extraction in the Gulf of Mexico, can be read as a "history of small decisions," a product of human agency, and thus evidence of our ability to construct other worlds. The "vast underwater fields of suspended oil," in other words, are beautiful—bad forms that signal good possibilities. In an allied register, Lerner observes that we, as a society, repress our affective response to the spill's devastation, because we recognize the power of our collective emotion, its capacity to impact stock prices and the trajectory of the economy at large. "Let our fear of our anger," the poem intones, "be a figure, however negative, for our capacity to bring what now appear as impersonal forces within the domain of the will, redescribing them as historical decisions." At the "end of history," when our volition finds its most obvious expression in the mundanity of market choice, this is a radical sentiment, which envisions the denaturalization of commodity rationality and reclamation of futurity. If "nature is bad art, affirming our non-response, good art, when it exists, will say: 'you have resigned yourself to an economy wherein you exchange your ability to respond for the ability to exchange your ability to respond, which is pathetic.'" The commoditization of everything, and the generalization of the sphere of exchange, has disabled our agency, diminished our historical power. The ideology of the market is a "strategy of containment [that] misplaces concreteness." The fetishism of the commodity, as Marx observed, personifies things and reifies people. But "good art," Lerner insists, can help hasten the plural "you," the "good collectivity," the "communal body," that will realize its humanity and volition and remake the world, beyond and in opposition to the ascendance of the commodity form. Ben Lerner, "Plume," *The Claudius App* 2 (August 2017).

112. Lerner, *10:04*, 133–134.

113. Lerner, *10:04*, 156.

114. Tao Lin, "An Interview with Ben Lerner," *The Believer*, no. 110 (September 2014).

115. Althusser, "Ideology and the Ideological State Apparatuses," 116; Fredric Jameson, *Postmodernism, or, The Cultural Logic of Late Capitalism* (Durham, NC: Duke University Press, 1991), 51.

Chapter 3

1. Rosa Luxemburg, *The Accumulation of Capital*, trans. Agnes Schwarzschild (New York: Routledge Classics, [1913] 2003), 257.

2. See David Harvey, *The New Imperialism* (Oxford: Oxford University Press, 2003), 137–82.

3. Stuart Hall, Chas Critcher, Tony Jefferson, John Clarke, and Brian Roberts, *Policing the Crisis: Mugging, the State, and Law and Order* (London: Macmillan Press, 1978), 217.

4. Lauren Berlant, "Precarity Talk: A Virtual Roundtable with Lauren Berlant, Judith Butler, Bojana Cvejić, Isabell Lorey, Jasbir Puar, and Ana Vujanović," in Jasbir Puar, ed., *TDR: The Drama Review* 56, no. 4 (Winter 2012): 166.

5. Karl Marx, *Grundrisse: Foundations of the Critique of Political Economy*, trans. Martin Nicolaus (New York: Penguin, [1857–58] 1993), 676, 677.

6. Marx, *Grundrisse*, 749–50.

7. Karl Marx, *Theories of Surplus Value*, trans. Renate Simpson (Buffalo, NY: Prometheus Books, [1862–63] 2000), 496.

8. Karl Marx and Friedrich Engels, *The Communist Manifesto*, trans. Samuel Moore ([1848] 1888), https://www.marxists.org/archive/marx/works/1848/communist-manifesto/.

9. Rosa Luxemburg, cited in Henry Tudor and J. M. Tudor, eds., *Marxism and Social Democracy: The Revisionist Debate, 1896–1898* (Cambridge: Cambridge University Press, 1988), 252–54.

10. Luxemburg, cited in Tudor and Tudor, eds., *Marxism and Social Democracy*, 253.

11. Luxemburg, cited in Tudor and Tudor, eds., *Marxism and Social Democracy*, 253.

12. Cédric Durand, *Fictitious Capital: How Finance Is Appropriating Our Future*, trans. David Broder (London: Verso, 2017), 66.

13. In the simplest terms, fictitious capital, as Durand has defined it, "represents claims over wealth that is yet to be produced." Marx highlighted three forms of fictitious capital: credit, government bonds (public debt), and corporate stocks and bonds. Credit money is a form of fictitious capital because, in Durand's explanation, it "is an advance on a future revenue and essentially does not come from previously saved funds." Government bonds, meanwhile, are simply an advance on future tax revenues. They do not, as Durand notes, "have any counterpart in capital valorized through production processes." This is not true of corporate shares, which do represent the capital invested by firms in the production process. But as Marx recognized, capital "does not exist twice over"—as a share, and as the "actual capital invested or to be invested in the enterprises in question." In reality, "it exists only in the latter form, and the share is nothing but an ownership title . . . to the surplus-value which this capital is to realize" (*Capital*, vol. 3, 597; cited in Durand, *Fictitious Capital*, 53). The power of fictitious capital, Durand contends, is an effect of its liquidity. Even if, for example, public or private bonds represent a claim on a future receipt or surplus, they can at any moment be translated into real money, at a price determined by the market's estimation of expected future returns. This liquidity heightens the intrinsic

volatility of speculation, and periodically results in economic crises occasioned by the mass offloading of securities or a run on bank deposits. Durand, *Fictitious Capital*, 1, 51, 52, 54.

14. The distinction between real and fictitious capital, and the analytic ascent of "speculation," has recently been scrutinized by Martijn Konings, in *Capital and Time: For a New Critique of Neoliberal Reason* (Stanford, CA: Stanford University Press, 2018). Therein, Konings persuasively argues that financial speculation produces economic order as much as it facilitates its undoing; and the state does not simply regulate financial processes but is itself "deeply implicated in the speculative dynamics of economic life" (jacket copy).

15. Joseph Schumpeter, *Capitalism, Socialism, and Democracy* (New York: Harper Perennial Modern Classics, [1950] 2008), 82.

16. Schumpeter, *Capitalism, Socialism, and Democracy*, 82–83.

17. Schumpeter, *Capitalism, Socialism, and Democracy*, 83. In one sense, Schumpeter's quarrel here is with those neoclassical economists who interpret capitalism as if it were a static phenomenon, that "accept the data of the momentary situation as if there were no past or future" (84). More particularly, Schumpeter resisted the normative notion of perfect competition and, relatedly, argued for monopoly as a potentially productive force, rather than an impediment to market efficiency and harbinger of crisis. Monopoly, in Schumpeter's formulation, is not only the consequence of the progressive concentration of capital, but an ephemeral and productive moment that results from the innovative interventions of the entrepreneur. When the entrepreneur introduces a new commodity or productive apparatus, he may enjoy, for a time, monopolistic profits. But eventually, other enterprises will mimic the new product or method, and the dynamism of the market will be renewed. Monopoly, Schumpeter suggested, is a spur toward generative competition rather than a sign of its absence.

18. Karl Polanyi, *The Great Transformation: The Political and Economic Origins of Our Time* (Boston: Beacon Press, [1944] 2001), 31.

19. David Harvey, *The New Imperialism* (Oxford: Oxford University Press, 2005), 141.

20. Harvey, *The New Imperialism*, 141.

21. Marx, *Capital*, 627.

22. Marx, *Capital*, 919, 1125.

23. This transition has been illuminatingly chronicled by Elizabeth Hinton, in her book *From the War on Poverty to the War on Crime: The Making of Mass Incarceration in America* (Cambridge, MA: Harvard University Press, 2016). In one sense, and as the prevailing historiographic tendency assumes, President Lyndon Johnson's Great Society programs existed on a continuum with the social innovations of the New Deal while attempting to redress the racial disparities of that legislation and provide greater "opportunity" for those on the margins of the labor market. As Hinton observes, though, Johnson's "War on Poverty" contained within it the discursive and institutional foundation of what would become the "War on Crime" (later joined,

under President Ronald Reagan, to the "War on Drugs")—a federal mandate that pathologized and criminalized poverty and blackness, heightened the punitive culture and policy of the "criminal justice" system, and deepened the police occupation of urban Black communities. The Law Enforcement Assistant Act of 1965, passed in the wake of the urban uprisings of 1964, and the Safe Streets Act of 1968 combined, Hinton notes, to encourage "a significant expansion of America's carceral state" (2). As the declension of the welfare state began in earnest in the 1970s and '80s, "law enforcement agencies, criminal justice institutions, and jails [became] the primary public programs" in poor communities of color. This transition has accelerated in pace with the intensification, over the past three decades in particular, of synthetic forms of dispossession. Today, 2.2 million people are incarcerated in American prisons, a figure that represents a greater than 900 percent increase over the past half century. And the logics of confinement have dovetailed with other forms of punitive social exclusion and control—from predatory lending that binds indebted citizens to their creditors and prevents poorer people from accumulating wealth, to states of "emergency" governance enacted in response to real or fabricated financial crises (which impose austerity conditions and dispossess marginalized jurisdictions of any democratic power). The prison itself, meanwhile, has not merely functioned to absorb those deemed disposable by the market, but has acted, as Ruth Gilmore has argued, as a key site of investment for overaccumulated capital, and as a lever for the transfer of public money to private developers and landowners. The extraordinary growth over the past several decades of the for-profit prison industry in particular clarifies the unique synthesis of depredation and repression at work in the moment of synthetic dispossession: the privatization of the social commons, the invention of new outlets for surplus capital and financial speculation, and the expansion of the police state.

24. Stuart Hall, Chas Critcher, Tony Jefferson, John Clarke, and Brian Roberts, *Policing the Crisis: Mugging, the State, and Law and Order* (London: Macmillan Press, 1978), viii.

25. Hall et al., *Policing the Crisis*, 217.

26. Lauren Berlant, *Cruel Optimism* (Durham, NC: Duke University Press, 2011), 3.

27. Berlant, *Cruel Optimism*, 4.

28. For an illuminating consideration of "crisis" thinking, as it bears upon the conjoined problems of history and temporality, see Amin Samman, *History in Financial Times* (Stanford, CA: Stanford University Press, 2019). In accord with my own account, Samman resists the historiographic and theoretical tendency that grasps the history of capitalism as a chronological progression of distinct stages. He outlines how the figure of "crisis," in the moment of finance capital's ascendance especially, clarifies an alternative understanding of history as repetition or reverberation, and heightens our attention to the "recursive action of the past on the present" (Introduction; accessed at https://www.sup.org/books/extra/?id=30045&i=Introduction.html).

29. Berlant, *Cruel Optimism*, 11.

30. Elizabeth Povinelli, *Economies of Abandonment* (Durham, NC: Duke University Press, 2011), 3.

31. Povinelli, *Economies of Abandonment*, 22.

32. Povinelli, *Economies of Abandonment*, 4.

33. Povinelli, *Economies of Abandonment*, 8, 9.

34. Povinelli, *Economies of Abandonment*, 10.

35. Povinelli, *Economies of Abandonment*, 100.

36. Judith Butler, "Bodies in Alliance and the Politics of the Street" (September 2011), http://eipcp.net/transversal/1011/butler/en.

37. Judith Butler, "Bodies in Alliance and the Politics of the Street."

38. Judith Butler, "For and Against Precarity," *Tidal*, no. 1 (December 2011), accessed at http://tidalmag.org/pdf/tidal1_the-beginning-is-near.pdf.

39. I am referring here to the short film *The BLM Bridge Protest: One Year Later* (2017), directed by Yolanda M. James, which interviews several participations in a 1,000-person demonstration that shut down the Hernando de Soto Bridge in Memphis, Tennessee, in 2016, following the police killings of Alton Sterling and Philando Castile.

40. Gabriel Winant, "We Found Love in a Hopeless Place: Affect Theory for Activists," *n+1*, no. 22 (Spring 2015), accessed at https://nplusonemag.com/issue-22/essays/we-found-love-in-a-hopeless-place/.

41. Winant, "We Found Love in a Hopeless Place."

42. Alison Shonkwiler, *The Financial Imaginary: Economic Mystification and the Limits of Realist Fiction* (Minneapolis: University of Minnesota Press, 2017), xxxii.

43. Shonkwiler, *The Financial Imaginary*, xxxii.

44. Leigh Claire La Berge, *Scandals and Abstraction: Financial Fiction of the Long 1980s* (New York: Oxford University Press, 2014), 11.

45. Arne De Boever uses the term "psychosis" to distinguish the pathology of finance capital. In *Finance Fictions*, he argues that, "with the abolition of the gold standard, the creation of complex financial instruments, the rise of high-frequency trading, and the unbridled intensification of speculative economic practices, we have moved from an era in which neurosis was the dominant affliction into an era in which psychosis has become prevalent." Fictitious capital, De Boever argues, has a "psychotic," "reality-disavowing" quality, which thus exists in tension with realist literary forms. If the novel, De Boever writes, brings "a degree of realism to psychosis, it is nevertheless also important to insist on the question of degree; a novel, after all, always remains a fiction, and thus it always also maintains a degree of what could be called 'psychosis', in relation to, say, the dry, actual reality that—in relation to the psychotic loss of reality—it can be said to write. Fiction mediates, in other words, between psychosis and realism." Arne De Boever, *Finance Fictions: Realism and Psychosis in a Time of Economic Crisis* (New York: Fordham University Press, 2018), 14–15.

46. The contest between the speculations of finance and the radical speculative acts of those dispossessed by financial capital has been generatively examined by Aimee Bahng. Her book *Migrant Futures: Decolonizing Speculation in Financial Times* describes, in particular, the "financial colonization of the future," which intensifies

"preexisting disparities of wealth held over from earlier histories of empire and neocolonial enterprises"; and the alternative futurities built by those who are at once dispossessed by financial capital and illegible as rights-bearing subjects within capitalist political order—"the undocumented, unbanked, and state-less workers . . . the colonized, displaced, and disavowed," who exist, or signal a way beyond, "the purview of statistical projection." Aimee Bahng, *Migrant Futures: Decolonizing Speculation in Financial Times* (Durham, NC: Duke University Press, 2018), 5, 7, 6.

47. Dave Eggers, *A Hologram for the King* (New York: Vintage, 2013), 4.

48. Eggers, *A Hologram for the King*, 13.

49. Eggers, *A Hologram for the King*, 12, 10.

50. Eggers, *A Hologram for the King*, 13.

51. Eggers, *A Hologram for the King*, 13.

52. Eggers, *A Hologram for the King*, 17.

53. Eggers, *A Hologram for the King*, 14.

54. Eggers, *A Hologram for the King*, 49.

55. Eggers, *A Hologram for the King*, 49.

56. Eggers, *A Hologram for the King*, 59.

57. Eggers, *A Hologram for the King*, 184.

58. Eggers, *A Hologram for the King*, 77.

59. Rafael Chirbes, *On the Edge*, trans. Margaret Jull Costa (New York: New Directions, 2016), 6.

60. Chirbes, *On the Edge*, 5.

61. Chirbes, *On the Edge*, 25–26.

62. Chirbes, *On the Edge*, 26.

63. Chirbes, *On the Edge*, 210–11.

64. Chirbes, *On the Edge*, 268.

65. Chirbes, *On the Edge*, 212.

66. Chirbes, *On the Edge*, 225.

67. Chirbes, *On the Edge*, 224.

68. Chirbes, *On the Edge*, 225.

69. Chirbes, *On the Edge*, 225.

70. Chirbes, *On the Edge*, 66, 67.

71. Chirbes, *On the Edge*, 131, 133.

72. Chirbes, *On the Edge*, 73, 397.

73. The Spanish boom of the early 1990s was concentrated in cities such as Barcelona and Sevilla; "all the money," Esteban observes, "flowed down those two great drains" (246). The cities themselves, though, are not simply sites of generalized prosperity, but spaces wherein the contradictions of capital are clarified and contested. The absorption of the surplus through urbanization, as David Harvey highlights, has always depended upon processes of "creative destruction" that evict and degrade the city's poorer residents. In the city, in other words, the intimacy of expanded reproduction and synthetic dispossession is brought into stark relief. And it is precisely this intimacy, and the inequities of its effects, that the Indignados critiqued.

74. Barbara Browning, *The Gift* (Minneapolis: Coffee House Press, 2017), 5.

75. Ben Lerner, *10:04* (New York: Picador, 2015), 47.

76. Browning, *The Gift*, 6–7.

77. Browning, *The Gift*, 7.

78. Browning, *The Gift*, 7, 24.

79. Browning, *The Gift*, 30.

80. Browning, *The Gift*, 51.

81. Browning, *The Gift*, 191.

82. Browning, *The Gift*, 202.

83. Eugene Lim, *Dear Cyborgs* (New York: FSG Originals, 2017), 3.

84. Lim, *Dear Cyborgs*, 5.

85. Lim, *Dear Cyborgs*, 11.

86. Lim, *Dear Cyborgs*, 7.

87. Lim, *Dear Cyborgs*, 18.

88. Lim, *Dear Cyborgs*, 21.

89. Lim, *Dear Cyborgs*, 22.

90. Lim, *Dear Cyborgs*, 22–23.

91. Lim, *Dear Cyborgs*, 24.

92. Hua Hsu, "Eugene Lim's Uncanny Sense of What It's Like to Be Alive Right Now," *New Yorker* online (June 7, 2017).

93. Lim, *Dear Cyborgs*, 56–57, 58.

94. Lim, *Dear Cyborgs*, 63.

95. Lim, *Dear Cyborgs*, 27.

96. Lim, *Dear Cyborgs*, 32.

97. Lim, *Dear Cyborgs*, 36.

98. Lim, *Dear Cyborgs*, 40.

99. Lim, *Dear Cyborgs*, 105.

100. Lim, *Dear Cyborgs*, 107.

101. Lim, *Dear Cyborgs*, 75.

102. Lim, *Dear Cyborgs*, 76.

103. Lim, *Dear Cyborgs*, 135.

104. Lim, *Dear Cyborgs*, 136.

Chapter 4

1. Warwick Research Collective (WReC), *Combined and Uneven Development: Towards a New Theory of World-Literature* (Liverpool: Liverpool University Press, 2015), 10.

2. Karl Marx, *Capital*, vol. 1, trans. Ben Fowkes (London: Penguin Books, [1867] 1990), ch. 31.

3. Marx, *Capital*, 876.

4. For an illuminating account of Gramsci's treatment of the problem of uneven and combined development, its cultural-political implications in Italy, see Stephen Shapiro and Neal Lazarus, "Translatability, Combined Unevenness, and World Literature in Antonio Gramsci," *Mediations* 32, no. 1 (Fall 2018): 1–37.

5. José Carlos Mariátegui, *Seven Interpretative Essays on Peruvian Reality*, trans. Marjory Urquidi (Austin: University of Texas Press, [1928] 1988), 6.

6. Mariátegui, *Seven Interpretative Essays*, 66–67.

7. Mariátegui, *Seven Interpretative Essays*, 70.

8. Frantz Fanon, *The Wretched of the Earth*, trans. Constance Farrington (New York: Grove Press, [1961] 1963), 38.

9. The above two paragraphs first appeared, in different form, in the following article: Eli Jelly-Schapiro, "Historicizing Repression and Ideology," *Mediations* 30, no. 2 (2017).

10. Walter Rodney, *How Europe Underdeveloped Africa* (London: Verso, [1972] 2017), 16.

11. Rodney, *How Europe Underdeveloped Africa*, 16.

12. Rodney, *How Europe Underdeveloped Africa*, 172.

13. Rodney, *How Europe Underdeveloped Africa*, 168.

14. Stuart Hall, "Race, Articulation, and Societies Structured in Dominance," *Sociological Theories: Race and Colonialism* (Paris: UNESCO, 1980), 306.

15. Hall, "Race, Articulation, and Societies Structured in Dominance," 306.

16. Hall, "Race, Articulation, and Societies Structured in Dominance," 324–29.

17. Hall, "Race, Articulation, and Societies Structured in Dominance," 320.

18. Hall, "Race, Articulation, and Societies Structured in Dominance," 322.

19. Hall, "Race, Articulation, and Societies Structured in Dominance," 341.

20. Harold Wolpe, "The Theory of Internal Colonialism" (1975), quoted in Hall, "Race, Articulation, and Societies Structured in Dominance," 322.

21. Hall, "Race, Articulation, and Societies Structured in Dominance," 322.

22. Immanuel Wallerstein, *The Essential Wallerstein* (New York: New Press, 2000), 133.

23. Wallerstein, *The Essential Wallerstein*, 134.

24. Wallerstein, *The Essential Wallerstein*, 86.

25. Wallerstein, *The Essential Wallerstein*, 89.

26. Michael Hardt and Antonio Negri, *Empire* (Cambridge, MA: Harvard University Press, 2000), 335.

27. Massimiliano Tomba, "Historical Temporalities of Capital: An Anti-Historicist Perspective," *Historical Materialism* 17, no. 5 (2009): 63.

28. *Baku: Congress of the Peoples of the East* (stenographic report) (London: New Park, 1977), 51; quoted in Ian Birchall, "The Communist International and Imperialism," *Viewpoint Magazine*, February 1, 2018.

29. *Baku*, 11, quoted in Birchall, "The Communist International and Imperialism."

30. Charles R. Holm, "Black Radicals and Marxist Internationalism: The IWMA to the Fourth International, 1864–1948" (PhD diss., University of Nebraska–Lincoln, 2014), 103. https://digitalcommons.unl.edu/cgi/viewcontent.cgi?article=1071&context=historydiss.

31. Aimé Césaire, *Discourse on Colonialism*, trans. Joan Pinkham (New York: Monthly Review Press, [1955] 2000), 78.

32. Fanon, *The Wretched of the Earth*, 37–38.

33. Fanon, *The Wretched of the Earth*, 129, cited in Stefan Kipfer, "Fanon and Space: Colonization, Urbanization, and Liberation from the Colonial to the Global City," *Environment and Planning D: Society and Space* 25, no. 4 (2007): 715.

34. Fanon, *The Wretched of the Earth*, 129.

35. Hall, "Race, Articulation, and Societies Structured in Dominance," 341.

36. Michael Hardt and Antonio Negri, *Multitude: War and Democracy in the Age of Empire* (New York: Penguin, 2004), 109.

37. David Harvey, *Spaces of Global Capitalism: A Theory of Uneven Geographic Development* (London: Verso, 2006), 113.

38. WReC, *Combined and Uneven Development*, 22.

39. Franco Moretti, "Conjectures on World Literature," *New Left Review*, no. 1 (January/February 2000): 55–56. Moretti's key insight is that literature, like all culture, is a product of encounters between different traditions or forms, which is never precisely symmetrical. That convergence might be defined by dispossession, or indebtedness, or simple compromise. But it is always marked by unevenness. Most crucially, Moretti argues, "in cultures that belong to the periphery of the literary system (which means: almost all cultures, inside and outside Europe), the modern novel first arises not as an autonomous development but as a compromise between a western formal influence (usually French or English) and local materials." This synthetic process—which is both an effect of and evinces political-economic asymmetry—is, historically, the *rule* of the novel's emergence; and the story we tell ourselves about discrete national traditions, developing in relative isolation, is very much the exception. And it is not simply a case of British or French forms being imposed on and adapted by novelists in, say, India and Senegal. The cultural forms of the periphery also impact upon the evolution of the novel in the metropole—just as the expanded reproduction of capital in the advanced capitalist world was and continues to be conditioned by economic processes unfolding on the periphery (58, 61).

40. WReC, *Combined and Uneven Development*, 8.

41. WReC, *Combined and Uneven Development*, 12.

42. WReC, *Combined and Uneven Development*, 16.

43. Massimiliano Tomba, *Marx's Temporalities* (Chicago: Haymarket Books, 2014), xiv.

44. That the dynamics of uneven and combined development are expressed within multiple spatial scales—the city, the nation, the world at large—is central to the work of geographers such as David Harvey and Neil Smith; and it is demonstrated as well by WReC, in their consideration of the literary registration of uneven development.

45. Pitchaya Sudbanthad, *Bangkok Wakes to Rain* (New York: Riverhead Books, 2019), 3–4.

46. Sudbanthad, *Bangkok Wakes to Rain*, 5.

47. Sudbanthad, *Bangkok Wakes to Rain*, 17–18.

48. Sudbanthad, *Bangkok Wakes to Rain*, 330.

49. Sudbanthad, *Bangkok Wakes to Rain*, 31.

50. Sudbanthad, *Bangkok Wakes to Rain*, 32.

51. Sudbanthad, *Bangkok Wakes to Rain*, 111.

52. Sudbanthad, *Bangkok Wakes to Rain*, 88.

53. Sudbanthad, *Bangkok Wakes to Rain*, 157.

54. Sudbanthad, *Bangkok Wakes to Rain*, 160.

55. Sudbanthad, *Bangkok Wakes to Rain*, 164.

56. Sudbanthad, *Bangkok Wakes to Rain*, 109.

57. Sudbanthad, *Bangkok Wakes to Rain*, 196.

58. Sudbanthad, *Bangkok Wakes to Rain*, 276.

59. Sudbanthad, *Bangkok Wakes to Rain*, 298.

60. Neel Mukherjee, *The Lives of Others* (New York: Norton, 2015), 10.

61. Mukherjee, *The Lives of Others*, 1.

62. Mukherjee, *The Lives of Others*, 3.

63. Mukherjee, *The Lives of Others*, 32.

64. Mukherjee, *The Lives of Others*, 33.

65. Mukherjee, *The Lives of Others*, 96.

66. Mukherjee, *The Lives of Others*, 126.

67. Mukherjee, *The Lives of Others*, 146

68. Mukherjee, *The Lives of Others*, 153.

69. Mukherjee, *The Lives of Others*, 174.

70. Mukherjee, *The Lives of Others*, 173.

71. Mukherjee, *The Lives of Others*, 199.

72. Mukherjee, *The Lives of Others*, 394.

73. Mukherjee, *The Lives of Others*, 394.

74. Mukherjee, *The Lives of Others*, 505.

75. Mukherjee, *The Lives of Others*, 449.

76. Mukherjee, *The Lives of Others*, 498.

77. Mukherjee, *The Lives of Others*, 497.

78. Rachel Kushner, *The Flamethrowers* (New York: Scribner, 2013), 3.

79. Kushner, *The Flamethrowers*, 30.

80. Kushner, *The Flamethrowers*, 92–93.

81. Kushner, *The Flamethrowers*, 97.

82. Kushner, *The Flamethrowers*, 201.

83. Kushner, *The Flamethrowers*, 166.

84. Kushner, *The Flamethrowers*, 266.

85. Kushner, *The Flamethrowers*, 250.

86. Kushner, *The Flamethrowers*, 215.

87. Kushner, *The Flamethrowers*, 214.

88. Kushner, *The Flamethrowers*, 367.

89. Kushner, *The Flamethrowers*, 217.

90. Antonio Gramsci, *The Southern Question*, trans. Pasquale Verdicchio (Chicago: Guernica, 2005 [1926]), 70.

91. Kushner, *The Flamethrowers*, 275–76.

92. Kushner, *The Flamethrowers*, 288.

Conclusion

1. Karl Marx, *Capital*, vol. 1, trans. Ben Fowkes (London: Penguin Books, [1867] 1990), 926.

2. Stuart Hall, "When Was 'The Post-Colonial'? Thinking at the Limit," in Iain Chambers and Lidia Curti, eds., *The Postcolonial Question: Common Skies, Divided Horizons* (London: Routledge, 1996), 242–46. For the arguments to which Hall is responding, see Anne McClintock, "The Angel of Progress: Pitfalls of the Term 'Post-Colonialism,'" *Social Text*, no. 31/32 (1992): 84–98; Ella Shohat, "Notes on the 'Post-Colonial,'" *Social Text*, no. 31/32 (1992): 99–113; and Arif Dirlik, "The Postcolonial Aura: Third World Criticism in the Age of Global Capitalism," *Critical Inquiry* 20, no. 2 (1994): 328–56.

3. Hall, "When Was 'The Post-Colonial'?," 249–50.

4. Hall, "When Was 'The Post-Colonial'?," 246.

Selected Bibliography

Adorno, Theodor. *Aesthetic Theory*. Translated by Robert Hullot-Kentor. London: Bloomsbury Academic, [1970] 1997.

Althusser, Louis. "Ideology and Ideological State Apparatuses." In *Lenin and Philosophy and Other Essays*. Translated by Ben Brewster. New York: Monthly Review Press, 2001.

Apter, Emily. *Against World Literature: On the Politics of Untranslatability*. London: Verso, 2013.

Arendt, Hannah. *Origins of Totalitarianism*. New York: Schocken, 1951.

Arrighi, Giovanni. *Adam Smith in Beijing: Lineages of the 21st Century*. London: Verso, 2009.

———. *The Long Twentieth Century: Money, Power, and the Origins of Our Times*. London: Verso, 1994.

Bahng, Aimee. *Migrant Futures: Decolonizing Speculation in Financial Times*. Durham, NC: Duke University Press, 2018.

Balibar, Étienne. "On the Basic Concepts of Historical Materialism." Translated by Ben Brewster. In *Reading Capital*. Edited by Louis Althusser. London: Verso, 1997.

Bastani, Aaron. *Fully Automated Luxury Communism: A Manifesto*. London: Verso, 2020.

Beckert, Sven. *Empire of Cotton: A Global History*. New York: Penguin, 2014.

Benjamin, Walter. "Theses on the Philosophy of History." Translated by Harry Zohn. In *Illuminations: Essays and Reflections*. Edited by Hannah Arendt. New York: Schocken, [1955] 2007.

Beranav, Aaron. *Automation and the Future of Work*. London: Verso, 2020.

Berlant, Lauren. *Cruel Optimism*. Durham, NC: Duke University Press, 2011.

Blaut, J. M. *The Colonizer's Model of the World: Geographical Diffusionism and Eurocentric History*. New York: Guilford Press, 1993.

Bloch, Ernst. *Heritage of Our Times*. Translated by Neville Plaice and Stephen Plaice. New York: Polity, [1935] 2009.

Boltanski, Luc, and Eve Chiapello. *The New Spirit of Capitalism*. Translated by Gregory Elliott. London: Verso, 2005.

Brenner, Robert. *The Economics of Global Turbulence: The Advanced Capitalist Economies from Long Boom to Long Downturn, 1945–2005*. London: Verso, 2006.

Brouillette, Sarah. *UNESCO and the Fate of the Literary*. Stanford, CA: Stanford University Press, 2019.

Brown, Nicholas. *Utopian Generations: The Political Horizon of Twentieth-Century Literature*. Princeton, NJ: Princeton University Press, 2005.

Brown, Wendy. *Undoing the Demos: Neoliberalism's Stealth Revolution*. New York: Zone Books, 2015.

Browning, Barbara. *The Gift*. Minneapolis: Coffee House Press, 2017.

Casanova, Pascale. *The World Republic of Letters*. Translated by M. B. DeBevoise. Cambridge, MA: Harvard University Press, [1999] 2004.

Césaire, Aimé. *Discourse on Colonialism*. Translated by Joan Pinkham. New York: Monthly Review Press, [1955] 2000.

Chakrabarty, Dipesh. *Provincializing Europe: Postcolonial Thought and Historical Difference*. Princeton, NJ: Princeton University Press, 2000.

Chambers, Iain, and Lidia Curti, eds. *The Postcolonial Question: Common Skies, Divided Horizons*. London: Routledge, 1996.

Chirbes, Rafael. *On the Edge*. Translated by Margaret Jull Costa. New York: New Directions, 2016.

Chow, Rey. *The Protestant Ethnic and the Spirit of Capitalism*. New York: Columbia University Press, 2002.

Cooper, Melinda. *Family Values: Between Neoliberalism and the New Social Conservatism*. Princeton, NJ: Princeton University Press, 2017.

Coulthard, Glen Sean. *Red Skin, White Masks: Rejecting the Colonial Politics of Recognition*. Minneapolis: University of Minnesota Press, 2014.

De Boever, Arne. *Finance Fictions: Realism and Psychosis in a Time of Economic Crisis*. New York: Fordham University Press, 2018.

De Loughry, Treasa. *The Global Novel and Capitalism in Crisis*. London: Palgrave Macmillan, 2020.

Denning, Michael. *Culture in the Age of Three Worlds*. London: Verso, 2004.

Diaz, Hernan. *In the Distance*. Minneapolis: Coffee House Press, 2017.

Durand, Cédric. *Fictitious Capital: How Finance Is Appropriating Our Future*. Translated by David Broder. London: Verso, 2017.

Eagleton, Terry. *The English Novel: An Introduction*. Hoboken, NJ: Wiley-Blackwell, 2004.

Egan, Jennifer. *A Visit from the Goon Squad*. New York: Anchor, 2011.

Eggers, Dave. *A Hologram for the King*. New York: Vintage, 2013.

Endnotes 2: Misery and the Value Form, 2010.

Engels, Friedrich, and Karl Marx. *The Communist Manifesto*. New York: Penguin Classics, [1848] 2015.

———. *The German Ideology* (1845–46). Translated by S. Ryazanskaya. In *The Marx-Engels Reader*. Edited by Robert C. Tucker. New York: Norton, 1978.

Fanon, Frantz. *The Wretched of the Earth*. Translated by Constance Farrington. New York: Grove Press, [1961] 1963.

Federici, Silvia. *Caliban and the Witch: Women, the Body, and Primitive Accumulation*. New York: Autonomedia, 2004.

Felski, Rita. *The Gender of Modernity*. Cambridge, MA: Harvard University Press, 1995.

Fisher, Mark. *Capitalist Realism: Is There No Alternative?* London: Zero Books, 2009.

Forter, Greg. *Critique and Utopia in Postcolonial Historical Fiction: Atlantic and Other Worlds*. Oxford: Oxford University Press, 2019.

Foucault, Michel. *The Birth of Biopolitics: Lectures at the Collège de France, 1978–1979*. Translated by Graham Burchell. New York: Picador, 2008.

Franzen, Jonathan. *Freedom*. New York: Farrar, Straus & Giroux, 2010.

Ghosh, Amitav. *The Great Derangement: Climate Change and the Unthinkable*. Chicago: University of Chicago Press, 2017.

———. *Sea of Poppies*. New York: Picador, 2008.

Gramsci, Antonio. *Prison Notebooks*. Vol. 1. Translated by Joseph A. Buttigieg and Antonio Callari. New York: Columbia University Press, [1929–35] 2011.

Greenwald Smith, Rachel, and Mitchum Huehls, eds. *Neoliberalism and Contemporary Literary Culture*. Baltimore: Johns Hopkins University Press, 2017.

Hall, Stuart. "Race, Articulation, and Societies Structured in Dominance." In *Sociological Theories: Race and Colonialism*. Paris: UNESCO, 1980.

Hall, Stuart, Chas Critcher, Tony Jefferson, John Clarke, and Brian Roberts. *Policing the Crisis: Mugging, the State, and Law and Order*. London: Macmillan, 1978.

Hannaford, Ivan. *Race: The History of an Idea in the West*. Baltimore: Johns Hopkins University Press, 1995.

Hardt, Michael, and Antonio Negri. *Empire*. Cambridge, MA: Harvard University Press, 2001.

———. *Multitude*. New York: Penguin, 2004.

Harootunian, Harry. *Marx after Marx: History and Time in the Expansion of Capitalism*. New York: Columbia University Press, 2015.

Harvey, David. *A Brief History of Neoliberalism*. Oxford: Oxford University Press, 2005.

———. *The Limits to Capital*. Chicago: University of Chicago Press, 1982.

———. *The New Imperialism*. Oxford: Oxford University Press, 2003.

———. *Spaces of Global Capitalism: A Theory of Uneven Geographic Development*. London: Verso, 2006.

Hinton, Elizabeth. *From the War on Poverty to the War on Crime: The Making of Mass Incarceration in America*. Cambridge, MA: Harvard University Press, 2016.

Holt, Elizabeth. *Fictitious Capital: Silk, Cotton, and the Rise of the Arabic Novel.* New York: Fordham University Press, 2017.

Inwood, Michael. *A Hegel Dictionary.* Hoboken, NJ: Wiley-Blackwell, 1992.

Irr, Caren. *Toward the Geopolitical Novel: U.S. Fiction in the Twenty-First Century.* New York: Columbia University Press, 2013.

James, C. L. R. *The Black Jacobins.* New York: Vintage, [1938; 1962] 1989.

James, Marlon. *The Book of Night Women.* New York: Riverhead Books, 2010.

Jameson, Fredric. *Postmodernism, or, the Cultural Logic of Late Capitalism.* Durham, NC: Duke University Press, 1991.

———. *A Singular Modernity.* London: Verso, 2002.

Karatani, Kojin. *History and Repetition.* Edited by Seiji M. Lippit. New York: Columbia University Press, 2011.

———. *Transcritique: On Kant and Marx.* Translated by Sabu Kohso. Cambridge, MA: MIT Press, 2005.

Kennedy, Liam, and Stephen Shapiro, eds. *Neoliberalism and Contemporary American Literature.* Hanover, NH: Dartmouth College Press, 2019.

Kinkle, Jeff, and Alberto Toscano. *Cartographies of the Absolute.* London: Zero Books, 2015.

Klein, Naomi. *The Shock Doctrine: The Rise of Disaster Capitalism.* New York: Picador, 2008.

Konings, Martijn. *Capital and Time: For a New Critique of Neoliberal Reason.* Stanford, CA: Stanford University Press, 2018.

Kornbluh, Anna. *Realizing Capital: Financial and Psychic Economies in Victorian Form.* New York: Fordham University Press, 2013.

Kunkel, Benjamin. *Indecision.* New York: Random House, 2006.

Kushner, Rachel. *The Flamethrowers.* New York: Scribner, 2013.

La Berge, Leigh Claire. *Scandals and Abstraction: Financial Fiction and the Long 1980s.* New York: Oxford University Press, 2014.

Lebowitz, Michael. *Beyond Capital: Marx's Political Economy of the Working Class.* New York: Palgrave, 2003.

Lerner, Ben. *10:04.* New York: Farrar, Straus & Giroux, 2014.

Lesjak, Carolyn. *The Afterlife of Enclosure: British Realism, Character, and the Commons.* Stanford, CA: Stanford University Press, 2021.

Lim, Eugene. *Dear Cyborgs.* New York: FSG Originals, 2017.

Lowe, Lisa. *The Intimacies of Four Continents.* Durham, NC: Duke University Press, 2015.

Lukács, Georg. *History and Class Consciousness.* Translated by Rodney Livingstone. Cambridge, MA: MIT Press, [1923] 1971.

———. "Realism in the Balance." Translated by Rodney Livingstone. In *Aesthetics and Politics.* London: Verso, 1980.

———. *The Theory of the Novel.* Translated by Anna Bostock. Cambridge, MA: MIT Press, [1916] 1971.

Luxemburg, Rosa. *The Accumulation of Capital*. Translated by Agnes Schwarzschild. New York: Routledge Classics, [1913] 2003.

Lye, Colleen, and Christopher Nealon, eds. *After Marx: Literature, Theory, and Value in the Twenty-First Century*. Cambridge: Cambridge University Press, 2022.

Mariátegui, José Carlos. *Seven Interpretative Essays on Peruvian Reality*. Translated by Marjory Urquidi. Austin: University of Texas Press, [1928] 1988.

Marx, Karl. *Capital*. Vol. 1. Translated by Ben Fowkes. New York: Penguin Books, [1867] 1990.

———. *The Eighteenth Brumaire of Louis Bonaparte*. Translated by Daniel De Leon. New York: International, [1852] 1963.

———. *Grundrisse: Foundations of the Critique of Political Economy*. Translated by Martin Nicolaus. New York: Penguin, [1857–58] 1993.

———. *Theories of Surplus Value*. Translated by Renate Simpson. Buffalo, NY: Prometheus Books, [1862–63] 2000.

McClanahan, Annie. *Dead Pledges: Debt, Crisis, and Twenty-First Century Culture*. Stanford, CA: Stanford University Press, 2016.

Moretti, Franco. *The Bourgeois: Between History and Literature*. London: Verso, 2014.

Mujila, Fiston Mwanza. *Tram 83*. Translated by Roland Glasser. Dallas: Deep Vellum, 2015.

Mukherjee, Neel. *The Lives of Others*. New York: Norton, 2015.

Nealon, Christopher. *The Matter of Capital: Poetry and Crisis in the American Century*. Cambridge, MA: Harvard University Press, 2011.

Negri, Antonio. *Insurgencies: Constituent Power and the Modern State*. Translated by Maurizia Boscagli. Minneapolis: University of Minnesota Press, 1999.

Nixon, Rob. *Slow Violence and the Environmentalism of the Poor*. Cambridge, MA: Harvard University Press, 2011.

Ondaatje, Michael. *In the Skin of a Lion*. New York: Vintage, 1997.

Osborne, Peter. *The Politics of Time*. London: Verso, 1992.

Palumbo-Liu, David, Nirvana Tanoukhi, and Bruce Robbins, eds. *Immanuel Wallerstein and the Problem of the World: System, Scale, Culture*. Durham, NC: Duke University Press, 2011.

Polanyi, Karl. *The Great Transformation: The Political and Economic Origins of Our Time*. Boston: Beacon Press, [1944] 2001.

Postone, Moishe. *Time, Labor, and Social Domination: A Reinterpretation of Marx's Critical Theory*. Cambridge: Cambridge University Press, 1993.

Povinelli, Elizabeth. *Economies of Abandonment: Social Belonging and Endurance in Late Liberalism*. Durham, NC: Duke University Press, 2011.

Rancière, Jacques. *Dissensus: On Politics and Aesthetics*. Translated by Steven Corcoran. London: Bloomsbury, 2015.

Robinson, Cedric. *Black Marxism: The Making of the Black Radical Tradition*. Chapel Hill: University of North Carolina Press, [1983] 2021.

Rodney, Walter. *How Europe Underdeveloped Africa*. London: Verso, [1972] 2018.

Samman, Amin. *History in Financial Times*. Stanford, CA: Stanford University Press, 2019.

Schumpeter, Joseph. *Capitalism, Socialism, and Democracy*. New York: Harper Perennial Modern Classics, [1950] 2008.

Scott, David. *Conscripts of Modernity*. Durham, NC: Duke University Press, 2004.

Shonkwiler, Alison. *The Financial Imaginary: Economic Mystification and the Limits of Realist Fiction*. Minneapolis: University of Minnesota Press, 2017.

Singh, Nikhil Pal. *Race and America's Long War*. Oakland: University of California Press, 2019.

Slobodian, Quinn. *Globalists: The End of Empire and the Birth of Neoliberalism*. Cambridge, MA: Harvard University Press, 2018.

Smith, Jason. *Smart Machines and Service Work: Automation in an Age of Stagnation*. Chicago: University of Chicago Press, 2020.

Sudbanthad, Pitchaya. *Bangkok Wakes to Rain*. New York: Riverhead Books, 2019.

Tomba, Massimiliano. *Marx's Temporalities*. Chicago: Haymarket Books, 2013.

Tombazos, Stavros. *Time in Marx: The Categories of Time in Marx's Capital*. Chicago: Haymarket Books, 2015.

Tucker-Abramson, Myka. *Novel Shocks: Urban Renewal and the Origins of Neoliberalism*. New York: Fordham University Press, 2018.

Tudor, Henry, and J. M. Tudor, eds. *Marxism and Social Democracy: The Revisionist Debate, 1896–1898*. Cambridge: Cambridge University Press, 1988.

Wallerstein, Immanuel. *The Essential Wallerstein*. New York: New Press, 2000.

The Warwick Research Collective. *Combined and Uneven Development: Towards a New Theory of World Literature*. Liverpool: Liverpool University Press, 2015.

Weber, Max. *The Protestant Ethic and the Spirit of Capitalism*. Translated by Talcott Parsons. New York: Scribner, [1905] 1958.

Williams, Eric. *Capitalism and Slavery*. Chapel Hill: University of North Carolina Press, [1944] 1994.

Williams, Raymond. *Marxism and Literature*. Oxford: Oxford University Press, 1978.

Winant, Gabriel. *The Next Shift: The Fall of Industry and the Rise of Health Care in Rust Belt America*. Cambridge, MA: Harvard University Press, 2021.

Index

CURRENCIES

New Thinking for Financial Times
STEFAN EICH AND MARTIJN KONINGS, SERIES EDITORS

Jakob Feinig, *Moral Economies of Money: Politics and the Monetary Constitution of Society*

Charly Coleman, *The Spirit of French Capitalism: Economic Theology in the Age of Enlightenment*

Amin Samman, *History in Financial Times*

Thomas Biebricher, *The Political Theory of Neoliberalism*

Lisa Adkins, *The Time of Money*

Martijn Konings, *Capital and Time: For a New Critique of Neoliberal Reason*

CPSIA information can be obtained
at www.ICGtesting.com
Printed in the USA
JSHW081124250123
36802JS00004B/4

9 781503 635432